The author writes with passion and author Jean's sixteen years of missionary experien stand the problems of unhealthy dependen "I want to plant the gospel and allow the cl..........

The book is a treasure of interesting personal incidents as well as the gleanings from other like-minded experts in the field of missions. I enthusiastically endorse her book as a convincing incentive to review our mission vision and to modify our mission efforts!

STEVE SAINT, SON OF MARTYRED MISSIONARY NATE SAINT; MISSIONARY TO THE (ECUADORIAN) WAODANI TRIBE; FOUNDER, INDIGENOUS PEOPLE'S TECHNOLOGY AND EDUCATION; AUTHOR OF END OF THE SPEAR AND WALKING HIS TRAIL; NARRATOR OF "BEYOND THE GATES OF SPLENDOR."

We Are Not the Hero is a rare combination of original metaphors, unique comparisons, and mind-challenging illustrations. Jean Johnson's sensitivity to culture and church planting goes beyond mere understanding. If I had to describe it in one word, I'd say "heart." She brings you along with her into striking settings and moving adventures, some from her experiences in Asia, others aptly chosen from history. New Testament guidelines for multiplying churches leap out with startling larity from sharp, action-packed examples that need no abstract explanation. Had I read this before going to the field, I'd have avoided serious and painful cultural errors.

DR. GEORGE PATTERSON, ORIGINATOR OF TRAIN AND MULTIPLY; AUTHOR OF CHURCH MULTIPLICATION GUIDE

Jean Johnson has, out of her own hard-won experience and copious reading and research, distilled for the rest of us what we might struggle to gather, compile, and make sense of over several lifetimes—a way forward. In We Are Not The Hero, the author presents, in an eminently readable style, church planting gold. She takes on tradition, institutionalism, dependency, and scores of the other enemies of church multiplication in a manner that allows any believer to grasp and apply these crucial lessons. This is no ivory tower book of pontification and pronouncement; this is a field manual smeared with mud from front-line trenches. Get it. Read it. Use it. And see your people, neighborhood, region, even your world, transformed.

BRIAN HOGAN, ASSISTANT DIRECTOR, YOUTH WITH A MISSION'S CHURCH PLANTING COACHES; AUTHOR OF THERE'S A SHEEP IN MY BATHTUB: BIRTH OF A MONGOLIAN CHURCH PLANTING MOVEMENT

Jean Johnson speaks from real-life, hard-earned experience. She has seen first-hand the unintended consequences of ministry meant to help the poor that actually deepens their poverty. Her book provides important insights for those who desire to serve effectively, engaging both their hearts and their minds.

DR. ROBERT LUPTON, PRESIDENT OF FCS URBAN MINISTRIES; AUTHOR OF *TOXIC CHARITY*

Transitioning a cross-cultural ministry into the hands of national workers is an important but delicate process. After five years of creating a ministry organization with Haitian Evangelists, the Lord impressed my wife and I to transfer the work entirely into the hands of reliable Haitian leaders. Through *We Are Not the Hero*, Jean Johnson empowered me to more clearly understand, explain, and begin to flesh out important indigenous ministry principles necessary for us and our Haitian friends to take this step of faith. Jean's gift of story telling and illustration makes everything she touches come alive and move from the head to the heart. My only disappointment is that I never had the opportunity to read a book like Jean's ten years ago when I first moved to Haiti with very little cross-cultural ministry training. I recommend this book to every new missionary preparing to enter a cross-cultural field, as well as any veteran missionary who would like to take steps towards indigenizing an existing ministry.

DANIEL CARL, MISSIONARY TO HAITI; CO-FOUNDER OF INTERNATIONAL LIVING STONE MINISTRIES, OMAHA NE

WE ARE NOT
THE
HERO

A MISSIONARY'S GUIDE
FOR SHARING CHRIST,
NOT A CULTURE OF DEPENDENCY

JEAN JOHNSON

Deep River
BOOKS

WE ARE NOT THE HERO

A Missionary's Guide for Sharing Christ, Not a Culture of Dependency

© 2012 Jean Johnson

Published by
Deep River Books
Sisters, Oregon
www.deepriverbooks.com
ISBN- 13: 9781937756451
ISBN 10: 1937756459
Library of Congress: 2012946977
Printed in the USA
Cover design by Jen Thomas

DEDICATION

To those who "do" missions with the desire and intentionality to keep god-complexes out of their mission efforts for the outcome of indigenous movements for Christ throughout the world.

To the local champions around the world who dare to break out of the confinements of unhealthy dependency to carve a path of dignity, creativity, mobilization, local community interdependence, and God-dependence.

Contents

PART I

A CALL TO PREMEDITATE MULTIPLICATION, INDIGENEITY,
AND SUSTAINABILITY

PART II

REFLECTION FOR PREMEDITATING MULTIPLICATION,
INDIGENEITY, AND SUSTAINABILITY

PART III
MULTIPLICATION, INDIGENEITY, AND SUSTAINABILITY IN ACTION

FOREWORD

This book is a remarkable gift to the twenty-first century Christian missionary movement. I cannot help but think how different my missionary experience would have been if I could have read this before going to Africa in 1961.

Filled with page after page of common-sense missiology, the author writes with an abundance of both cultural and spiritual sensitivity. More than that, this is the record of a field missionary who learned the hard way that some things work and others do not. What she is doing here is shortening the learning curve for anyone who is launching out in cross-cultural ministry. Everyone doing cross-cultural ministry owes her a debt of gratitude.

The author's immersion into Cambodian culture is worth noting up front. She felt called to a country which was not open to American missionaries at the time (the late 1980s). A closed country did not stop her from getting involved. Knowing that there were thousands of Cambodian refugees living in her home area of Minneapolis, she decided to use this ready access to her advantage. After six years of close interaction with these families, the country of Cambodia opened up once again to the outside world. In one sense, culturally and linguistically, she hit the ground running.

But Jean's story has many more interesting twists and turns. While in Cambodia, she quickly applied herself to the hard work of enculturation, while at the same time importing Western cultural Christianity. This dichotomy made her restless and caused her to reach back into her missionary training to see what she might discover that would help her.

About five years into her missionary service in Cambodia, Jean stumbled onto the eight-hour video series which I prepared in 1996 called *Dependency Among Mission-Established Institutions*. She ordered so many sets that I wondered if she realized that it was mostly about dependency in Africa. When I asked her about it, she replied that Cambodia had a huge problem of dependency that needed to be addressed. This set her on a path of figuring out not only how the dependency syndrome was created, but how to address the issue for the benefit of churches and other institutions in Cambodia.

One of her observations, spelled out in the pages of this book, is that the horrific government and military actions of the Khmer Rouge destroyed the *initiative* and *ability* of people to do things for themselves. If that were not bad enough, following the end of this horrible period, many missionary and aid agencies poured into the country with financial aid programs, virtually paying people to do what they could or should have been able to *at least start doing* for themselves. If the Cambodian people had any remaining dignity and self-respect, it was not being helped by the well-meaning outsiders who were reinforcing the feelings of inadequacy that gripped this nation.

Thankfully, there is more to the story—at least for the author herself. After sixteen years in Cambodia as a missionary, Jean decided to step back for two years to reflect on her experience and to do some teaching in a Christian university in North America. All the while she was asking, "What should my future contribution be to the Christian movement around the world?" In the end, Jean decided to make herself available to others struggling with issues of unhealthy dependency in cross-cultural church planting. Following her years at the university, she began a ministry of writing, speaking, and consulting, sharing what she had learned with those who want to see the church stand on its own feet with the presence of the Holy Spirit as their guide and Jehovah Jireh as their provider. In the past several years she has traveled to England, East Africa, India and various places in North America, sharing what she has learned. Instead of returning to Cambodia, she has helped hundreds who live and work cross-culturally, to do their job better.

One of the things that inspired me greatly was the term "premeditated sustainability" which Jean coined while writing this book. Premeditated sustainability means strategizing from the beginning how churches in the Christian movement should support, govern, and reproduce themselves. It is *not* just working hard and hoping for the best! Imagine how resources could be multiplied in cross-cultural evangelism if sustainability were built into the process from the beginning.

As missionaries and church leaders we do not need to reinvent the wheel, as it were—making many unnecessary ministry mistakes. This book will help Christian workers start right—or to transition toward healthy sustainability in situations that need to be reversed. It should be required reading for all those contemplating missionary service.

GLENN J. SCHWARTZ
EXECUTIVE DIRECTOR, WORLD MISSION ASSOCIATES

HEROES AND PREMEDITATION
𝕎 𝕎 𝕎

COWBOY BOOTS! RED, WHITE, AND BLUE SOCKS! A STANCE OF PRIDE!

Americans love heroes, and if we are willing to admit it, we like to be heroes. The actress Aisha Tyler frames her thoughts about heroes: "There's a part of every person that is entertained by the idealistic, the fantastic."[1] We thoroughly enjoy when the idealistic captures us and takes us away for a couple hours through movies like *War Horse*, in which man and animal sacrifice for the greater good, or *Extremely Loud and Incredibly Close,* which allows us to embrace a father hero who died in the Twin Towers on September 11 through the eyes of his son. The movie *The Avengers,* a 2012 film, brought together American superheroes Thor, Captain America, Black Widow, Nick Fury, Iron Man, Hawkeye, and the Hulk to save the earth from Loki, their terrifyingly powerful enemy. This film tied a record for the fastest film to gross $1 million worldwide.

Beyond desiring to go on journeys with heroes in the movies or celebrating real-life role models, everyone entertains thoughts of being fantastic on behalf of someone else (if they are willing to admit it).

Missionaries aren't immune to the lure of heroism. The movie *City of Joy* had a huge impact on me. I was amazed at how Dr. Max Lowe (Patrick Swayze), originally from Texas, and his mentor, an Irish woman (Pauline Collins), heroically involved their lives with the slum dwellers and lepers of Calcutta. There is something about their *fantasticness* that makes one say, "I want to do that too!" But after serving as a missionary in my own *City of* Joy—war-torn Phnom Penh, Cambodia—I have come to believe that these places do not need more Western heroes.

I led a class discussion at a university on the topic of global perspectives. The students and I had just completed reading an article about how an American missions team in northern Mexico made assumptions based on their own cultural experience and operated out of those assumptions. This dialogue led to the question, "Why do American Christians have a propensity to enter other countries as experts instead of learners and as heroes instead of servants?" A student quickly retorted, "Because Americans think they own Christianity!" The student's statement was quite profound, and much was packed in that short response. How would people act if they thought they owned Christianity? Perhaps as heroes. We are here to bring you God! We are here to use North American dollars to make you better! We will show you how to do church the right way! Here is what I think! This is how you alleviate poverty!

Steve Saint developed a DVD series called *Missions Dilemma: Is There A Better Way To Do Missions?* Within this series, Steve interviewed Christian leaders from around the world. One of the questions he asked was, "If there is one piece of advice you could give to North Americans of how to do missions better in your part of the world, what would it be?" Steve's first interviewee, Oscar Muriu, a leader and pastor in Kenya Africa, responded in the following manner:

> You have an amazing capacity to resolve problems. Now, it's a great thing about Americans: the ability to innovate and to resolve problems. The downside of that is that when you come to our context, you don't know how to live with our problems. You see our poverty. You see our need. You see the places we're hurting. And, you have a great compassion to come and solve us, but life can't be solved that way. Many times well-intentioned Americans will come into our context and they try to fix my life. You can't fix my life! What I need is a brother who comes and gives me a shoulder to cry on and gives me space to express my pain, but doesn't try to fix me. When Jesus comes into the world he does not try to fix all the poverty, all the sickness, all the need, the political situation. He allows that to be, but he speaks grace and he speaks salvation and redemption within that context because there is a greater hope than this life itself. Now, this tendency to fix it has become a real issue so that some of the reserve we feel as Africans or as two-third worlders is so many people have come to fix us that O' Lord, please don't bring another person to fix us. We have been fixed so many times we are a real mess now. Please allow us to be us. Allow us to find God and to find faith in the reality of our need.[2]

Ever since I watched the DVD and listened to Muriu's responses, I can hear his gentle but convincing voice in my head: "We have been fixed so many times we are a real mess now." As I travel around the world, I am hearing the same sentiments expressed by Oscar Muriu, especially among those cultural groups Americans have tried to fix too many times.

Through our mission methods and attitudes, we do not want to shove others into a mindset that says, "We must wait for a hero from far away to come and fix us!" Margaret Wheatly and Deborah Frieze, in their book, *Walk Out Walk On,* describe communities that have created meaningful change in their communities by fixing themselves from the bottom up rather than waiting for experts and heroes from the outside to fix them from the top down:

> They may have been told they're "backward" or don't possess the requisite expertise to solve their own problems. Had they accepted current thinking, they would have sat back waited passively for help to come from the outside—from experts, foreign aid and heroic leaders.[3]

Let us take off our cowboy boots and ease our stance of superiority. Rather, let us adhere to Oscar Muriu's words by giving others a shoulder to cry on, space to express themselves, and opportunity to find faith and God within their reality.

Let us do this—and let us do it in a deeply premeditated, deliberate, and humble way.

What comes to mind when you hear the word "premeditated"?

"Your honor and members of the jury, there is no doubt that Jack is a scorned lover who premeditated the murder of his wife. He calculated every step and detail, not only to succeed in killing his wife, but also to cover up the murder and elude the police."

We most often hear the word premeditated associated with first-degree murder. In many circumstances, premeditation is not a good thing. But when it comes to Great Commission endeavors, I am convinced that we need to premeditate our motives, actions, and desired outcomes. We need people to say, "You are guilty of premeditation: the display of willful purpose, intentional reflection, and advance planning."

My goal in writing this book is to assist those who fulfill the Great Commission cross-culturally to do it in such a way that they premeditate multiplication, indigeneity, and sustainability among the respective people groups whom they serve. Below are down-to-earth, brief explanations of four key words that shape this book:

People Groups: "For evangelization purposes, a people group is the largest

group within which the Gospel can spread as a church planting movement without encountering barriers of understanding or acceptance."[4]

Multiplication: 2 x 2 = 4; 4 x 4 = 16; 16 x 16 = 256; 256 x 256; 65,536
"And the Lord added to their number daily those who were being saved."
(Acts 2:47)

Indigeneity: God works within cultures and through cultures, not in spite
of them, and so should we. "Paul then stood up in the meeting of the
Aeropagus and said, "Men of Athens! I see that in every way you are very
religious. For as I walked around and looked carefully at your objects of
worship, I even found an altar with this inscription: TO AN UNKNOWN
GOD. Now what you worship as something unknown I am going to pro-
claim to you." (Acts 17:22–23)

Sustainability: Possessing motivation and a work ethic like the little engine
that could, who repeated the phrase "I-think-I-can; I-think-I-can!" "The
Little Engine That Could" is a classic story about a long train that could
not make it over a mountain. The only engine that had the vision and
willingness to pull the long train was a very small one. The small engine
succeeded in the enormous task of pulling the train over the mountain
by repeating the mantra, "I-think-I-can; I-think-I can!" Every church,
church movement, and people movement for Christ has the privilege
and duty to pull its own train without being unduly dependent on outsiders. "Make it your ambition to lead a quiet life, to mind your own
business and to work with your hands, just as we told you, so that your
daily life may win the respect of outsiders and so that you will not be
dependent on anybody." (1 Thessalonians 4:11–12)

In the case of being participants of the Great Commission, may we stand
accused of and clearly found guilty of premeditation.

PREFACE

ψ ψ ψ

A few days after my graduation from North Central Bible College, I began the journey of planting a church among Cambodians in St. Paul-Minneapolis, Minnesota. According to my training in cross-cultural communications, my first strategic action steps were obvious to me: move into a Cambodian community and "do life" with them.

For six years, I lived among the Cambodians. I ensured that my income was no more nor less than that of the Cambodians with whom I lived. Their family struggles became my family struggles; their weeping became my weeping. I lived in the Cambodians' only housing choice: a-should-have-been-condemned building, rat and cockroach infested, with drunks passed out on the floor after wandering in from outside. I saw a Cambodian boy's troubled eyes and beaten body after a man who snuck into the building raped him. I was manhandled and robbed in a dark space between the first and second doors to the building. The Cambodians and I watched the drug deals outside our windows the way some people watch nightly television. I did not come and go and merely hear about the Cambodians' everyday trials as refugees in an overwhelming context; rather, I experienced many of these challenges with them.

Furthermore, the Cambodians' celebrations became my celebrations, and their laughter became my laughter. I enjoyed sitting in small groups in the hallways of the apartment building, exchanging stories and humor. Sharing Cambodian meals together was the highlight of my day. I felt as though I was living in a Cambodian village right in the middle of an American city. I did not and could not fix their problems as a rich helper from the outside; rather, I entered into their struggles with life, and we worked as a team to find solutions and faith in Christ.

My training at North Central Bible College had prepared me to enter into this mission field of Cambodian refugees with willful purpose and advance planning for the purpose of making disciples who make disciples. I learned to work intimately within the culture and not in spite of it through an incarnational lifestyle.

After six years of living and ministering among the Cambodians in St. Paul-

Minneapolis, I headed to Cambodia to serve as a missionary. I spent another sixteen years there among these beautiful people. I have come a long way, both in literal travel and in life's journey. I fulfilled many of my dreams in Cambodia—many of which were generated in my heart before ever setting foot in that part of Asia.

Interestingly, about four years into my mission term in Cambodia, something critical occurred to me: I had grown lax in my "premeditated" way of doing missions, as I had practiced among the Cambodians in the U.S. Instead, I had slid into operating out of instinct. In other words, I was unconsciously allowing my cultural and church experiences to dictate my strategies, rather than forming strategies through an intimate understanding of the worldview and culture at hand. This lapse in strategic discipline caused me to neglect making disciples among unreached people groups who could in turn make disciples in their own "Jerusalem, Judea, and Samaria." Rather than setting aside my *ethnocentric[1] influence* and *economic affluence*, I used these privileges and positions to my advantage—or so I thought. For example, I used my expertise and money acquired from the USA to accelerate the growth of the church, while completely ignoring the fact that the Cambodians did not have ongoing access to such resources and that such a deficit would eventually lead to a "I-think-I-can't; I-think-I-can't!" mentality.

Even as I write this paragraph, this question comes to mind: What happened? Why did I set aside some of my convictions of how to do missions according to my cross-cultural communications training and experience among Cambodians in the USA? I am not sure, to tell you the truth. Perhaps Cambodia's post-genocide desperation sucked me into wanting to be a mini-savior. Perhaps the American drive for expediency and tangible success put me on the path of shortcuts. Maybe the "goodies" (vehicles, technology, supplies, and money) that were accessible to me as a foreign missionary were too hard to decline. Perhaps I settled too quickly into the missions patterns that I saw unfolding around me. Or maybe the reason for compromising was a combination of all of these elements.

Whatever the reason, a deep dissatisfaction began to grow within me, like a seed of conviction that sprouts and grows stronger each year. I tried to ignore it, justify it, and dismiss it as a rude interruption to my thought patterns. But it would not leave me alone. In hindsight, I believe God allowed my dissatisfaction to bring me back to what I had learned and implemented in Minnesota.

This description may sound confusing to those who have visited or heard about the first church that I planted in Phnom Penh, the capital city of Cambodia.

The church presently has over three hundred people, functions with Cambodian leadership, and the members support their own leaders. It is a wonderful church in so many ways, but that amount of success does not negate the fact that I had some inherent weaknesses to my missions approach. Using my cultural influence and my economic affluence allowed me to plant and to build "successful" churches and ministries through my own missions efforts, yet it robbed the Cambodians of birthing, sustaining, and multiplying their own indigenous churches and ministries. In other words, I led the Cambodians to believe that they needed to be well financed and semi-American in their approach in order to spread the gospel. Sure, I modeled prayer and dependency on the Holy Spirit. But I showed them with my right hand what they could readily access—the Holy Spirit—and with my left hand what they could not—material resources from affluent countries.

Jonathan Bonk wraps up what I am trying to share in a succinct manner:

> Material and economic abundance has been the hallmark of the modus operandi of Western missionaries throughout the past two centuries. In sharp contrast to their apostolic counterparts of the first century, portrayed by St. Paul as being "on display at the end of the procession," like men condemned to die in the arena (I Cor. 4:9).[2]

When Western missionaries use their ethnocentric influence and economic affluence in ministry, they inevitably birth ministries that are carbon copies of their expensive, Western forms of Christianity. This action makes it nearly impossible for local disciples of Christ to implement effective evangelism, discipleship, worship, acts of compassion, leadership training, and church planting by mobilizing their own local resources and cultural expressions.

Peter and John told the crippled beggar, "Silver or gold I do not have, but what I have I give you" (Acts 3:6). Peter and John did not pass on their cultural influence or affluence. Rather, the two disciples gave the crippled man a far better gift: they gave him Jesus Christ of Nazareth himself, through a miraculous healing from the hand of God. Sometimes in Cambodia, I felt so unlike Peter and John. My experience was much more like, "Silver and gold I have; look what I can do for you!"

One evening, I was preparing for an important speaking opportunity among North American missionaries. As part of my preparation, I reread the book The Indigenous Church by Melvin Hodges. I sought God with this question: "Have I, have we, wandered too far from Melvin Hodges's advice about how to grow the indigenous church?"

In answer, God practically hit me over the head with Ezekiel 27:12: "Tarshish did business with you because of your great wealth of goods." Immediately, I restated the verse in this manner: "Tarshish did *spiritual* business with you because of your great wealth of goods." I could hear it in my mind: "Cambodia did spiritual business with you because of your great wealth of goods. Haiti did spiritual business with you because of your great wealth of goods. Uganda did spiritual business with you because of your great wealth of goods." Would we not rather have nations say, "We did spiritual business with you because of your great wealth of faith?"

We have such an opportunity to exemplify our deep faith in God—a faith that draws people of other nations into a desperate dependence on God. But do we truly make the most of this opportunity?

While it may seem that our North American influence and economic affluence makes us good missionaries, others beg to differ:

> But when white people come in with a lot of money or "know-how" and try to make things "better," that's when things go to hell. Why can't white people just visit? Why must they always meddle? It's as if you were invited to dinner at someone else's house and during your brief visit you insisted on rearranging all the furniture in the house to suit your tastes.[3]

About mid-journey in Cambodia, I decided to stop rearranging other people's furniture. This book is born out of my season of God-given dissatisfaction, asking evaluative questions and discovering ways to implement missions that intentionally submit my ethnocentric influence and economic affluence before God for the purpose of cultivating indigenous movements for Christ that both sustain and multiply over the long term.

The Bible itself supports this approach to missions. The story told in Acts 17:16–34 is a prime example. While in Athens, anxiously waiting for Timothy and Silas to arrive, Paul found himself in a city full of idols. The numerous idols spoke volumes to Paul's heart about the disconnect between the Creator and those living in Athens. Paul went to the cultural centers of this city, such as the markets and synagogues, to instill in the Athenians a faith in God through Jesus Christ instead of faith in their philosophies discovered through endless debates.

At first, the people of Athens called Paul a babbler. Then, they claimed that Paul was promoting a foreign god of some kind. Finally, their defensiveness and inquisitiveness turned into a request: "May we know what this new teaching is that you are presenting?" Paul filled their request by meeting in their comfort zone, the Areopagus—a rock outcropping that served as the high court of appeal in Athens and where the citizens conducted their philosophical debates. Paul started to talk on topics that were familiar to his listeners, and then he moved to the unfamiliar: "Men of Athens! I see that in every way you are very religious." Instead of bringing some abstract concept to their ears, Paul used an existing altar to introduce them to God:

> Athenians, I am a new visitor to your beautiful city. As I have walked your streets, I have observed your strong and diverse religious ethos. You truly are a religious people. I have stopped again and again to examine carefully the religious statues and inscriptions that fill your city. In one such temple, I read the inscription: "TO AN UNKNOWN GOD." I am not here to tell you about a strange foreign deity, but about this One whom you already worship, though without full knowledge. This is the God who made the universe and all it contains. (Acts 17:22–24, *The Voice*)

Paul earnestly told them about the true God, sprinkling in poetry familiar to the Athenians. There were some definite scoffers in the crowd, but there were also men who asked to hear more on a later day. Others believed and became followers of Jesus Christ.

I see the role of a missionary all wrapped up in Paul's experience. When we enter a new city, we see all the symbols of disconnect between God and the people. The residents of that city view us as babblers and people who are advocating a foreign god. But we do our best to talk intelligently within their culture. We take every measure to present God in a culturally relevant manner so that our hosts begin to see God as their God, not as the god of the foreigners. We live, work, and pray among them until several people inquire, "May we hear more about what you are teaching?"

With that door opened, we share by emphasizing the familiar to introduce the unfamiliar: the God of heaven and earth, who made the world and everything in it. We describe God's character and actions as we sprinkle in indigenous poetry. We receive an invitation to expound more, and eventually several people believe and become followers of God through faith in Jesus Christ. Paul did all of this by working within the Athenians' culture (leaving his ethnocentrism at home) and living a simple lifestyle (instead of maneuvering through economic affluence).

As a missionary, I did a lot of things right and a lot of things wrong. On these pages, I share both experiences as a way to provide you a tool for your missions journey. As I pass the baton, may it be durable and light, and may it empower you to run your lap around the missions track like one who will cross the line and break the winner's tape.

Beyond sharing my own stories, experiences, and insight, I have intermixed other missionary practitioners' experiences and insights. Although this book is tailored for North American missionaries and many of the examples are from Cambodia, I believe the content, principles, and practical suggestions will be beneficial for those who do missions in various stages of ministry, in a variety of contexts, with varying lengths of service, and a range of sending countries.

I hope and pray that this book will stimulate your motivation and creativity as you strive to avoid creating unhealthy dependency for the purpose of cultivating indigenous movements for Christ—movements that have multiplication, indigeneity, and sustainability at the core.

PART I

A CALL TO PREMEDITATE

Multiplication, Indigeneity, and Sustainability

CHAPTER ONE

CLOSING THE GAP

> "A thousand, thousand would not suffice and
> a dozen might be too many."
>
> ROLLAND ALLEN

> "It isn't the proliferation of missionaries that produces the
> healthiest churches. It is the quality of the missionary and the
> soundness of his or her practice which determines the outcome."
>
> GLENN SCHWARTZ

I woke up lazily in the morning and decided to take a walk through the streets of Phnom Penh, Cambodia. As I watched people making their way to the market, I heard a familiar sound—an out-of-control motorcycle skidding across the blazing hot pavement. I had that sinking feeling as I glanced in the direction of the commotion—that feeling of wanting to look, but fearing what I might see.

Two people lay strewn upon the ground. One person moved, the other did not. I felt the tension in the air. As is typical, a crowd gathered to gawk at the scene. I did my share of staring as well. The driver of the cycle remained listless, lying in a puddle of blood that seemed to shout at us, "This is serious!" I whispered to myself, "As always, no one will lend a hand due to the complications of being a good neighbor in Cambodia!"

As I wrestled with my own thoughts, a man ran toward the unconscious driver. *Finally, some compassionate person is going to help, I thought.*

The determined bystander reached the victim and jumped over his body, back and forth several times as if he were playing a game. Then he walked away, never touching the bleeding and desperate man. I asked a bystander, "What just happened?" The man replied, "He is calling the soul back into the body."

Bewildered and feeling hopeless, I walked away with a plaguing question: "How can I as an American even begin to understand a worldview completely alien to my own and serve with any degree of effectiveness?" Nonetheless, I found myself there in Cambodia as a twenty-eight-year-old missionary, naïve and over-whelmed, yet committed to staying for the long haul.

When I first arrived in Cambodia in 1992, I had all the passion in the world, but I lacked wisdom—despite my missions experiences in cross-cultural ministry in the USA. There existed a huge gap between my passion and my ability to put into practice sound missiological[1] principles. This gap is normal for any mission-ary who has freshly arrived in a region and among a people, but the rate at which cross-cultural communicators close that gap varies from person to person.

Missionaries who operate out of passion and yet lack strategic wisdom may find themselves in a dilemma similar to the monkeys described in a Tanzanian folktale I once read:

The rainy season that year had been the heaviest ever and the rivers had broken their banks. There were floods everywhere and the animals were all running up into the hills. The floods came so fast that many drowned except the lucky monkeys, who used their proverbial agility to climb up into the treetops.

They looked down on the surface of the water where the fish were swimming and gracefully jumping out of the water as if they were the only ones enjoying the devastating flood.

One of the monkeys saw the fish and shouted to his companion: "Look down, my friend, look at those poor creatures. They are going to drown. Do you see how they struggle in the water?"

"Yes," said the other monkey. "What a pity! Probably they were late in escaping to the hills because they seem to have no legs. How can we save them?"

"I think we must do something. Let's go close to the edge of the flood where the water is not deep enough to cover us, and we can help them to get out."

So the monkeys did just that. They started catching the fish, but not without difficulty. One by one, they brought them out of the water and put them carefully on the dry land.

After a short time, there was a pile of fish lying on the grass motion-less. One of the monkeys said, "Do you see? They were tired, but now they are just sleeping and resting. Had it not been for us, my friend, all these poor people without legs would have drowned."

The other monkey said, "They were trying to escape from us because they could not understand our good intentions. But when they wake up, they will be very grateful because we have brought them salvation."[2]

This folktale teaches that what one thinks is good from his frame of reference is not necessarily good from another's, an important lesson to remember when working cross-culturally. The monkeys' encounter with the fish reflect some of my own experiences in Cambodia. I saw. I empathized. I reacted, and I messed up. Bottom line? I now do many things differently, as hindsight serves as my guide.

Although it is not easy, the ongoing process of recognizing, evaluating, and embracing my mistakes has been very important. Embracing a mistake is like embracing a friend who is willing to tell me the truth. Morris Kline, a professor of mathematics, once wrote: "The most fertile source of insight is hindsight."[3] Erwin McManus eloquently states, "Problems, obstacles, and challenges can either become the markers of our limits and limitations, or they can become the spring-board into a whole new world."[4]

A devastating yet true story that occurred in Cambodia in the 1990s mirrors the Tanzanian folktale. An American evangelist came to Cambodia during a very delicate and politically charged time. Some local pastors and missionaries feared that a high-profile evangelistic crusade in the stadium of the capital city was pre-mature and anti-strategic for Cambodia. Nonetheless, the event occurred as planned. Advertisements about the crusade led Cambodians to believe that heal-ing was guaranteed to all who attended. Many people sold all their land or animals to secure transportation to this event. Those who didn't receive healing began rioting, along with other disgruntled instigators. The evangelist was escorted back to his five-star hotel, and he eventually rushed out of the country. With the North American evangelist gone, the local churches suffered the repercussions of gov-ernment crackdowns. The outsiders ministered; the insiders suffered.

This event and the evangelist's name became a way to demean Christianity. A whole ten years later, I was watching local television when a Cambodian polit-ical leader, who was running for a key position in the government, delivered a campaign speech. To emphasize his integrity to potential voters, he exclaimed, "I will not lie to you like Mr.— did!" Let that sink in: an evangelistic method imple-mented in the '90s fueled such animosity toward Christianity in the culture that ten years later, a political leader was able to use this "Jesus event" as an example of fraudulence.

Why do I tell this story? To drive home the point that what we do as cross-cultural ministers can have a powerful effect on a country either for or against a movement for Christ. Although our cross-cultural ministry strategies are almost always well intended, they can actually hinder genuine growth of the church of Jesus Christ within nations. Our imprint upon another culture cannot be instantly recalled. As missionaries, our words and actions carry weight for years to come—the good, the bad, and the ugly. Am I trying to scare you? Yes and no. I am not trying to scare you from sharing your life and faith with others in different parts of the world. However, I am trying to scare you into soaking yourself in as much practical training about the indigenous church as possible.

Sixteen years in Cambodia have given me the rare opportunity to observe the effects of missions within an unreached people group from the pioneer stage to the birth and development of an existing church and ministries within Cambodia. My long-term experience has developed within me an understanding of missions in a long-term sense—had I not stayed in Cambodia for a significant length of time, I believe I would have a completely flawed understanding of the working out of missions. I will forever be on a learning curve, but at this point in time, I desire to draw you into the journey and pass on some of my lessons to those who are preparing to serve on the mission field, those who are presently serving on the mission field, those who are praying and giving on the home front, and those who influence missions in any form or fashion—for we all intrinsically impact the Great *Com-mission* together.

Some teachers prefer to take people forward and let the past remain in the past. But I believe that the vulnerabilities of our yesterdays help shape fresh alternatives for our todays. Let's learn from yesterday to make tomorrow even better.

CHAPTER TWO

COMMON GROUND

One of my favorite coffee shops is called Uncommon Grounds. It operates out of a two-story historic home in uptown Minneapolis. At first glance, it looks like an odd place to ground coffee beans and sip on a latte, but there is nowhere more ideal to sit at a table and read a good book. Uncommon Grounds has become a common place for many to gather, rest, or study while enjoying their favorite coffee.

Before we plunge into the meat of this book, I desire to take some time to establish "common ground" regarding a few key terms and phrases throughout this book. So I invite you to enjoy a cup of coffee or tea while you read.

WHAT IS "CHURCH"?

My personal definition of *church* has nothing to do with buildings, budgets, or butts in seats (Jim Henderson's words, not mine).[1] Rather, I think of church as a group of people who mutually support one another in their transformational journey under the lordship of Jesus Christ, multiplying within and beyond their community.

Acts 2:42–47 and Matthew 28:18–20 reveal the communal, transformational, and multiplying components of the church:

> They devoted themselves to the apostles' teaching and to the fellowship, to the breaking of bread and to prayer. Everyone was filled with awe, and many wonders and miraculous signs were done by the apostles. All the believers were together and had everything in common. Selling their possessions and goods, they gave to anyone as he had need. Every day they continued to meet together in the temple courts. They broke bread in their homes and ate together with glad and sincere hearts, praising God and enjoying the favor of all the people. And the Lord added to

their number daily those who were being saved. (Acts 2:42–47)

Then Jesus came to them and said, "All authority in heaven and on earth has been given me. Therefore go and make disciples of all nations, baptizing them in the name of the Father and of the Son and of the Holy Spirit, and teaching them to obey everything I have commanded you. And surely I am with you always, to the very end of the age." (Matthew 28:18–20)

Because "fellowship of believers" is an unwieldy term, I use the words *church* and *church planting* throughout this book. At times, context will dictate that church refer to buildings, budgets, and butts in the seats, but in general, I invite you not to allow the terms church or church planting to lock you into any preconceived prescription of how church has to be based on your experience.

WHAT IS "INDIGENOUS"?

Missionaries originally borrowed the term *indigenous* from agriculture. Different species of plants are conditioned to grow naturally and abundantly within specific environments. Context, such as type of soil and weather patterns, enables the plants to thrive. Likewise, the term indigenous partnered with the word church refers to the process of churches growing naturally and abundantly within their given cultural contexts. In other words, an indigenous church should be influenced by and relevant to the local context.

The term *nonindigenous church* refers to a church within a local context that becomes merely a projection of the missionary or church planter's context and therefore struggles to grow and impact its own surroundings.

I once read a statement that maintained a ministry could be completely indigenous before being fully administered by locals within a respective context. The key word here is "administered." What does *administer* mean? According to dictionary.reference.com, it means "to manage (affairs, a government, etc.); have executive charge of." I would not deem a ministry indigenous while foreign missionaries have administrative authority. The ethos of a ministry often flows out of the leader. If the administrator is foreign, most likely his ethos will be foreign.

On the other hand, a local church may operate with local leadership, but still rely on foreign funds to implement core biblical functions such as evangelism, support for internal leaders, meeting needs within the body, showing compassion to their communities, and teaching the Word of God. This dependency on out-siders is equally detrimental to a truly indigenous church.

Below, I have written a three-part characterization of *indigenous* derived from three missiologists. These characteristics form my framework of understanding and are core to this book.

1) "Reflects the cultural soul of the society,"[2] as stated by Donald McGavran.
2) "Generated from within,"[3] as shared by David Garrison. Garrison explains that within an unreached people, an outsider may plant the first church or churches, but as promptly as possible, insiders should drive church planting.
3) Evidence of self-image, self-functioning, self-determining, self-support-ing, self-propagating, and self-giving, as taught by Dr. Alan Tippett.[4]

I summarize the experts' definitions of the indigenous church in the following manner: *An indigenous church is a community of believers under the lordship of Jesus Christ who culturally reflect the soul of the society around them and who have the desire and ability to sustain and multiply themselves in every facet of life and ministry.*

Dr. Alan Tippett's six "self principles" often cause resistance in people who feel that the emphasis on "self" is imposing a value of Western individualism that is not common in much of the world. Others conclude that emphasizing self undermines dependence on God.

"Self" may not be the best word choice, but that does not negate the effec-tiveness of Dr. Tippett's principles. Self-control is one of the fruits of the Spirit listed in Galatians 5:23, and Paul instructs Timothy to exercise self-discipline in 2 Timothy 1:7. In both of these cases, it does not mean that we can exercise self-control and self-discipline without the Holy Spirit or other believers in Christ. By contrast, Paul's instructions point to an intentional degree of self-commitment and self-surrender involved in the process.

Likewise, Dr. Tippett was not inviting disciples and churches in various nations of the world to be independent with the kind of independence that flows from selfishness and arrogance. Rather, he desired to see disciples and churches develop a healthy image of their own role within their cultural context and carry out that role with dependence on God rather than dependence on missionaries in areas of function, support, propagation, and giving.

Several entities who understand the heart behind the "self-principles" have tweaked the wording without dismissing the principles. Trans World Radio (TWR) and HJCB Global titled one of their symposiums "From Unhealthy Dependency to Faith-Reliance." Charles Brock, the author of *Indigenous Church Planting*, used the phrase "Christ-sustained ability"[5] instead of "self-sustaining," based on 2 Corinthians 3:4–6a: "Such confidence as this is ours through Christ before God. Not that we are competent in ourselves to claim anything for ourselves, but our competence comes from God. He has made us competent as ministers of a new covenant." All that to say, when it comes to the "self" principles, do not throw the baby out with the bathwater.

WHAT SELF-RELIANCE IS NOT

This book includes a significant amount of emphasis on self-reliance. Self-reliance in the context of indigenous church life does not mean living and working apart from God or the body of Christ. Rather, self-reliance encourages reliance on God and the indigenous body of Christ (the local community of believers) versus harmful dependence on the affluence of those far removed from a local context.

I use the words *self-reliance, self-supporting,* and *self-sustaining* throughout this book with an emphasis on local stewardship and local servanthood.

MOVEMENTS FOR CHRIST

Throughout this book, I will also refer to movements. In some parts of the world, the word *movement* has political connotations. (For that reason, it should be used cautiously outside of missions circles.) In the case of this book, I am using the term strictly in the realm of missions. There are three types of movements readily described by those who study and implement cross-cultural missions: insider movements, people movements, and church planting movements (CPMs).

An *insider movement*, according to Rebecca Lewis, is:

...any movement to faith in Christ where a) the gospel flows through pre-existing communities and social networks, and where b) believing families, as valid expressions of the Body of Christ, remain inside their socioreligious communities, retaining their identity as members of that community while living under the Lordship of Jesus Christ and the authority of the Bible.[6]

A *people movement*, according to David Hesselgrave, is a:

Phenomenon of a significant number of the people of one tribe, class, or caste converting to Christ together.[7]

A *church planting movement*, according to David Garrison, is:

...a rapid multiplication of indigenous churches planting churches that sweeps through a people group or population segment.[8]

Rebecca Lewis helps us see the difference between an insider movement and a church planting movement:

Please note that Garrison (2004) has defined "church planting movements," as opposed to "insider movements", in the following manner: "Church Planting Movements, though opting for indigenous house church models rather than traditional church structures, nevertheless make a clean break with their former religion and redefine themselves with a distinctly Christian identity. The resulting movement is indigenously led and locally contextualized." (Garrison 2004, "Church Planting Movements vs. Insider Movements, p.154, IJFM 21:4). So the main differences between "insider movements" and "church planting movements" lie in the nature of the "house churches" (pre-existing social networks turning to Christ rather than artificial aggregate groupings) and the social identity of those involved (retained versus changed). In both movements the churches are not institutionalized, and the people in both movements share a new spiritual identity as members of the Kingdom of God and disciples of Jesus Christ. In the case of "insider movements", however, this new spiritual identity is not confused or eclipsed by a new social identity.[9]

Another missional movement that is being written about, talked about, and implemented in the twenty-first century is the *apostolic movement*. Alan Hirsch and Dave Ferguson define such a movement this way:

A missional church will always express itself as a reproducing church that multiplies new sites and new churches. A missional people involves Christ followers sent as agents of good news in every sphere and domain of life (work, play, politics, economics, education, and so on). When you add these two together, you have the missional equation of an apostolic movement.[10]

Hirsch and Ferguson have created a simple equation to explain the above:

Multiplication Church Planting + The Missions of All People Everywhere
= Apostolic Movement.[11]

One of my yearnings is that all missionaries and indigenous peoples contribute to movements—the act or process of moving. The kingdom of God should be spontaneously and intentionally moving and taking root in every person and people group throughout the nations—to the ends of the earth.

My goal in writing this book is not to promote one type of movement over another, but rather to share how North Americans who do missions can hinder and/or cultivate movements for Christ in countries not their own. So as not to lock anyone into one type of movement, I am going to use the phrase "movement for Christ" when speaking of movements, unless the context deems otherwise.

GLOBALIZATION

Failing to address globalization in a book on cross-cultural missions would be like trying to ignore the fact that my nose exists on my face. Globalization is a complex reality which makes my head spin.

As a little girl, I pictured oceans as individual bodies of water, almost like water continents. It took me awhile to realize that the oceanic divisions created by men and women are actually connected. If I were a fish, I wouldn't have to take a plane to travel from the Indian Ocean to the North Atlantic Ocean. Globalization reminds me of the ocean. People all over the world are becoming interconnected at a fast pace and throughout a vast territory. Professor and author David Held, who has great experience in the field of international relations and is a prime resource person on globalization, states:

Drugs, crime, sex, war, disease, people, ideas, images, news, information, entertainment, pollution, goods, and money now all travel the globe. They are crossing national boundaries and connecting the world on an unprecedented scale and with previously unimaginable speed. The lives of ordinary people everywhere in the world seem increasingly to be shaped by events, decisions, and actions that take place far away from where they live and work. Cultures, economies, and politics appear to merge across the globe through rapid exchange of information, ideas, and knowledge, and the investment strategies of global corporations.[12]

In the 1990s, life was much slower and less connected in Cambodia. I remember the days when everyone in my organization had access to only one phone, located in an office. Our mail was hand-carried from Thailand on a monthly basis. On the flip side, when I was in America for furloughs, I had little, if any, contact with Cambodians. Today, I am connected with many friends in Cambodia through Facebook. Wow! The earth is still a big globe, but we have figured out how to connect ourselves. Globalization is a part of all of us in one form or another.

Although globalization is upon us, the world is not tamed. Globalization itself has a wild side that is impossible to predict: we cannot know how this change will intricately affect all lives upon this earth. World scholars busy themselves trying to describe and express their opinions about globalization. In terms of missions and the gospel, we have much to think about! For the most part, I do not plan to tackle globalization in this book. But recognizing that globalization is a context in which we all now operate, I will leave you with a few thoughts about it.

Globalization can be both the heads and tails side of a coin—good and bad; hopeful and fearful; embraced and shunned. Globalization can be the King Kong of the world or its Florence Nightingale—maybe both at the same time. Globalization is a paradox. On the one hand, easy access to one another throughout the world has caused people to respect and explore each other's differences. At the same time, accessibility increases prejudice and the drive to preserve one's territory. While missionaries are excited about how many countries are open to the ways of the West, other countries are becoming diametrically opposed to the West and Christianity. Globalization offers amazing opportunities and unprecedented ways to efficiently connect, communicate, and influence one another. Unfortunately, globalization also allows the rubbish and icky stuff of different societies to cross boundaries at a rapid and influential pace.

What does this mean to us? First, while we take advantage of the opportunities of globalization, we need to leave our icky stuff at home as much as possible. Second, we should take steps to ensure that globalization does not become another excuse for the West to practice paternalism in the disguise of advancing God's kingdom.

Let's keep in mind the Golden Rule for Missions according to Dutch missiologist Hendrik Kraemer as our feet bring good news:

To have a genuine and untiring interest in the whole of people's lives—their ideas, sentiments, religion and institutions—for Christ's sake, and for the sake of the people themselves…[13]

And how can they preach unless they are sent? As it is written, "How beautiful are the feet of those who bring good news!" (Romans 10:15). I want to ensure that my feet are indeed beautiful by not trampling over other people's cultures with a mindset that America has arrived on the scene.

CHAPTER THREE

"THE THINNING" REVISITED

In the early 1960s, there were approximately two thousand followers of Christ in Cambodia. The country was home to viable and growing churches guided by both trained pastors and lay leaders. Shockingly, something happened which thinned out the Cambodian church to three hundred adherents. What could have possibly thinned out the church so radically: persecution, natural disaster, a surge in Buddhism?

I know of no better way to set the stage for this book than by sharing with you the story of "The Thinning," as author Don Cormack calls it in his book *Killing Fields Living Fields*, and its bearing on today. At the same time, how my life intersects and interlocks with the survivors of the Killing Fields is a huge component of my story and the words written in this book.

In *Killings Fields Living Fields*, Don Cormack traces the history of the Cambodian (Khmer)[1] evangelical church from the 1920s to the 1990s, sharing heartfelt testimonies and the church's historical and political backdrop. Below, I share several stages of Cormack's account of the Cambodian evangelical church and then look at how eventually my own life intersected with the *Killing Fields Living Fields* story of Cambodia.

THE BEGINNING OF THE CAMBODIAN EVANGELICAL CHURCH AND BIBLE SCHOOL

The Cambodian Evangelical Church had her humble beginnings among rice farmers in the mid-1920s. A farmer and his three male companions purposely headed on a seven-kilometer hike to Battambang, a province in northwestern Cambodia, to hear about a God called Jesus.

As the men walked, they passed by everything that represents life for Cambodians. I can picture their trek even now as I reflect on the quaintness of Cambodia in my early years of living there. Young rice seedlings peek up after the dry season. A boy leads his cows as an ornery one tries to go the other direction. The monks in their saffron robes go from house to house collecting donated rice in an effort to help Buddhist followers make merit. Spirit houses of every shape and size are as common as the stone water jars in front of each family home.

The man leading the way, Uncle Has, and his three friends, finally reached the place where a missionary was sharing about Jesus. After listening and ample conversation, the farmers began their walk home, pondering everything they had heard. Upon arriving home, Uncle Has shared all he could remember with household members and several onlookers. Uncle Has and his extended family read and talked about Jesus from the Gospel of Luke, which had been translated into the Khmer language, into the late hours of the night.

Has and his family continued that conversation as part of a lifetime of sharing Christ with others. Uncle Has, who had dared to seek out a strange foreign man who talked of Jesus, became the firstfruits of the gospel in Cambodia.

In the following years, the gospel spread through Has's network of relationships, and house churches were formed. As the church grew, there came a demand for capable leaders. In 1925, missionaries started a Bible school/seminary in their home in Battambang to meet this demand. The seminary became a focal point of Cambodian church life because it was the place leaders and lay leaders were sent out from and came to in order to regroup. For the next fifty years, the Bible school provided a central location for studying, administrating, gathering, and recuperating. Amazingly, the church increased to two thousand adherents by the '50s and early 1960s.

THE THINNING

In the mid 1960s, something happened to thin out this expanding church. During this season of steady growth, the key foreign missions board relating to the Cambodian evangelical church made an impacting decision. I will quote Cormack's thorough description:

It was at this time that the foreign mission board announced it was phasing out its monetary aid to the churches in order to encourage them to become self-supporting. This action was received with considerable dismay and reluctance by the Khmer workers and their congregations. For a few difficult and testing years it appeared that practically every worker might be lost to the church, as one by one they left their ministries to accept more lucrative employment elsewhere. Although it was a painful decision, and some might argue a time bomb which should never have been left so long before defusing, the mission stuck to its resolve in the interest of developing a strong and healthy indigenous church, and not one forever tied to the apron strings of the foreign missionary society...

It is little wonder, therefore, that all those who had "entered the ministry" primarily because they saw it as a secure and respectable career, in which they could always rely on the patronage of wealthy foreigners for support or for other material or social perks, soon became disillusioned with the reality of grueling and thankless toil with no substantial reward. These were among the first to be thinned out, returning to secular employment or taking up positions with other organizations willing to pay them well enough. The education, social skills and English language they had acquired at the Bible School did open other doors to them. This hireling mentality would continue to plague the church in later years, indeed right up to the present day. Beginning in the early 1970s Christian relief organizations and various cults all eager for recruits, workers, and instant "indigeneity" to impress the homeside support base. With half-digested and popular missiological slogans, they were willing to pay well for Khmer "membership." This patronage syndrome, so entrenched throughout Khmer social, political and military culture, was to become a fundamental weakness in the Cambodian Church, stunting its true indigenous growth, distorting its perception of Christian discipleship and service; exposing it to attack and ridicule, and endlessly dividing it by creating all manner of jealousies and misunderstandings within the community of believers.[2]

"The Thinning" was not due to some uncontrollable force such as persecution, but rather the harmful effects of "growing a church" to be dependent on outside initiative and funds.

A REMNANT OF THREE HUNDRED BELIEVERS AND PASTOR YEAH'S PROCLAMATION

There was one positive side to the Thinning: the strategy of the missionaries to overcome unhealthy dependency on foreign resources sifted out superficial believers from sincere believers and left the evangelical church with three hundred tried-and-true members. As Gideon's numerically whittled army of three hundred became an effective force, so did the three hundred faithful Cambodian disciples. Pastor Yeah was one of those three hundred believers, and he determined in his heart not to allow the church to be thinned out again. Cormack records:

> ...men like Pastor Yeah were determined that it should never be allowed to slip back into a state of lethargy and dependence. Surely after forty years they were ready to stand mature in Christ! If and when the missionaries returned, their relationship with the church and their responsibilities would have to be carefully negotiated. It would be necessary to emphasise the importance of the Khmer church managing its own affairs, fully supporting itself, and realising its obligation to take the gospel to all Cambodians, both within and around the country's borders.[3]

REVIVAL IN THE MIDST OF TURMOIL

In the early 1970s, the sights and sounds of civil war and political upheaval caused a revival among the body of three hundred believers in Christ. The beloved king of Cambodia, Sihanouk, began to hold hands with the Vietnamese government, a no-no for Cambodians who considered Vietnam a historical enemy. Sihanouk allowed the North Vietnamese to move weapons in Cambodian territory to aid them against the South Vietnamese, who were backed by America. The American military unjustly dropped bombs on innocent Cambodian villagers who lived near the border of Vietnam. National approval of King Sihanouk began to wane, and this once godlike king was overthrown by a military-led coup d'état. A dark cloud of uneasiness spread over Cambodia.

In the midst of this chaos, a rebel group of Cambodians decided it was time for them to strike—like a snake patiently waiting in the bushes for its prey. Commanded by their leader, Pol Pot—who was influenced by communism in the 1950s in Paris—this rebel group slowly cooked their own porridge of communism, adding secret ingredients like anti-intellectualism and agrarianism. This communist regime, referred to as the Khmer Rouge—meaning Red Khmer—fervently worked to unleash their plan of turning the country back to year zero upon an unsuspecting people.

The Khmer Rouge started on the outskirts of Cambodia and made its way inward, village by village, saying, "You are the 'old people!' Anyone who lives in the city or is unlike you, they are 'new people.' They are your enemies!" The Khmer Rouge put weapons in children's hands and planted seeds of hate for the city dwellers. Those countryside people who eluded the grip and mind control of the Khmer Rouge flooded into the capital city of Phnom Penh. These exhausted refugees brought nothing with them except for horrific stories of suffering experienced under the fist of the Khmer Rouge.

American carpet bombing, a coup, Vietnamese animosity, civil war, and rumors of a mysterious communist Khmer regime produced a restlessness and unnerving fear among the Cambodians. Whereas in the past Cambodians had persecuted Christians, they now sought them out to find some sort of relief from the insanity around them. The body of Christ experienced unprecedented growth. Over the next five years, churches, cell groups, and gatherings spontaneously multiplied due to the nation's spiritual vacuum and desperation to find hope. A spiritual awakening was upon Cambodia—but right on the heels of this spiritual blessing was the Khmer Rouge's aggressive arrival into the capital city.

The Killing Fields

April 17, 1975 became the day of a horrible nightmare for Cambodians. Odd-looking Cambodians, in black pajamas with identical haircuts, cradled weapons as they entered Phnom Penh. With mixed feelings, the Cambodians looked on as the Khmer Rouge announced the end of the civil war and their instant rule. On the one hand, the drawn-out civil war was over. On the other hand, Cambodians didn't know what to expect from this imposing regime.

The Khmer Rouge designed a festive parade to act as a smoke screen and gain favor with the Cambodian masses. The bogus parade worked, and Cambodians let down their guard. The country was suddenly under the spell of Pol Pot's madmen. When the parade was barely over, the Khmer Rouge announced an immediate evacuation of the city. "America is going to bomb the city," they warned. Three million people, confused and frantic, evacuated the city at the mere word of this new regime.

As students of recent history know, the seeming rescue operation was really a trick to carry out an evil worse than genocide. The evacuation was nothing but a ploy to gain instantaneous control of a population and destroy city life and all forms of infrastructure. While the Cambodian people were vulnerable and defenseless, the Khmer Rouge organized the entire country into backbreaking egalitarian labor camps. If this wasn't sick enough, the Khmer Rouge systematically broke down the family system by separating family members and placing them in different work units. Children were taken away from their parents to be raised by the Angkar—the Khmer Rouge organization. "We have eyes of a pineapple," warned the Angkar. People lived in constant fear, always wondering when those eyes would fall upon them. Cambodians watched as friends and family members were marched away, knowing they would never see them again. "March ahead! We are moving you to a different work location. You are going to your new home and all is well," maintained the Khmer Rouge oppressors. What those words really meant was "You are going to be hit over the head, and your bodies will line the graves that we have dug for you."

The Khmer Rouge tortured and exterminated the educated and skilled: government officials, civil workers, doctors, lawyers, teachers, bankers, librarians, musicians, Buddhist monks, and the list goes on with no end in sight. Pol Pot's regime eventually executed people for the smallest infractions: singing out loud, snatching up a bug to eat, collapsing from hunger, or escaping to find a family member. The fields were stained with the blood of Cambodian men, women, and children, hence the label "The Killing Fields." Would this madness never end?

THE YEAR ZERO EXPERIMENT ENDS

The year zero experiment finally came to an end in 1979 due to an offensive attack by the Vietnamese troops which forced the Khmer Rouge to relinquish power and hide out in the jungle. After five years of insanity and approximately two million dead, the international community finally took notice of the nightmare from which Cambodians could not awaken.

The dispersal of the Khmer Rouge opened the way for many Cambodians to flee to the border of Thailand. Cambodian refugees became dislocated people without a home. Eventually, some of these refugees settled in North America. It was then that my life intersected with the Cambodians, and the direction of my life was changed forever.

LIFE AMONG THE SURVIVORS

My Cambodian journey began as I walked through the energized halls of my high school in St. Paul, Minnesota, in 1980. I never imagined that my Cambodian classmates, who had been dislocated from their homes in Cambodia, would alter the path of my life so intensely that the place they once called home would become my home for sixteen years.

As my friends and I walked through the hall to our next class, we saw the new students. Our teachers had told us that our high school would receive a group of Cambodian refugees at some point; I guessed this was the day. The Cambodian new arrivals looked scared to death and stared straight ahead, not wanting to meet anyone's eyes. As my friends passed through the inquisitive stage, they turned into peer tormentors, making fun of every oddity. "Look, they have flip-flops on in the middle of winter!" a fellow student scoffed. The teasing continued in the lunchroom as the Cambodians struggled to eat American food or brought their own strange-smelling food. If students did not tease them, they stayed clear of them, forcing the Cambodian students into a very lonely state.

Unlike my classmates, I was stuck in the inquisitive stage. I talked with these new Cambodian arrivals, ate lunch with them, and overwhelmed them with questions. In time, an idea came to mind. I would start an English class during my study hour and teach these Cambodian students English. To be honest, I wasn't the best example to them—I taught my Cambodian friends how to ditch school and share their free lunch tickets with me. Nonetheless, I truly cared about their well-being as they adjusted to a new environment and culture.

While all of this was happening, I was growing in my newfound faith in Jesus Christ.

As I established trust with the Cambodian students, they told me their stories, and suddenly their plight impinged upon my comfort zone. I never in a million years could have imagined the horrors that my new friends had endured. One teenage boy told me about his experience.

"The soldiers accuse me of stealing a potato," he said. "I do not take potato, but no one listen to me. They drag me to a field, and I afraid so much. A soldier grab my arms and tie my hands behind my back. I do not know what is happening. Two soldiers pick me up and put me in large sack. I feel the ants bite me everywhere. I scream so loud. I can do nothing. The soldiers push me out of bag and I crawl forward. I almost die."

I understood the details of my fellow student's personal story, but I did not understand who those heartless soldiers were or what their mission was. Through more stories and ample conversation, I learned about what had happened to these precious Cambodians.

While the Cambodians' stories tore at my heart, my American friends tore at my self-esteem. They called me "The Asian Lover." Their words placed a crisis of choice in my life—and I chose my American friends. Their careless words swayed me, and I severed my relationships with the Cambodians. As far as I was concerned, my journey with Cambodians was a thing of the past.

After I graduated from high school in 1981, I attended North Central Bible

College in Minneapolis, Minnesota. From class to professors to chapel to fellow students, I received a feast of spiritual food. I had a talk with God that unfolded as follows:

"I am spiritually obese! I take in spiritual encouragement every day, but I do not give it out. God, is there some ministry or way in which I can serve others?"

The following day, a college friend approached me with a request. "Jean, how would you like to help me with a youth ministry?" I hadn't expected God to answer my prayer so quickly! Immediately, I asked my friend, "Who is in the youth group?"

His reply made my body tingle: "Mainly Cambodians, Hmong, and Vietnamese." God had given me a second chance! I vowed in my heart, *I will pick up from where I left off and rebuild relationships with Cambodians. God, forgive me for my detour.*

Every Friday, a group of anywhere between twenty and forty Southeast Asian youth gathered in a home, and I had the opportunity to tell them about the gospel. Throughout my college years, I rarely missed a Friday evening. I spent time in their homes and joined them in their celebrations. The interaction with Southeast Asians caused more questions to rise up within my heart: "Who is going to tell the Hmong that chicken sacrifices pale in relationship to God's sacrifice of his only Son? Who is going to tell the Cambodians that idols have eyes but cannot see and ears but cannot hear?"

These were dangerous questions to ask God, questions that God used to guide me into cross-cultural ministry. As soon as possible, I changed my major. In 1986, I graduated with a major in cross-cultural communications.

After college in 1986, I discovered that I could not go to Cambodia as I had hoped due to the postwar instability of the country. The Vietnamese occupation, communist rule, and Khmer Rouge attempts to regain power made it difficult for outsiders to visit or reside in Cambodia. As I felt discouraged, God redirected me with this thought: "Think of a people, not a place." This meant that I should start building relationships and sharing my faith with the approximately four thousand Cambodians who lived practically in my backyard in Minneapolis-St. Paul, Minnesota.

That year, I went to a Cambodian New Year celebration to purposefully build relationships with Cambodian people. At length, I conversed with Somaly, a Cambodian woman who was a teacher in Cambodia before the war broke out. Somaly committed to teach me the Cambodian (Khmer) language. Like a small child, I learned to recite the Cambodian alphabet, the largest alphabet of any language in the world. Within weeks, I met Somaly's extended family: eight members living in a one-bedroom house in the inner city.

With fear and trepidation, I asked Somaly's older sister, the head of the household, "Could I live with you?" This Cambodian family of eight was completely bewildered as to why I wanted to live with them, yet they welcomed me into their family. I put my bed in the hallway, the passageway from the kitchen to the only bedroom. I taped note cards on every object in the house, displaying the Khmer word for each object. This Cambodian family became my classroom for learning the language and culture.

After experiencing life with Somaly's family, I moved to an apartment building with approximately thirty refugee Cambodian families. I was the only non-Asian living among them. For six years, I lived among the refugee Cambodians in Minneapolis-St. Paul, inviting them to do life with God.

Finally, in 1990, I received notice from a friend that the Assemblies of God had pursued an opportunity with the Cambodian government to send a couple of missionaries there in a humanitarian capacity. Instantly, I called the powers that be and told them about my story and desire to go as a missionary to Cambodia. After I hung up the phone, I realized that, in the midst of my excitement, I had totally forgotten about any type of protocol or official channels. Even more amusing, I failed my language aptitude test with the Assemblies of God missions sending organization. What could they say? I already knew the Cambodian language. After raising funds, in July of 1992 I was in a plane on my way to Cambodia—a place referred to as the Killing Fields.

"THE THINNING" REVISITED?

I wasn't the only one who entered Cambodia in July of 1992. While 90 percent of the Christian Cambodians had been killed during the Khmer Rouge genocide, some believers had escaped to Thailand. Others joined the faith in the refugee camps. A portion of these believers returned to Cambodia and served as the foundation of the body of Christ. Furthermore, Christian humanitarian workers and missionaries like myself from various sending organizations began pouring into Cambodia.

After about six years in Cambodia, I began to see some of the same issues of unhealthy dependency that the first Cambodian evangelical church had experienced in the mid-1960s. I wondered if somehow we were revisiting or recreating the consequences of the Thinning through our own actions. Were we listening to Pastor Yeah, who had remained faithful through the self-supporting efforts of the Cambodian evangelical church in the 1960s and had determined to do things differently? Don Cormack's words became a haunting echo:

> ...and men like Pastor Yeah were determined that it should never be allowed to slip back into a state of lethargy and dependence. Surely after forty years they were ready to stand mature in Christ! If and when the missionaries returned, their relationship with the church and their responsibilities would have to be carefully negotiated. It would be necessary to emphasise the importance of the Khmer church managing its own affairs, fully supporting itself, and realising its obligation to take the gospel to all Cambodians, both within and around the country's borders.[4]

Did I learn from the foreign missions board that discovered its outside funding to be "a fundamental weakness in the Church of Cambodia, stunting its true indigenous growth"? Did I come alongside the remnant of believers and say, "You can manage your own affairs, support yourself, and take the gospel to all Cambodians, relying on God and his timetable. I am here to cheer you on," or did I outpace the fragile church and erect ministries at my pace and with my resources?

With half a decade of service in Cambodia already behind me, these types of questions began to bounce around in my mind like ping-pong balls in a spirited match. The questions didn't scare me, but drove me to become a forever student, constantly searching for ways to grow the indigenous church. From 1998 onward, I slowly but surely adjusted my missions practices to work more intentionally toward planting and affirming the indigenous church. This book is a by-product of my taking seriously the history of the Thinning and allowing Pastor Yeah's words to influence my ways of thinking and doing missions. I certainly do not have missions all figured out in this vast and complicated world, but I do strive to think and think again so as to improve my contribution to the Great Commission.

At the end of the day, apostolic pioneer missionaries have the responsibility to never cease thinking deeply and widely. A pioneer for the gospel of Christ will both start and prepare the way among the least reached and unreached of the world. Like John the Baptist, we have the grave responsibility to not promote our own agenda, but to step aside and allow Jesus to be visible as the dove descends upon him.

The next day John saw Jesus coming toward him and said, "Look, the lamb of God who takes away the sins of the world! This is the one I meant when I said, 'A man who comes after me has surpassed me because he was before me.' I myself did not know him, but the reason I came baptizing with water was that he might be revealed to Israel." Then John gave this testimony: "I saw the Spirit come down from heaven as a dove and remain on him." (John 1:29–32)

We have the awesome privilege to be a voice crying out in the wilderness: "Look, the Lamb of God who takes away the sins of the world!" How wonderful it is to point and then move aside as Christ brings the Spirit of God among a people, transforming them within their culture and not in spite of it.

In the next chapters, we will explore multiplication, indigeneity, and sustainability in detail. There are many words in this book, some based on good old-fashioned experience, some anointed by the Holy Spirit, and others mere opinion. I pray that the Holy Spirit will illuminate to you all that he has in mind for your role and context.

PART II

REFLECTION FOR PREMEDITATING

Multiplication, Indigeneity, and Sustainability

CHAPTER FOUR

PLAN FOR MULTIPLICATION:

MAKING DISCIPLES WHO MAKE DISCIPLES WITHIN EVERY COMMUNITY

"Pastor Veasna, my church is not motivated to plant other churches, and I am so busy implementing programs for the church members, I feel like I am plowing a field with no ox. Your church has planted numerous churches, which have planted other churches. Where does the motivation come from?"

"Pastor Sopheap, the vision was sown in our hearts and minds at the conception of our church. We have a mantra in our church: 'Bananas reproduce bananas and disciples reproduce disciples; mangoes reproduce mangoes and churches reproduce churches.' Multiplying is a part of our vision and is integrated into our practices as disciples of Christ and as a church. We pass this very mindset onto the churches we 'daughter' as well."

When I arrived in Cambodia in July of 1992, there were more landmines in the ground than people on it. Every way I turned, I saw the blatant red signs with a white skull and crossbones warning of danger. The landmines did not discriminate between animal or child, old man or militant. When stepped on, a mine mutilated its victims. Within post-genocide Cambodia, more than forty thousand amputees live without one limb or another, and sometimes without two limbs.

Disfigurement and missing limbs limit a person's mobility. As missionaries, we need to avoid burying missiological landmines. Missiological landmines are ways of perceiving and doing missions that maim the ability of first-generation disciples to multiply disciples among their own people and beyond. It does not matter how many unreached people groups missionaries minister among if they do their task in such a way that those respective people groups do not have the vision and capability to multiply themselves.

Dr. George Patterson, who has thirty-three years of missions experience in church planting movements, gives a clear description of what a movement for Christ includes:

> To start a movement for Christ among unreached people groups, which includes the planting of churches and the training of leaders that from the beginning have the spiritual authority, vision, and capability to multiply themselves without any necessary reference to the missionaries.[1]

Based on the conversation between Sopheap and Veasna at the opening of this chapter, we can see that multiplication does not just happen. Rather, missionaries need to aim for and plan for multiplication every step of the way. In this chapter, I reveal how I planted missiological landmines which robbed the first-generation Cambodian believers of the spiritual authority, vision, and capability to multiply themselves—and to invite us to be premeditators of multiplication.

MY GREATEST ASSET BECAME MY GREATEST STUMBLING BLOCK

Many people have said to me, "Knowing the Cambodian language and culture upon arriving in Cambodia must have been a great asset." My response is "yes and no." In some ways, my greatest asset became my greatest stumbling block. After I had waited to go to Cambodia for so long, I wanted to release years of pent-up passion. With the Cambodian language skills I had acquired while living among Cambodian refugees in the USA, I went to work almost immediately, sharing the gospel of Jesus Christ with the intention to plant a church in the capital city of Cambodia.

The drive *to do*, coupled with the *ability to do*, became a hindrance to me. My American mentality of redeeming the time and producing results influenced me to plant my first church in such a way as to hinder that local church's ability to daughter churches as part of its ongoing DNA. I was driven and impatient, which can be a dangerous combination no matter how well-intentioned!

I indeed did plant a church in Phnom Penh after only being in Cambodia for a short time. Today, that church has Cambodian pastors who are completely supported by the congregation, and they have planted a few churches here and there. I am thankful to God that he was faithful and blessed the labor of my hands in planting a sizable and influential church. But since then, I have come to learn what ingredients lead to the planting of churches and the training of leaders that from the beginning have the spiritual authority, vision, and capability to multiply themselves without any necessary reference to the missionaries—and what ingredients hinder such planting and training.

Rather than diving in immediately just because I could, I should have observed and involved myself in the culture much more intently and deeply. Worldview and the ingredients of multiplication, rather than instinct, should have guided my cross-cultural actions. In this way, I could have operated out of trained passion, rather than charging ahead in untrained passion that was roughly shaped by my exposure to Cambodian culture in an American setting and my North American church experience. If I could do my early missions years all over again, I would do nothing but be and learn before I dared to try anything formally.

The best way I can summarize my church planting experience in those initial years is with this phrase: "elephant churches."

Elephant Churches

In my early years in Cambodia, my friend Diane and I headed to a remote province called Ratanakiri in northeast Cambodia, home to mostly hill tribes. We had heard that some hill tribes used elephants for work, and we wanted to ride one. Unable to speak the hill tribe languages, we asked a Cambodian to introduce us to the Khmer Leou—"highlanders."

"Could you negotiate a ride on elephants for us?" we asked. The Cambodian gentleman politely led us to a Khmer Leou village. After arriving in this quaint village and exchanging pleasantries, we saw a man leading three elephants toward us—an actual family of three! Like a little kid, I could barely speak over the excitement rising up in my throat. The village leader pointed toward the elephants as a sign for us to mount these mammoth animals.

As if kneeling to pray, the mother and father elephant descended. Diane and I mounted the adults with ease, using their bended knees as stepladders. Off we rode, sitting in rough-woven baskets, with boys straddled around the necks of each elephant. True to its nature, the baby elephant plodded along behind us. Feeling like the queen of the jungle—without Tarzan—I surveyed the tribal houses and surrounding jungle as the elephants trotted along with authority.

This road is a bit narrow; I certainly don't want to share it with a vehicle, I said to myself. Before the thought even left my mind, there was sudden movement around me. The boys turned the full bodies of the adult elephants so their heads were facing into the thick bush and kept them as still as possible. Going forward was not an option, nor was backing up. I sat quietly, hoping my stillness would somehow keep the elephant from heading straight into the ravine. I heard the rumbling of a truck and realized the boys were keeping the elephants calm as this odd creature with four wheels came bouncing down the road. Forget balance!

Suddenly, I heard earsplitting sounds coming from the elephants. I turned to seek comfort from Diane. Diane? I don't think so! Her elephant was standing upright on its back two feet as if ready to ride into battle. Diane's eyes were bulging from her head, and before I could say something reassuring, her elephant took off on a wild run through the jungle. I broke into uncontrollable laughter as my elephant casually plodded along. Chiding myself—I might never see my friend again!—I bit my lip and searched for her down the path of broken trees and torn leaves. Finally, I saw her off in the distance. She was safe, but blood was trickling down the elephant's forehead. Diane explained, "The boy could not get the elephant to stop, and he accidentally hit the elephant with the sharp end of the ax instead of the dull end!"

Eventually, we reached a enchanting waterfall. The boys invited us to dismount the elephants to give us an opportunity to get closer. We were above the waterfall, so we stood as close to the edge as possible in order to see the water hit the rocks below. While Diane and I were thoroughly enthralled with the awe-inspiring view, I saw the baby elephant running toward us in a sideways strut. I knew this wasn't a circus act, and I wondered if it signaled a problem. Before we could discern the situation, the baby elephant shoved his backside into our backsides, nearly pushing us over the cliff. We staggered and quickly regained our balance. Before we could determine why this elephant wanted to murder us, he repositioned himself to make another hit. I shouted with all my might, "Run!" As we were running and trying to act composed at the same time, the boys motioned for us to remount the elephants. What a relief to be out of reach!

As we headed back, my physical-therapist friend adjusted her gluteus maximus due to a bit of soreness. When I saw the edge of the village, I knew—with a mixture of gladness and sadness—that our ride was almost over.

The mother and father elephant pulled right up to the veranda of a stilted house. Like Olympian gymnasts, we delicately walked across the backs of the elephants and onto the veranda. While we chatted with the village chief, who knew a little of the Khmer language, we heard an odd commotion. As we peered down, the baby elephant wrapped his trunk around the bamboo ladder—the only way down from the stilted house—and the little thief ran away in the other direction! Certainly, that elephant was in his terrible twos! What an adventure, and much more exhilarating than a predictable tourist elephant ride.

Church planting practitioners have recently been using the reproductive system of elephants and rabbits to speak about multiplication. An elephant is fertile four times a year. The elephant has one baby per pregnancy, and she carries the baby for twenty-two months (we women think we have it bad!). An elephant reaches sexual maturity at the age of eighteen, so our baby elephant friend would be with its parents for quite some time yet! An elephant couple would add merely one member to the family after three years. Elephants eat a large amount. One baby is plenty!

Rabbits, on the other hand, are much more active! Rabbits are fertile most of the time. No curfew is going to prevent the inevitable. A female rabbit has an average of seven babies per pregnancy, with a one-month gestation period. Female rabbits reach sexual maturity at four months. (Forget the curfew. Lock them up!) According to experts, one rabbit family consisting of one male and one female could optimally increase to 460 million rabbits within just three years.[2]

Apply this to church growth, if you will: an elephant church reproduces very slowly, if at all. It plods along, adding members and losing members in spurts—the revolving-door syndrome. The needs, plans, and maintenance of the existing church always take precedence over reproducing new churches. An elephant church lacks the spiritual authority, vision, and capability to reproduce disciples and plant other churches. In contrast, rabbit churches have the DNA to multiply rapidly.

In my early years of missionary work in Cambodia, I settled for a ministry of planting elephant churches. The first church I planted was and is successful in adding members, conducting ministries, and teaching the Word of God. Yet, due to the way I planted the church, the church is stuck in elephant mode. I did not encode them with the DNA that mangoes reproduce mangoes, churches reproduce churches, disciples reproduce disciples, and pastors reproduce pastors.

One day after teaching on multiplication and comparing the process to the reproduction of elephants and rabbits, I was given a silver pendant of a rabbit for a gift—symbolic of my key lesson. Enough people mistook it for the Playboy bunny that the pendant is now safely tucked away in my jewelry box, but my vision and understanding of multiplication is now a part of my DNA, and I will continue to pass it on whenever I can.

CONGLOMERATE CHURCH PLANTING SPELLS E-L-E-P-H-A-N-T

How did I go about planting my first church? As a missionary in a new context,

I formed friendships with my language teacher, a seller at the market, relatives of my Cambodian friends in America, and several others. I said to myself, "These will be the members of my first church plant!", and sure enough, I gathered them together to learn from the Word of God, pray, and worship. Some people came with mixed motives, such as to find a job or to learn English; many people came and went; but several people developed a sincere relationship with God through Jesus Christ. I sat back many times and smiled about the great potential of this Cambodian church. The church grew, and eventually this group of believers settled into a church building within a neighborhood where they had no prior relationships. This looked like an incredible opportunity to reach more people in a new area!

Unfortunately, the method I had used to pioneer this church partially paralyzed it. Missiological landmines stole the arms and legs necessary to multiply disciples.

Let's retrace my steps. I started the church by extracting individuals from their everyday network of relationships to experience God in an imposed community. Their church friends, from a variety of communities, in some ways became more important than their own communities. Yet, in actuality, the members of the church only saw each other once a week. The community members viewed those who attended the church as seekers of the foreigner's god, thus a dichotomy of "us" and "them" developed. The believers in Christ were reluctant to share their faith outside the walls of the church with families and friends. Additionally, the believers practiced their faith in the church setting, but struggled to live out their faith in everyday life with the people they did life with. Moreover, the church members had difficulty developing relationships with people surrounding the actual church building because the community saw them as believers in a foreigner's god who had just plopped into their community uninvited.

Unwittingly, I had implemented a church planting approach which Donald McGavran calls the "one-by-one out of the social group" method or the "conglomerate church" approach. An experienced missionary, author, and former professor of missions at Fuller Theological Seminary in Pasadena, California, McGavran states that approximately ninety out of one hundred missionaries plant churches in this manner. Steven Hawthorne, in The Perspectives Study Guide, summarizes McGavran's description of how conglomerate churches are planted:

> He calls it the "one-by-one out of the social group" method. "Extraction" is the practice of urging an individual or family to divorce themselves

from their family and culture in order to follow Christ. The impetus for extraction can come from a combination of missionaries and local churches pulling the convert toward a foreign or Christianized sub-culture. Alternatively, extraction can take place when members of the local culture ostracize or "squeeze out" the follower of Christ from their society. Either way, it's extraction. It invariably slows down, and often entirely freezes, a movement to Christ.[3]

Keeping in mind that the ultimate goal is a movement for Christ, extraction is indeed an enemy of multiplication. In contrast, Donald McGavran urges us to implement a "people movement" approach:

> The goal is not one single conglomerate church in a city or a region...
> The goal must be a cluster of growing, indigenous congregations, every
> member of which remains in close contact with his kindred.[4]

If I had read Donald McGavran's article before I went to Cambodia, I would have been equipped to implement a "people movement" approach. Instead, I fumbled around way too much in the dark, doing that which came naturally to me as a North American.

THE TEST OF ANY WORK

As missionaries, it is important that we implement ways to evaluate our progress. Robert E. Coleman, in his classic book *The Master Plan of Evangelism*, motivates us to use multiplication criteria to measure our effectiveness:

> Are those who have followed us to Christ now leading others to him and teaching them to make disciples like ourselves? Note, it is not enough to rescue the perishing, though this is imperative; nor is it sufficient to build up newborn babes in the faith of Christ, although this too is necessary if the first fruit is to endure; in fact, it is not sufficient just to get them out winning souls, as commendable as this work may be. What really counts in the ultimate perpetuation of our work is the faithfulness with which our converts go out and make leaders out of their converts, not simply more followers...
>
> The test of any work of evangelism thus is not what is seen at the moment, or in the conference report, but in the effectiveness with which

the work continues in the next generation. Similarly the criteria on which a church should measure its success is not how many new names are added to the roll nor how much the budget is increased, but rather how many Christians are actively winning souls and training them to win the multitudes.[5]

Rabbit churches do not just happen. McGavran echoes the words of Robert Coleman:

> It is usually easy to start one single congregation in a new unchurched people group. What is truly difficult, but essential, is planting not one church, but a cluster of growing churches which reflects the cultural soul of society.[6]

If we want to plant indigenous movements for Christ that multiply within their own context and beyond, we need to be intentional about the process. Today, we often hear about the carbon footprint our generation is leaving for the next generation. The cry of the forward-thinking is that we must not leave behind a mess for others to clean up after we leave this earth. As missionaries, it is essential to consider what type of footprint we are leaving in the various countries we set foot in. We need to measure and assess the direct and indirect consequences of our presence and missions efforts. Do we need to revise our strategies so as to reduce our "foreign emissions" and "paternal footprints," and instead stimulate indigenous movements for Christ that have the God-given authority, vision, and capability to sustain and multiply these movements without dependency on missions entities?

The Great Commission involves multiplication: "Make disciples of all nations …teaching them to obey everything I commanded." Included among Jesus's commands is the command to make disciples.

As a prime scriptural example, Philip made a disciple of an Ethiopian dignitary, a process which included the prompting of the Holy Spirit, the Scriptures, the proclamation of Jesus, a relationship, the dignitary's chariot, a believing heart, and a body of water near the road. Nothing was imposed into the experience; rather, it unfolded naturally: two people in the right place at the right time, one person seeking and one person sharing. Is it possible that we complicate the discipleship-making process? Do we add on so many extras that we stifle the spontaneous work of the Holy Spirit? Do we create numerous static programs and expect people to come to us?

I personally miss the simplicity of multiplication occurring through natural relationships, which has often been replaced by program-focused ministries both in North America and around the world. I recall how John the Baptist, upon seeing Jesus, shouted, "Look, the Lamb of God, who takes away the sins of the world!" Andrew was drawn to Christ through John, and Andrew immediately found and led his brother, Simon Peter, to Jesus. When Philip encountered Jesus, like Andrew, he found Nathanael and told him all about Jesus (John 1:35–51). This chain reaction of find and tell is essential to the process of multiplication.

There is in nature a phenomenon called tonic immobility. Some animals, such as sharks and snakes, will enter a state of paralysis to mislead their predators. The predators assume the animals to be dead and move on to other possibilities. The basic concept is to become literally motionless to trick the enemy. While this works in the animal kingdom, it does not work in God's kingdom. In regard to movements for Christ, immobility becomes a permanent death, not a temporary state of paralysis.

Jesus was always on the move. The disciples were on the move. Paul was on the move. Multiplication involves movement. We tend to program the process of making disciples and then try to fit people into that program's mold. The more program-oriented we become, the more immobile we become. Exclusive Christian communities dependent upon buildings and programs within those buildings are not the answer to movements for Christ around the world.

Recently, I read about an urban garage-church movement among Hindus.[7] Instead of building a church and inviting people to come to it, the missionaries modeled house church within existing garages. One devoted Hindu man came to Christ in this garage setting. He became a follower of Christ, shared constantly among his network of relationships, and baptized those who believed in Jesus. These churches multiplied and were often referred to as "garage church." The missionaries did not plant a church by erecting a building and extracting people from here and there to function as church. The churches met in garages and were available and tangible to the neighbors of each respective garage. Garages were readily available from house to house, which enabled the church to grow with mobility and multiplication.

Mission Frontiers contains an article about Mir-Ibn-Mohammad, a Muslim-background believer who facilitated a movement for Christ in his birth village. "There are now thousands of home groups of those who have given their lives to Jesus, with each group serving about ten families. It is my passion to see all Muslims following Jesus within Islam," Mir-Ibn-Mohammad stated.[8] Mir-Ibn-Mohammad dedicated his life to Jesus because of the miraculous intervention of Jesus. While he was drowning, Jesus held him up in the water. Mir-Ibn-Mohammad had heard of Jesus and called out his name.

This man could have joined the ranks of Christians in some formal setting such as a church or Bible school, but God called him back to live out his faith among his own people. Due to Mir-Ibn-Mohammad's desire to integrate with the people of his socioreligious identity and another God-given dream, the chief of his tribe became a follower of Jesus. When that chief became seriously ill, he gave his turban to Mir-Ibn-Mohammad as a sign that he would serve as the chief in his place. Now, from an influential position within the tribe, Mir-Ibn-Mohammad actually uses the Bible to lead his tribe. Amazingly, he prevented a woman in his tribe from being stoned to death by sharing the story of the woman who was caught in adultery, as described in the Gospel of John.

Knowledge of Mir-Ibn-Mohammad's methods of leadership has spread to adjacent villages. A couple of those leaders tried to shoot Mir-Ibn-Mohammad, but he did not die, despite the many bullets that nicked his skin and the one bullet that entered his body. His survival caused fear among his persecutors. They knew the tribal rules. Mir-Ibn-Mohammad had the right to take revenge. Once again, Mir-Ibn-Mohammad modeled governance of a tribe by living out Jesus's principles, in this case the principles of forgiveness.

God led Mir-Ibn-Mohammad on an intentional journey of multiplying disciples. Mir-Ibn-Mohammad demonstrated that movements for Christ include the process of entering into a people's socioreligious identity through an incarnational lifestyle, rather then disrupting the community identity through missions programs that divide and extract. Thousands of home groups, living out their faith in Jesus within this Muslim people group, are a result of premeditated multiplication.

I shared with you why "rabbit" multiplication of churches did not happen under my watch during my early years of missionary work in Cambodia. However, multiplying is not about giving up, it's about giving over—giving over our mistakes to God, learning vital lessons, and continuing to do what we do in a new light. Jesus died; Peter went back to fishing in the seas. The resurrected Jesus recommissioned Peter three times; Peter returned to fishing for men. We all can get lost in our boats, fishing for that which is temporary, but God can and will redirect us. As quoted early in this chapter, let us respond to Robert Coleman's challenge to "actively win souls and train them to win the multitudes." Let us perpetuate the work that Peter started after Jesus reminded him:

"We still love one another" (John 21:15–17).

Each "reflection for premeditation" chapter within this section of the book has a partner chapter in Part 3, "Multiplication, Indigeneity, and Sustainability in Action." The partner chapter offers suggestions about how to apply what you read in this section. According to what you are reading now, the reflection topic is multiplication, and its practical application is located in chapter 11. I suggest that you read chapters 1–10 in order to gain a foundational and holistic understanding of the concepts and how they connect before tackling actual implementation. Once you complete those chapters, reread chapters 4–10, one at a time, alongside the corresponding action chapter.

> "We could list hundreds of helpful items to start churches, but we can count on our fingers and toes those few essentials that make the crucial difference between reproductive and sterile churches. Blessed is the Christian worker who knows the difference."
>
> DR. GEORGE PATTERSON

CHAPTER FIVE

STRATEGIC FROM THE BEGINNING:

RECOGNIZING HOW DAY 1 AFFECTS DAY 100, 1000, 10,000 . . .

"Believers within my congregation bring people to church, but do not invest in the discipleship of those people. They seem to think that it is their role to invite people to church and my role to keep them here. Pastor Veasna, could you please give me some direction?"

"Brother Sopheap, a lot has to do with how a church is started. I have seen where a missionary will arrive and rent a building. Then, he invites people to attend a church service in which he evangelizes through a sermon. The mentality of merely inviting people to church was inbred into their minds from the beginning. These habits are hard to change. In our situation, discipleship was modeled to us as a lifestyle and a mandate for every believer. When we plant churches, we stay away from the professional complexities found in many churches. We emphasize and build up local lay leaders and encourage the priesthood of all believers. Sopheap, if you were to plant a new church from scratch, what would you do differently from the beginning to avoid the problem you are having now?"

I did not become interested in the World Cup until I lived in Asia. (American NFL football has no place in most of the world.) Since I value narratives, I was reading a variety of narratives used for business training. This particular business website, which provides online learning, presented a case study of the English football team that did not play satisfactorily in the FIFA 2010 World Cup.[1] The website said that when something goes amiss in the business world, some people look for current causes instead of foundational strategies. In other words, they look for the wind, rain, and hail instead of identifying cracks in the foundation. In this case, football analysts should not blame England's weaknesses in the FIFA World Cup on incidental circumstances or seasonal setbacks in 2010. Rather, they need to look at the foundational core of English football.

The website suggested several foundational weaknesses of England's football organization that captured my attention. Firstly, they stated that most of the teams are owned, managed, and coached by companies from outside the UK that have conflicting interest in their own national football teams. Secondly, two thirds of England's football players are from other nations, which wreaks havoc on promoting and discovering local talent. To summarize, *outside control and funding undermine the indigenous motivation and mobilization* of English professional football. One could coach day and night to improve the football players or matches of England, but it will be to no avail if they ignore these fundamental weaknesses.

Does this analysis sound familiar? It should! The scenario in England football echoes a similar weakness in the foundational strategies of missions. When we see believers in other nations lacking indigenous motivation and mobilization capabilities, we often look for circumstantial influences or seasonal setbacks. Yet, it is our very foundational strategies of outside ownership, funding, and managing of local efforts that impair the motivation and mobilization capabilities of the indigenous church.

At the opening of this chapter, Pastor Veasna revealed foundational strengths and strategic beginnings to the church movement that involved his effort and experience. In this chapter, we will explore how the beginning of every missions effort is the time to strategize for indigenous movements, including multiplication, indigeneity, and sustainability.

INSIGHT FROM TRAGEDY

The streets were somewhat quiet after dark, which was typical of Cambodia during the 1990s. There was an unspoken curfew within the capital city of Phnom Penh, so the majority of people stayed close to home. My friend and I were driving down a main street called Mao Tse Tung Boulevard. An elderly gentleman had started to cross the road and stopped in the middle to wait for our vehicle to pass. As we focused on the road ahead, we saw a pickup truck speeding toward us in the opposite lane. I commented to my friend, "I sure hope they slow down for him!" The driver of the truck didn't even begin to step on his brakes. He hit the elderly man at full speed. The man catapulted over the top of our vehicle. We heard his bones crack on impact as he landed on the road behind us like a rag doll. The truck smashed into a tree, and the two men responsible fled from the scene. We pulled over and ran to the wounded man's side. I became instantly nauseous as I saw the man's brain protruding from his skull.

Though we had not intended it, our lives now intersected with this man's life. We had a choice to make. How extensively did we want to get involved? Within moments, neighbors and family members gathered around the seriously injured man; technically, we could have walked away. Instead, we rushed the man and his family to the hospital. While the injured man gasped for air like a wounded bird, the doctors ironically cleansed his superficial wounds. Within a couple of hours, this grandfather, father, and husband died. We could have justified our departure at that time too. Who would blame us? There was nothing else we could do. But we did not depart. We went to the home of the deceased man. There we sat, offering condolences to the family, feeling terribly out of place. The monks arrived, and the body was brought home from the hospital. For the next several hours, we intimately entered into the heart of the Cambodian worldview—how Cambodians respond to the death of a family member.

We could have withdrawn ourselves from this experience at any point. However, if we sincerely wanted to be learners in the midst of a people group's worldview, we needed to stay—the longer we stayed, the more we would learn. There was definitely something within our workaholic Western nature that made us feel that a drawn-out and unplanned event such as this was an intrusion into our busy ministry schedule. As missionaries, we felt a pressure to get to the real work—Bible studies and evangelistic programs. This disturbs me as much as the next Christian, but the truth is, most North Americans are in a hurry to finish one activity to get to another. We have a drive within us that wants end results fast. We often squander our beginnings to get to the end. The problem is that the beginning shapes the end.

For us, the encounter with this grieving family was a beginning—a beginning to understanding how a culture interprets life and death. Such experiences are windows into understanding the worldview, and they can function as bridges to eventually help others understand God. We can waste these beginning opportunities to get to our real work, or we can allow these opportunities to be our real work.

In my early years, how many beginning opportunities did I squander? I am learning, and I desire to keep learning, to be strategic from the beginning. God is a genesis God. In the beginning, he did everything with the future in mind.

We need God's intuition as we apply ourselves with the beginning and future in mind.

DAY 1 AFFECTS DAY 100

I have created a saying that guides my cross-cultural work: "Day 1 affects day 100." In other words, what I do from the very beginning (on day 1) will either impede multiplication or enhance it within a given cultural context down the road (on day 100). In my early years serving as a cross-cultural church planter, I thought multiplication was something to be communicated when the church was more mature. I was wrong. The reality is that *everything* I say and do from that very first day onward will either empower indigenous believers with the spiritual authority, vision, and capability to multiply, or it will stifle them.

Allow me to share two generic examples of "doing missions" which reveal how the beginning affects the process and outcome.

A missionary is anxious to gather new believers on a regular basis, to study the Bible and to worship. He decides to kindly open his own home for what he calls a "Sunday church service." From his perspective, times together at his home are meaningful and productive. Eventually, the missionary determines that the participants are capable of conducting the service themselves while he makes a trip to his home country for two months. Upon returning, the missionary discovers that only a few believers met while he was gone, and those were people who worked for the missionary. Why?

Though he did not intend them to, assumptions had settled into the minds of the people:

- The missionary is the leader and supplier of this ministry, which he started.
- We exist and function as a church based on the missionary's presence.
- Our meager homes are not adequate as a place to meet and worship.

What the missionary *did not* realize is that what he implemented on day 1 would indeed affect day 100. The missionary led the local believers to assume that the function of the church is about what the foreign missionary provides and does. It is nearly impossible to undo such a mindset, and the impact will negatively affect the church for years to come.

Now for another example: A missionary plans his first informal Bible study with six local new believers in Christ. They meet outside on a woven mat under a shady tree at one of the participant's homes. The missionary tells a Bible story in accordance with existing local mediums of communication. He facilitates a participatory learning style for discovering key principles from the Bible story. These new believers share their faith with others in their community by retelling the Bible stories. They really have a sense of ownership. The local believers express sentiments such as:

- My mother will truly relate to this Bible story, as she is a widow and struggling with life.
- I sense God is so real when I have the opportunity to talk about the characters and their experiences in the Bible story.
- I can do this! I can tell others about Jesus!

What this missionary *did* realize is that what he implemented on day 1 would affect day 100. He purposefully implemented a method of teaching, storytelling, and participation to build the believers' capacities to be presenters of the gospel from the beginning. Talking about their faith enabled them to internalize the message and verbalize it, unlike hearing a lecture, which creates spectators. Additionally, the local believers were able to easily share Bible stories because the method of communication was natural to their culture. From these two examples, we see that what missionaries do at the birthing stage and throughout subsequent stages significantly affects the development and health of the church in the long run.

Mothers often read to their babies in the womb. I have never seen a newborn baby quoting the poetry of Maya Angelou; nonetheless, experts say that there are benefits to doing this which become evident after the baby is born. First of all, due to the fact that unborn babies are able to receive outside stimulus by their seventh month of development, the baby outside the womb will recognize the voice patterns of the mother, which soothes and comforts the baby. Secondly, some experts say that the habit of reading to babies in the womb helps the educational development of the child.

What mothers do on day 1 affects day 100. When we have the opportunity to birth a church movement for Christ, we must consider every word spoken and every action taken while the church is still in the womb.

BEGINNING STAGES IN MONGOLIA AND THAILAND

Throughout my service in Cambodia, I had the chance to visit Mongolia to teach on church planting and observe ministry there. Mongolia is a place that is dear to my heart. Marku Tsering is a missionary who works among the Tibetan Buddhist peoples in Asia. He shares some thoughts relating to the birth of the modern Mongolian church:

> From a mission's strategy perspective, in 1990, Mongolia was a clean slate. The country had no recent history of missions, no western colonial history, no established church, no recognizable Christians, and no Bible. It was a grand opportunity to get evangelistic strategies right. It was also a tempting venue to experiment. It was significant that the two key evangelistic tools in the early days were non-sectarian and interdenominational. The early missionaries of the 1990s and the Mongolian Christians were all keen to evangelize Mongolia as quickly and effectively as possible. It was no surprise that the period from 1990 to 1993 was characterized by a flurry of activity.[2]

After reading Tsering's description about the clean slate, I asked myself, "What did missionaries do with that clean slate? What was their flurry of activities, and what were the results?"

To seek answers to these questions, I must turn to the Leatherwoods, Hogans, and other teammates who were part of the beginning in Mongolia. Rick Leatherwood entered Mongolia as one of the first American tourists in the late 1980s during a time when Mongolia was just opening its door a crack to the outside world. In his book *Glory in Mongolia*, Rick reveals how God used him and others to lead one Mongol man to the Lord and eventually launched a movement for Christ that includes more than 40,000 believers.

There are several noteworthy beginning actions that I believe contributed to the movement. First, when Rick made his first visits to Mongolia, he brought with him Native Americans who are followers of Christ. He strategically allowed the Native Americans and the Mongols to exchange their stories, which revealed amazing similarities between them such as some shared words, modes of dwellings, physical features, and much more. This common ground created a bridge to allow them to bring God's big story into their conversations.

Second, the young and growing Mongolian church during this time formed "gering groups." A ger is the traditional, nomadic-style house of the Mongols. So instead of using the term "house churches," they referred to their groups as gering groups. The missionaries did not force a church building culture upon the Mongol followers of Christ, but rather allowed them to meet in their organic settings—drinking tea, fellowshipping, singing, and sharing the Word of God.

Related to the gering groups, I was very impressed to find that in the early stages, the missionaries along with the local believers made a tough beginning decision for the sake of multiplication, sustainability, and indigeneity. Brian Hogan, the author of *There's a Sheep in My Bathtub: Birth of a Mongolian Church Planting Movement,* shares about a time in Erdenet, Mongolia, when the believers met only in small groups. Eventually, the small groups held a "big meeting," which is a Mongolian way to say "celebration"—a key term common to cell-church models. The believers and elders enjoyed the comradeship and encouragement they received in the big meetings and decided to conduct big meetings every Sunday. This change caused the house churches to stop growing because new people were more drawn to the big meetings. At a glance, this exchange of venues seemed to be worthwhile, since the big meetings were growing. But key ingredients to making disciples—intimacy, participation, and accountability—were sacrificed for the big group atmosphere. The Mongolian leaders, with the support of the missionaries, canceled the Sunday big meetings. Brian elaborates on the positive outcome of this vital decision:

> The fruit of this drastic action was dramatic. Within a couple of weeks all of the groups needed to multiply as they were too big. The new believers were being taught to obey Jesus at last, and new life flushed through the celebration meeting once a month—and it was good.[3]

From time to time, the delicate balance of when to have big meetings to accompany house groups became an issue. But the bottom line remains the same—what the early missionaries and Mongolian believers did in the beginning would have its impact one way or another.

Third, Rick and his family lived in a ger within a local community, learning and using the heart language of the people. Not every missionary readily practiced living on a local hashaa (land plot) in a Mongolian ger that housed the kitchen, living room, dining room, and den in one room. Yet the Mongols warmed up when they saw the missionary members of the household doing outdoor chores right along with them. Others, such as the Hogans, intentionally used public transportation and lived in apartment buildings with Mongol neighbors instead of on mission compounds as they did life in Ulaanbaatar, and eventually they launched a church planting movement among the Halkh Mongolians.

Fourth, Rick and his cohorts allowed room for the Mongol believers to use and adapt their own forms and expressions of faith and worship. Rick gives a charming example:

> Take the Mongols transition during the morning milking. Today, as you read this page, literally thousands of mothers, daughters, and grandmothers, milked their family's cow or goat, to provide for their family's staple nourishment of milk or tea, and as they did this, they threw a cup of milk into the air as an offering to God. Is this wrong? How should a missionary respond to this? Should he try to stop it? No. This is not wrong. It is merely a form of worship. The question the missionary should ask is, "To whom are you throwing the milk?" It is not the missionary's role to question whether throwing milk is a legitimate form of worship (simply because it is different from his own), but his attention should be directed to the content of the worship, not the form …God does not expect everyone around the world to worship Him in exactly the same way. Jesus does not come to abolish the cultures of the world, but to fulfill them.[4]

Fifth, many of the early missionaries to Mongolia used and affirmed the usage of drama and storytelling, which was a natural form of communication among the Mongols. Can you imagine how many Bible stories relate to the pastoral people of Mongolia? For example, wrestling is one of the major sports and part of an annual festival in Mongolia called *Naadam*—the three games of men: wrestling, horse racing, and archery. Picture the Mongols' heart connection to God as they hear the story of Jacob wresting with the angel of God (Genesis 32:23–34), or of Jesus riding on a horse at his glorious appearing (Revelation 19:11–21), or of how the prophet Nathan used a story about a herdsman who dearly loved his sheep to confront David (2 Samuel 12), or of how Jonathan shot arrows as a way to secretly communicate with David (1 Samuel 20). Rick describes this heart connection best:

> When the little old ladies heard the teaching about milking one's cow, which they do every day of the year, they were overjoyed. They rushed forward at the close of the meeting saying thank you, thank you. God

loves them just the way they were, and they could worship God just the way they had been doing since they were little girls, only now with greater and more fulfilled meaning.[5]

Sixth, Rick and others prayed and trusted God to perform signs and wonders. God's supernatural work connected the movements to his glory and not to any one missionary or foreign entity. Seventh, indigenous churches were emphasized instead of denominational churches that often impose their own cultural forms and structures.

A flurry of activities conducted by missionaries—especially activities done from the beginning, at the foundational level—can either make or break an indigenous movement for Christ. The Leatherwoods and their companions (although they made their mistakes just like the rest of us) worked hard to ensure their flurry led to multiplication. Brian Hogan told me that the Mongolian church sends out more missionaries per capita than anywhere else in the world.

Jesus spent thirty years experiencing the culture of Israeli men and women before he launched his public ministry. Shortcuts for the sake of expediency are destructive to the foundation and expansion of indigenous ministry. I have seen impressive apartment buildings go up in record time in Cambodia, only to collapse with the first sign of stress—and in this case, what is true in natural architecture is also true in spiritual architecture. I believe in the rapid-growth characteristic of church planting movements, but true rapid multiplication occurs because indigenous principles are carefully applied in the beginning, rather than neglected for the sake of instant results.

Alan and Lynette Johnson learned valuable lessons while planting churches in Thailand. During my first years of missionary service, when I could not receive mail in Cambodia, my mail was sent to Thailand and then hand-carried into Cambodia. Since Alan and Lynette had the same last name, I often received their mail, and they received mine. Similar to my journey, Alan Johnson grew into an indigenous paradigm after ministering for many years in Thailand. Upon being assigned to help a local Thai pastor replant a fledgling church, Alan immediately implemented what he had experienced in the North American church. He and the Thai pastor endeavored to conduct programs and events such as crusades, English classes, passing out tracts, prayer walks, and showing the Jesus movie.

After much effort and plenty of finances spent, the missionary couple and the Thai pastoral couple were worn out—and only thirty-five people had been added to the church. Alan found comfort in the fact that others were equally stuck in their ministries throughout Thailand. Many of those Christian workers have concluded that the greatest obstacle to church planting is the resistance of the Thai people. Yet his experience has led Alan Johnson to believe there are other fundamental issues at play.

> Missionaries involved in church planting among Buddhist populations wrestle with the problem of very slow church planting and church growth among existing congregations. One response to this has been to deal with issues of contextualization to see how the Gospel message and church life can be made to better fit the local context and thus become more relevant to the people. I personally believe that this is a very important piece of the explanatory "puzzle" as to why it is so difficult to plant churches among Buddhist peoples.
>
> However, I have come to see this problem as being much more complex and multidimensional, with issues of contextualization being only one of a series of interrelated factors. I want to argue here that what may be the most significant reason for slow church planting and growth among Buddhist populations comes from the models of evangelism, ministry, church structure, and church life that are employed. I want to suggest that it is less a case of us not making sense to people from Buddhist backgrounds than it is one of perpetuating philosophies and models of ministry and ways of "doing church" that hinder our ability to plant and grow churches capable of multiplying rapidly and over long periods of time.[6]

Alan looked beyond the soil to the planter and caretaker of the soil. Likewise, let's look beyond the surface and discover what we can do in the beginning *to plant and grow churches capable of multiplying rapidly and over long periods of time.*

BEGINNINGS AFFECT ENDINGS

The book *Operation World* serves as a guide for people to strategically pray for every nation of the world. Within this book there is a section called "Challenges for Prayer" which reveals the specific prayer needs of each respective nation. Below are several excerpts related to specific prayer requests from different nations. As you read, notice the suggested root causes/beginnings that contribute to the existing challenges:

The Church in Belize

Many missions, especially short-term, have saturated this small nation. Much has been positive, particularly in the areas of medicine/health care (especially in the remote and poorer areas), literacy and training. But the never-ending presence of mission-trippers creates dependency, which actually undermines the national Church. Pray for fruitful partnerships that empower and require true sacrifice by all for Kingdom purposes.[7]

The Church in Botswana

Most mainline Protestant churches were established by Western missions in generations past, but now are generally in decline. Some suggest that the mainline churches' struggles today are a legacy from the early missionaries' failure to contextualize the gospel to local culture; this has resulted in pervasive nominalism. Both local congregations and denominational structures are affected. Pray for revival among these historic churches.[8]

The Church in India

The need for change in the Church is urgent and has never been greater. Pray for:

i.   Unity. The National United Christian Forum brings together the Catholic Bishops' Forum, the National Council of Churches and the Evangelical Fellowship. The All India Christian Council serves Christians of all denominations, with over 5,000 agencies, NGOs, denominations and institutions working for human rights, social justice, religious freedom and protection of minorities. A spirit of divisiveness characterized the past; now, unity is greater than ever before, in part due to hostility from external forces. Pray for unity to mature and to endure. Greater cooperation and accountability are needed between local churches and sending agencies.

ii. Indigenization of Church culture, structure and expression—for too long, churches have relied on foreign cultural forms.

iii. Greater reliance on an Indian model of cell/house churches rather than on Western-style modes and places of worship.

iv. Effective discipling—through coordinated, collaborative efforts—of the many being impacted by any one of the multiple methods of evangelism. Many new believers come to faith through large rallies, healings or miracles, but opportunities are few for Christian instruction to strengthen and sustain them in their faith.

v.   More relevance in impacting the mainstream of national life. The Church is seen as linked to the marginalized, deprived sections of society. Business, politics, arts, culture and the middle and upper classes—all shapers of Indian society—have not yet been impacted by the gospel.[9]

The Church in Myanmar

The retention of leaders. Far too many attend seminary in order to learn English, seen as a ticket out of the country. Others study abroad but don't return to the challenging life of ministering in Myanmar. Praise God for the establishment of Masters degree programmes at MEGST which enable aspiring ministry leaders to get equipped and remain in Myanmar.[10]

Issues such as dependency, nominalism, lack of indigenous churches, and difficulty retaining leaders did not just arise in a vacuum. Each one of these stated challenges reveals rough beginnings, such as an overdose of short-term teams; failure to contextualize the gospel; importing foreign forms, structures, and models; and offering training with Western perks. We could equally find "answers to prayer" within *Operation World* that reveal well-thought-out and strategic beginnings that led and lead to health and long-lasting fruit. The key is that those who do missions grasp that their beginning strategies will positively or negatively affect the middle and end results.

UNLOCKED MULTIPLICATION IN ONE SMALL STEP

In the book *Starting A House Church*, Larry Kreider, the director of DOVE Christian Fellowship International, tells of an experience where one key adjustment unlocked a barrier created in the beginning of their ministry. A man and his wife were responsible for leading a house church in the USA. The couple did everything by themselves to make this house church function productively. One day, Larry Kreider encouraged the couple to delegate responsibilities to others. Listen to what happened when the couple followed Larry's advice:

When we offered the other members of the group the opportunity to serve, he was shocked—they took everything! But that's not the end of the story. Over the course of about six months, the single group of believers multiplied into three groups—a prime example that God's people learn by doing![11]

The couple began the house church by doing all the work by themselves. On day 100, the couple was still doing everything. Wise words helped the couple unlock multiplication—and it only took one simple step.

One evening, I was watching the news on WCCO TV. The newscaster informed viewers that Baylor University Center in Dallas, Texas, has the lowest heart failure readmission rate of any hospital in the USA, 15.9 percent. As I listened, one of the cardiologists said, "From the beginning we prepare the patients for discharge." In other words, the cardiologists and staff intentionally plan from the beginning to ensure success—no relapses.

My hope is that the phrase "day 1 affects day 100" will stick in our minds and constantly serve as a voice to remind us to be intentional and thoughtful, designing everything we plant and nurture from the beginning with multiplication in mind—especially as we head to new fields of harvest.

"The beginning is the most important part of the work."

PLATO

CHAPTER SIX

MODEL FOR REPRODUCIBILITY:

MAKING THE WAY FOR INDIGENOUS PEOPLE TO
HAVE A REPRODUCIBLE MINISTRY

"Pastor Veasna, last week a medical team came from America. They visited families within our community who had sick family members. They gave checkups and shared medicines and vitamins with those who needed them. The interpreters helped them both to communicate and pray for people. After the visits, the medical team told us which families prayed to receive Jesus. We followed up and went to those very same homes. However, we had a completely different reception. They accused us of forsaking our culture. They were disappointed when we didn't bring medicine with us and asked when the Americans were returning. Why is it when the missionaries minister, they have so much success? I think we should let the missionaries plant the churches and we can just help."

"First of all, I wouldn't call repeating a 'sinner's prayer' after receiving medical attention from someone seemingly superior as successful. Your visits to their homes with a customary greeting revealed the true spiritual condition of the people. The missionaries are modeling methods that your church cannot reproduce. In some ways, their method causes your community to view you as inferior because you come empty-handed. Do not give up! Share the Gospel and plant churches with the resources God has placed around you and use methods that are appropriate for your context. Rely on the creativity and enablement of the Holy Spirit!"

As a church planting coach in Cambodia, I once brought lanterns for use in a drama, a contextualized performance of the Bible story about Ruth and Naomi. I say contextualized in that the Cambodian church planters allowed the surrounding context to influence the style and nuances of the play. The Cambodian farmers were only able to meet at night after they came in from the fields, so I thought it would be beneficial to provide artificial lighting. I also brought a few other resources from the city to enhance the drama and create a pleasant atmosphere in this village setting. I viewed the lanterns as a simple act of kindness and a way to increase the effectiveness of this friendly community event.

A couple of weeks later, the church planters and I were preparing for another storytelling gathering. The church planters gave me a list of things I could bring to the gathering: a tarp, a car battery, and a portable stereo. As I held the list, I realized that I had made a momentous mistake. I was thinking of the success of the immediate event. "What will make this ministry event that I am a part of succeed in a timely manner?" This short-term thinking was a problem for several reasons. One, I communicated through my actions that the local resources of that village were somehow inferior. Two, I conditioned the church planters to feel a need to access resources not readily available to them in order to succeed in this ministry and future church plants. Third, if the church-in-process were to daughter a church in the future, they would want to use external resources to do it, as I had modeled to them.

This whole method can be summed up in one word: *nonreproducible*.

As a missionary-coach, I desire every aspect of ministry to go as well as possible for the church planters and participants. I want the church planters to go to sleep with a smile on their faces and ruminate a passion within their hearts for the next day of ministry. Equally, I long for the participants to rest well while waiting with anticipation to gather again. If I'm totally honest, I like to rest well with a smile on my face too.

However, I cannot allow myself to think merely of the moment, the day, or the week—about what brings the most satisfaction and anticipation in the moment. I need to think about the future. When I use resources and methods local believers cannot easily reproduce, I create a roadblock for them. I make them feel powerless because they cannot do ministry "like Jean." As a result, local believers will often give up or find a missionary to do the work. This return to the missionary starts a chain of psychological and financial dependency on missionaries and churches abroad. I cannot even begin to emphasize how beneficial it is when I allow the organic context and the local people to supply the resources instead.

Using restraint for the sake of reproducibility does not come naturally. There will be times when withholding seems callous. Dr. Charles Brock, who is a veteran in healthy indigenous church planting, helps us get past the mindset of dodging reproducibility with his passionate words: "Stingy? No! A growth producing stewardship? Yes! Such growth is desirable wherein independent self-hood is realized with full dependence on Christ."[1]

When I finally resisted the temptation to bring in resources, the local church planters and community pitched in and made things happen. You should have seen the drama when the Cambodian gentleman who acted out the crafty snake in the garden of Eden situated himself in an actual tree! When I allowed the church planters to creatively use their local resources, those dramas were their most powerful and culturally relevant. More importantly, I was finally thinking and modeling reproducibility, which is a significant ingredient to multiplication.

Intentional Reproducibility from the Beginning

I am convinced that if missionaries were to only follow one missiological principle—the principle of reproducibility—they would avoid most of the problems that strangle indigenous churches and keep them from mobilizing themselves to fulfill the Great Commission in their own context and beyond. Once more, Dr. Charles Brock speaks purposely about reproducibility:

> One of the five major characteristics of an indigenous church is its ability, in Christ's strength, to reproduce itself. A church does not attain this characteristic easily nor by accident. The way a church is born will influence its ability to reproduce itself...
>
> Many may say this is not important; just get as many churches started as possible and don't worry about the way it is done ...One man who is able to plant a church so modeled that very few ever could approximate his success is not thinking world evangelization. He is nearsighted. There may be room for unique models which are not reproducible, but if the world is to be reached, it will be by multiplication and not by addition. Reproducibility speaks multiplication.[2]

Success for the sake of myself is not the end goal, and it never should be. We need to think beyond our desires for fulfillment. Otherwise, our own successes may lead those in our host culture to fail.

Many times I had to copy the key for my motorcycle in Cambodia. Whenever I handed the original key to the repairman, an exact copy was handed back.

Modeling in ministry works the same way; you will receive back a copy of whatever you hand over. DNA is passed on from the parents to the children, the trainer to the trainee, the mother church to the daughter church, and movement to movement.

With this in mind, we need to realize the intimate relationship between modeling and reproducibility. The following are important principles of reproducibility:

- You pass on a genetic blueprint by modeling.
- The effectiveness of modeling is directly proportional to its reproducibility.
- Consider reproducibility over the long term.
- Consider reproducibility in terms of "typical" target members.
- Remember, you are modeling the Who, What, How, When, Where, and Why of ministry.[3]

Our modeling speaks volumes over our words and theory. In other words, people watch what we do more than what we teach.

In many parts of the world, people are concrete learners; they learn by seeing and emulating what they see. Jesus taught the disciples in this manner: "Walk with me. See what I do and do what I do. Take nothing with you on your journey. Go from village to village preaching the gospel. Cast out demons and heal the sick" (see Luke 9; Matthew 10). How many grown children act just like their parents? How many daughter churches reflect their mother churches? How long does it take for Hollywood stars to promote a trend? It is true in all areas of life: *we pass on a genetic blue print by modeling.*

Modeling breaks down if the means are nonreproducible. If we use resources that are not available in the local context or are too expensive for the average local person to access, we have sabotaged reproducibility. If we dig a well for people, but do not empower them with the ability to maintain the well or capability to dig other wells, we have ignored reproducibility. *The effectiveness of modeling is directly proportional to its reproducibility.*

I have seen missionaries or visitors from North America teach Cambodians how to make greeting cards so they can generate an income. These greeting cards are created with a style that appeals to expatriates and tourists. It may meet a need in the short term, but this plan lacks reproducibility over the long term. The small pool of customers limits the progress and reproducibility of such a business plan in the extreme. Often, expats will buy certain crafts because they want to encourage the seller, but this motive eventually comes to an end. Once, I went to a quilt sale in Cambodia. I was anticipating lightweight quilts with Cambodian designs. Instead, I found bag after bag of thick quilts like those I would find on my grandma's rocking chair back in the USA. Locals were not attracted to winter quilts, and expats or tourists wanted items unique to Cambodian culture. *Consider reproducibility over the long term.*

Finally, what is reproducible for one group may not be for another. We need to ask what is typical for each group. For example, a Mongolian who lives in the capital city of Ulaanbaatar may consider it feasible to give money as part of his tithes and offerings. On the other hand, a Mongolian nomadic herdsman who lives off the land would find it nearly impossible to give money as his offering to God—his gifts must be more earthy. *Consider reproducibility in terms of typical target members.*

A missionary team worked hard to ensure that locals would lead all of the sessions and activities at a national family conference. In this case, they gave intentional thought to the who and what of reproducibility. On the other hand, the missionaries provided the funds necessary for transportation and the expensive rental fees for a place to gather. *When you desire to measure reproducibility, consider the who, what, how, when, where, and why.* If one of these categories is neglected, reproducibility is unlikely. For example, if the who is reproducible, but the where is not, the locals may never be able to emulate such an event. In this case, will the missionaries become indispensable?

EXCUSES, EXCUSES

I have heard well-meaning people say, "We never intended or expected the locals to reproduce what we did in their country." I struggle with this thought process. Recalling Pastor Veasna'a experience, the methods of evangelism that the locals could afford and implement appeared inferior to the means used by the visitors, damaging the witness of the locals in the long term. In that case, a medical team from abroad that assisted in launching or boosting the church plant gave the impression that the foreigners do all the good stuff. Outsiders can bring energy and encourage people to become part of a developing church through medical attention while at the same time subtly diminishing the local church planters' and leaders' motivation and creativity.

Another common statement—one I've often thought myself—is "If one or two people come to the Lord through our efforts, all is well!" I never want to diminish the beauty of souls being transformed by God. Yet, would it not be much better for several people to connect with Jesus in a way that can be perpetuated by those who live, eat, and share life in those communities? Modeling is fruitless if those under our tutelage cannot reproduce what we model with means accessible to them. Model the willingness to allow God to cultivate local people to use their creativity and God-given resources around them—that is worth emulating.

"Healthy churches are born to reproduce."

DR. GEORGE PATTERSON

CHAPTER SEVEN

FACILITATE THE GROWTH OF THE INDIGENOUS CHURCH:

ENSURING THE CHURCH REFLECTS THE SOUL OF THE CULTURE AND HAS PSYCHOLOGICAL OWNERSHIP OF ITS PURPOSE AND FUNCTION

"Pastor Veasna, yesterday I prayed for a sick man by placing my hands on top of his head. The man was a government official. He seemed upset that I touched his head in that manner. I realize this is disrespectful in our culture, but that is how they pray in the Bible."

"Brother Sopheap, that is how the missionaries often pray. But let me ask you a question: to pray for someone by laying hands on his head, is this a biblical mandate or a cultural tradition?"

The pain of suicide is unmistakable: "I feel as though I lost a part of me. Why did he go like this? I cannot make sense of life without him. I did not see the signs. If only I had been more attentive. Was it my fault? What could I have done differently? I feel like I betrayed him—or did he actually betray me? I know my questions will not bring him back. Oh, that my soul would feel alive again!"

This grieving man did not lose a son to suicide; he lost his own cultural identity. He committed cultural suicide, gaining Christianity but losing his own culture along the way. As missionaries, it's important that we recognize the tremendous negative impact on one who is forced to deny his or her cultural identity to become a Christian wrapped in someone else's culture. Cultural suicide visits many families throughout the world due to missions endeavors—and it is not something we should downplay or ignore.

When I was in West Bengal, India, a beautiful follower of Jesus Christ from Nagaland—located in the northeastern corner of India—told me a few details about her history. Uniquely, Nagaland is 95 percent Christian, unlike most of the subcontinent, which is predominantly Hindu and Muslim. The gospel of Jesus came to Nagaland in the twentieth century through missionaries, and as is common in missions history, it came cloaked in colonialism. (Colonialism was all about shoving one's culture down the throats of another cultural group while taking up residence and control in their territory.) My friend shared that Western nominal Christianity is now the state of her culture in Nagaland, but she feels as if something deep inside is missing. She is living with a sense of cultural suicide.

Glenn Schwartz, author of the book *When Charity Destroys Dignity: Overcoming Unhealthy Dependency in the Christian Movement*, shares some thoughts about the identity of churches within their respective cultures:

An Indigenous Church should look and sound like the society of which it is a part. In other words, it should not stand out as something culturally different or foreign. It should stand out in other ways. It ought to be seen as a group of people concerned to carry out God's priorities in their communities. Believers should stand apart from the average person in the neighborhood because of their obedience to God's Word. But the church should not look like a culturally foreign institution. Unfortunately, many mission-established churches simply look and sound foreign to the eyes and ears of local people around them.[1]

The greatest tragedy is that Christianity in Nagaland has already slipped into nominalism; many profess Christianity but do not possess a relationship with Jesus as their Lord and Savior. Sound familiar? Is it possible that conformity to an imposed form of cultural Christianity contributed to nominalism in Nagaland to some degree?

The phenomenon of cultural suicide started a long time ago. The apostle Paul talked about it in regard to the Jews and Gentiles. Initially, the Jewish believers didn't even think that Jesus's saving reconciliation was for the Gentiles. To get the message through, God had to practically knock Peter over the head with a sheet containing four-footed animals, reptiles, and birds. Believe me, it was no gourmet meal! On that sheet were creatures that Peter would never eat for dinner; they were unclean according to Jewish tradition. God had the audacity to command Peter to eat those nasty critters. And he had a way of making his point clear: he repeated the routine three times.

What was the God-point of this strange vision? God communicated to Peter that indeed, Jesus's saving reconciliation was for every tribe, tongue, and nation.

However, even when Peter and his comrades finally accepted that God had extended his grace to Gentiles, they expected the Gentiles to commit cultural suicide. The Jewish followers of Christ demanded that the Gentiles believe God with their hearts and become Jewish with every other aspect of their beings. The whole purpose of the council of Jerusalem recorded in Acts 15 was to address the problem of making Gentiles deny their cultural identity in order to become Jewish Christians. Paul told the assembly that God had done miraculous signs and wonders among the Gentiles, the uncircumcised Gentiles, without their becoming Jews—and he referred to this process of imposing your culture on others as "putting yokes on people's necks."

During my fist visit to a church in another country, I had the following sentiments: "Oh, I have goosebumps on my arms when I hear them singing songs from my country in their language! We really are one family in God!" I meant well, but can you see the cultural superiority in that comment?

One of the reasons we impose our culture on others through missions efforts, I believe, is that our Western culture has so meshed with our biblical faith that we struggle to discern the difference. In a letter addressing the problems of culture and faith, Paul shared that the faith journey in God is about being a new creation within your own culture and influencing that culture from the inside out (Galatians 6:12–16). Yet when making disciples in a cultural group other than our own, we often expect people to conform to our Western Christian culture—expecting them to change from the outside in.

The opposite of cultural suicide is cultivating the indigenous life of the church. There are several definitions of *indigenous*, but for now, I am going to use Kim Harrington's definition to set our course:

> Indigenous means the church in any given nation should be homegrown, a natural expression of Christ within its own culture; not unnecessarily influenced, controlled, or supported by foreigners, even though they may have originally introduced the Gospel.[2]

When God's kingdom touches a people, cultural changes are inevitable and good. Yet cultural suicide is deadly—deadly for a man's soul and deadly for the advancement of God's kingdom.

THE CHRISTIAN GOD WEARS A FOREIGN FACE

One day, a Cambodian Christian looked in the mirror. He saw a white man, six feet tall, with blue eyes and blond hair staring back at him. The more time he spent with Christians and North American missionaries, the more he outwardly behaved like an American. No wonder Cambodians call Christianity the "foreigner's god"! Beyond Cambodia, a Taiwanese man once stated, "The Christian God wears a foreign face."[3]

This conclusion, "Christianity is the Westerner's religion," rings out all over the world. And there is good reason for it. When I have visited churches in Myanmar, Thailand, Mongolia, Belize, Uganda, and other parts of the world, I have seen churches that smell, look, and feel like my home country, instead of an expression of their own respective cultures.

Alan Johnson and other colleagues who serve as missionaries in Thailand reveal that the response to the gospel among Thai people has been painfully slow. They point out several reasons for this resistance, but a major factor is that the gospel has been wrapped in a foreign culture. If Thai missionaries were to plant a church in North America with a Thai-ness to its styles and forms, we would exclaim, "Ludicrous; it will never work!" Yet missionaries from places like North America plant churches that are carbon copies of their own culture in cross-cultural settings and expect them to be effective. We comprehend it when it is happening to us, but we are slow to understand when we are making it happen.

Even though I have a bachelor's degree in cross-cultural communications, I still feel the pull to operate out of my own cultural experiences—it is so natural. Natural feels good to me. The problem is, I imagine natural feels just as good to my host culture! I am the cross-cultural communicator. I am the one who needs to allow what is unnatural to become natural to me, not the other way around. Recognizing this and asking for God's help in this area are important keys to showing indigenous people that our God does not have a foreign face.

WHY IS THAT MAN SO DIFFERENT?

One day while I was worshiping in a Cambodian church, I glanced over to the other side of the room where a Cambodian man caught my attention. I questioned myself, "What is different about him?" Immediately, I realized he was worshiping uniquely, with a style very different from the rest of the church participants. After a few moments of focusing on him, I realized that he was a blind man who attended the church. And it dawned on me: "Of course, because the man is visually impaired, he is worshiping in a way that is natural to him!"

This man was bowing his upper body as he worshiped, and his hands were clasped in a form that expressed deep reverence in the Cambodian culture. Due to his blindness, he had no basis to worship any other way than that which was innate. The other participants were worshiping in a style that had been modeled to them by missionaries from other countries—making eye contact with God and exposing their armpits as they lifted their arms upward. That is definitely not a posture of reverence in Cambodia!

Gene Edwards wrote a series of books in diary-narrative form to tell the story of Paul and his companions' missionary journeys. Each part of the narrative is told through the eyes of different people involved and influenced by those journeys. *The Silas Diary, The Titus Diary, The Timothy Diary, The Priscilla Diary* and *The Gaius Diary* are intended to give readers a lifelike experience of the book of Acts. In *The Silas Diary*, we travel with Paul and Barnabas after they are sent out from the church in Antioch—the first Gentile church (Acts 11:19–26; 17:1–4). Using his imagination and the biblical historical context, Edwards portrays Paul as having no desire to be lured into pampering Jewish believers with more biblical counsel and attention while they are virtually ignoring the spread of the gospel among Gentiles in their own neighborhoods. In the book, Paul and Barnabas often discuss where they should focus their attention and ministry. One such dialogue unfolds like this:

I have a problem with this:

Barnabas moved to the stern of the old freighter and stared back at the receding coast of Cyprus. "I'll return to this island if ever my people open themselves—and the churches—to the Gentiles," he said wistfully.

"Would it be to any great advantage?"

"What?" asked Barnabas, turning to face Paul.

"In the church in Antioch, during their first four years of its existence, a few Jews have become believers. But have they found it easy to be a part of an informal Gentile church?"

"No," replied a cautious Barnabas, already seeing that he had accidentally opened a very serious conversation.

"And did the Jews who came into the Antioch assembly try to change the Gentiles expression of the bride of Christ?"

"Yes."

"Did they succeed?"

"No."

"And did some get deeply hurt?"

Barnabas was silent.

"Did the Gentile believers change their cultural ways to satisfy the

Jewish believers who came among them? Could they even if they tried? No. They will always be Gentiles, not Jews. The Gentile way should prevail in an assembly of Gentiles gathering in a Gentile land.

"Now reverse that," Paul continued. "The churches on Cyrus are Jewish, Hebrew to the core. If the Gentiles were to come to the meetings of these Jewish churches—even if they eventually outnumbered the Jews—they would still be in a Jewish experience of the body of Christ, would they not?"[4]

Eph 5:21 Submit to one another out of reverence for Christ!

Paul goes on to tell Barnabas that when the Jews fled Jerusalem and found themselves in Judean villages and towns, they brought their Jewish ways of doing church with them. As they spread out into new areas, they made carbon copies of the church experience they came from. Many of us have experienced churches in settings far from North America, and yet we see that their experience of church is Americanized or Westernized. Thinking about Paul's mode of operation, we see that each people group should have the opportunity to be a unique expression of the bride of Christ without having to surrender their culture to another culture, especially one separated from them by an ocean.

I don't think you will ever find a missionary who does not agree that churches should be culturally relevant. Yet, churches upon churches inherit the culture of the foreign missionary. We need to ask ourselves, "What leads to this discrepancy between voiced intentions about planting the indigenous church and actual actions?"

It takes God-given discipline and patience for us to set aside our human drive to impose and control, but it is so worth the outcome—indigenous churches that have godly influence in their society.

FLASHBACKS

When missionaries and community developers initially worked in the rural areas of Cambodia after the Killing Fields genocide, they used meetings to disseminate information, call for cooperation, and propose projects. Outsiders would never have imagined that such a meeting could solicit negative feelings, but the meetings reminded attendees of the hard times endured during the genocide. After twelve or more hours of labor in near-death conditions, Cambodians under the control of Pol Pot's regime had to attend nighttime "livelihood meetings" within their various rural cooperatives. These meetings gave Pol Pot's cadres opportunity to spread their ideals and instill fear into the people. They warned the attendees to cooperate with one another under the sole authority of the Angkar, some mysterious ruling party that no one ever saw.

Beyond indoctrination, Cambodians were expected to confess their sins or reveal the sins of others in these meetings—any small fraction that opposed the communist ideology of Pol Pot. When individuals admitted their offenses, people applauded, and the cadres would even give them a hug combined with praise, but during the night, those very same people disappeared. An evening of redemption and hope of acceptance by Pol Pot's bullies ended in a mass grave. I call these public confessions and affirmations "Pol Pot altar calls."

Knowing that, we can now see how a development meeting or Christian meeting with any hint of similarity to the "livelihood meetings" could have turned the average Cambodian's stomach sour. My challenge to all of us is to not assume that what worked for us will work for others. We need to allow this inner voice to speak to us: "Be perceptive of the context around you, and allow the Spirit of God and what you learn to shape your way of cultivating the indigenous church."

Laying Hands on the Buttock: Deciphering What Is Biblical and What Is Culture

New believers within new cultural contexts will struggle to decipher what is the "gospel" and what is the culture of the missionary. Frequently, I have seen Cambodians who prayed for the sick by laying their hands on the head of the one seeking prayer. Sounds like normal behavior to us, but put this in cultural context: to touch the top of someone's head within the Cambodian culture is outstandingly disrespectful. Touching someone's head in the Cambodian context is like North Americans praying for people by laying hands on their buttocks. Not a good idea!

If placing one's hands on someone's head is so utterly impolite, why do Cambodians do it? Because a percentage of missionaries and Christian visitors prayed for the sick in this particular manner. Basically, they mingled their own cultural experiences with the gospel mandate of praying for the sick. The Cambodians assumed that if missionaries were praying in this manner, it was the biblical way to pray.

It is common practice for local Christians to emulate forms from the missionaries' cultures while assuming those forms are a mandate from Christ. As missionaries, we must endeavor to discern what is gospel and what is merely our own culture. Upon this discernment, we purposely refrain from functioning out of our own cultural frame of reference, but rather contextualize our efforts so that the indigenous church can be a natural expression of Christ within its own culture.

I once had a missionary tell me that we are not responsible for what we model. Rather, we should teach believers in the host culture how to think and evaluate in an analytical way—to discern for themselves what is biblical and what is merely the missionaries' culture. I agree with him to a degree, but I question the effectiveness of his approach. First of all, many people throughout the world are not analytical thinkers; rather, they are concrete thinkers. In this case, a cross-cultural communicator would need to spend a liberal amount of time retraining his students to analytically interpret and process life. If the cross-cultural communicator is successful in this endeavor, it will most likely be among the few and not the majority. There is a popular phrase that often rings true: "The majority rules."

A Ghanaian pastor who studied in a Western-style theological school (utilizing analytical, linear thinking) revealed how the majority ruled in his case:

> After all my training [in Bible college] was finished, I went back to the village and found that it did not fit.[5]

Western Christians cannot make the assumption that because we conduct Bible schools and train local leaders (the minority) in our Western ways, the majority within the country will respond and benefit. Maybe missionaries should open the net as much as possible. This is a Cambodian way of saying that missionaries should strive to achieve the best outcome in the best way possible. In other words, missionaries could train indigenous people to discern between what is biblical and what is merely one's own culture and at the same time do their very best to refrain from modeling forms that are imported from Western culture.

IT SEEMED SO UN-TIBETAN

The Tibetan Autonomous Region sits on a plateau, considered the highest region of the earth. One Christmas, a friend gave me a Tibetan copper horn, which is three feet and three inches long. Small turquoise stones accent the horn. No matter how hard I blow on the horn, only an anemic breathy sound comes forth. I cannot even stir my dog with the noise it makes. The horn stands in my house to remind me of a people who need to experience God through Jesus Christ. In the book *Sharing Christ in the Tibetan Buddhist World*, Marku Tsering shares about a missionary couple, John and Vivian, who befriended a Tibetan couple. As the friendship progressed, John and Vivian invited Dorje and Pasang to a Christian church. Dorje and Pasang described their experience this way:

The room is full of people, but bare of images except for a small cross at the front of the room. Dorje finds it strange that the Christians do not have statues or pictures of their God. As the service begins with prayer, Pasang notices that the worshippers do not seem very reverent. One or two of the foreigners present are leaning against the wall as they pray, and no one is making prostrations to the Christian God. When the congregation begins to sing, Dorje notices the words are Tibetan but the melody is a strange-sounding Western tune he has never heard before. He shifts uncomfortably as one song refers to the blood shed by Jesus Christ. "Does this foreign religion shed blood?" he wonders.

A few minutes later, the pastor stands up and begins his sermon. Dorje and Pasang have heard lamas teach before, but they seldom understood what the lamas said because the teaching was in hard to understand religious language. The Christian pastor gave a simple message in everyday language that was easy to understand. Once again there is prayer. Pasang notices that the Christians do not recite mantras. Instead, they pray as though they were talking to their God.

After they leave the service, Dorje and Pasang discuss the Christians and their religion. Vivian and John had talked with them about the Buddhist and Christian ideas of God, man, sin, and what happens after death, and both Dorje and Pasang realized that this Christian religion was very different from Buddhism. Not only were the teachings different, there seemed to be so many foreign ideas, foreign songs, and foreign people involved. It seemed so un-Tibetan.

Dorje and Pasang had heard that Christians were always trying to get people of other faiths to leave their own religion and become Christian. Friends had told them that wherever the Christians go, they start Western-style schools, hospitals, and development programs, and that this was the way they got people to convert to Christianity. Both Tibetans agreed that the Christians should not do this. From what they had seen, to become a Christian one would first have to stop being a Tibetan and become a foreigner. If that was the case, then it was better to remain a Buddhist.[6]

Who is the man in the mirror? In this case, it is indigenous people who see themselves as giving up their identity as Tibetans to take on a Western reflection when they become Christians. Missionaries should unfold ministry in such a way that Tibetans can become sincere followers of Christ, but still see their own reflection in the mirror. It is a shame that people living in Asia sometimes view Jesus as the foreigner's god, when Jesus was born in Asia!

I am not advocating syncretism (a blending of one's own cultural practices with faith in Christ to the point where those practices are actually in conflict with God's will revealed in the Bible), and I realize there will be changes within the worldview of a cultural group that follows Jesus Christ. Yet, we cannot fear syncretism to the point that churches become un-Tibetan, un-Cambodian, or un-Ugandan, just to name a few examples.

Western Christians often fear syncretism in other parts of the world while at the same time ignoring their own forms of syncretism. Have you been to a "Christian" wedding lately? The tradition of having bridesmaids originated to ward off evil spirits. The bridesmaids wore similar dresses to the bride's in order to attract the evil spirits away from her. The bouquet served similar purposes. Originally, the bouquet was made from garlic and other strong-smelling herbs to ward off any unwanted spirits.

The majority of wedding traditions practiced by Christians today have roots in the folklore and superstition of several different ancient cultures. Beyond adopting biblical practices syncretized with ancient forms, Westerners have added many cultural trappings to biblical mandates and practices to suit their culture. I can only imagine how sad Jesus would feel if he joined in with our fast-food-approach to communion. Our Western institutional way of conceptualizing and doing church comes more from Christianity shaped by the Roman Empire under Constantine than the Bible. As Westerners, we need to keep in mind that we do not possess the perfect way to do church—in fact, we may be guilty of syncretism in our own context. Thus, we must not be too quick to pass on our cultural trappings along with the gospel or to so fear syncretism that people of other nations view Jesus, born of Asia and sent from heaven, as an American or European.

THE FIVE SENSES OF THE INDIGENOUS CHURCH

How do we define a truly indigenous expression of church? Perhaps we could say that a church is indigenous when any given people group experiences Christ through its five senses—sight, hearing, touch, smell, and taste—and not the foreigner's five senses. Allow me to unravel a general scenario of what an indigenous experience in a Cambodian setting looks like:

A Cambodian husband, wife, and daughter go to their neighbors' house to join believers in Christ for their evening gathering. They are a bit anxious because this is their first time, and they do not know what to expect. As they arrive, they smell the typical aroma of rice porridge. Their mouths water as the garlic stimulates their taste buds. The group participants share a meal together and talk about everyday life. The father feels a weight lifted from his shoulders as he hears that others are struggling with their crops as well. He senses he is not alone. The father feels the texture of the mat under his feet and is aware that he is among his own. An elderly man quotes a poem from God's book about God's concern for nature and the harvest. The participants place the palms of their hands together and bow their faces to the mat and begin to pray that God would send rain. After their prayers, the mother and daughter immediately focus when they hear a man and woman sing a response-and-answer song about how God created everything.

The family leaves intrigued and encouraged. Beyond their five senses, their spirits have felt extraordinarily drawn to this Jesus. As they walk, the daughter is quietly singing a Cambodian style song, which the group sang together. The father is determined that his family will join their neighbors again for the next gathering.

The family's warm reaction is due to experiencing the Creator in an indigenous context. The opposite of indigenous is when a local church borrows imported theology, practices, structures, and forms from another culture. Missionaries—as outsiders working on the inside—need to be strategic and intentional about allowing the organic shaping of the indigenous church. Our natural propensity is to *do*, but "doing it our way" will surely impose foreign-ness on churches meant to be indige-nous.

UNDER THE TIP OF THE CULTURAL ICEBERG

When it comes to practicing this kind of intentionality, comments like this are typical: "From my observation, the people of this or that country seem very Western, so a strict indigenous approach is not necessary." This observation is rarely valid. When glancing at the tip of an iceberg, one only sees the jagged tips of the iceberg rising above the frozen water. However, the iceberg extends way below the water's surface.

Patty Lane, the author of *Crossing Cultures*, refers to the layer of ice above the water as the "objective culture" and the nonvisible ice as the "subjective culture." Nowadays, Cambodians living in the city have slowly put away their sarongs and silk skirts for MTV-style clothing. Many young females have begun to dye their hair red or blonde. Lotions galore are sold to whiten one's skin. A motorcycle that says "Pizza Company" heads toward a customer's house in which the youth are singing a Michael Jackson song in karaoke form. You will hear again and again Cambodians saying the North American cliché, "Oh, my god!"

All of these sights and sounds may cause a Western observer to conclude that Cambodians are quite Western. But in this case, all we see is the objective culture: changes in style, food, clothing, entertainment, and commodities. Below the surface is the subjective culture that is still very Cambodian: motivations, assumptions, interpretations, values, feelings, and beliefs—which makes up what is ultimately called a *worldview*.

Patty Lane gives us a tangible example about a Vietnamese refugee who settled in Houston, Texas. Ha Nguyen worked hard to learn enough English to go to a community college. The story unfolds:

> On his first day of class he decided to tell his professors and classmates that his name was John instead of Ha. He had learned that in English Ha was not a name but a laugh. He did not want people to laugh at him. He also decided to buy sandwiches in the student center for lunch instead of taking rice and spring rolls his aunt offered. Over the course of the next few months his clothing, speech, diet and mannerisms all began to look like those of the U.S.-born students at his college. One day his professor mentioned how remarkable it was that "John" had become an American so quickly.[7]

The professor came to his conclusion about John by merely looking at the objective changes—the tip of the iceberg. If the professor went to Ha's home, he would be surprised at how ethnically Vietnamese Ha really was. When it came to family matters, values, motives, beliefs, and decision-making, Ha was not Americanized.

As missionaries, we will have the tendency to form our strategies based on what we see on the objective level. Many missionaries who work with university students and campus ministries in other countries disciple students according to their university's culture, while ignoring their home-setting culture. Often these students conduct life as Christians on campus, but quickly abandon biblical principles and practices upon returning home. Logic works on campus, but witchcraft works at home. We cannot allow the observable culture to trick us into becoming lackadaisical in our genuine effort to proactively cultivate an indigenous church.

Globalization, easy access to one another around the world, makes Ha's story a reality in many countries—without people ever having to leave their homelands!

Globalization allows cultures to intimately touch other cultures. In light of globalization, we may be apt to mistakenly interpret a particular country's objective culture as their worldview. Culture runs deep, thus missionaries need to dig deep.

Mark Batterson's book *Primal* illustrates powerfully how much culture is an integral part of a person.[8] Batterson writes about a study which was conducted between a group of Mexicans and a group of North Americans. None of the people within their respective research groups had visited the other group's country. Those conducting the research developed a binocular that showed one image for the right eye and another for the left eye. One image was of a baseball scene, and the other was a bullfight. When the participants looked into the binoculars, their eyes were forced to focus on one image. The North American participants saw the baseball image, and the Mexicans saw the bullfight image. It is amazing to me that the brain immediately goes to and focuses on that which is familiar when offered a choice. As we live and work cross-culturally, we cannot allow the objective culture to mislead us from ministering at the subjective level.

DIFFERING DEFINITIONS

Indigenous means different things to different people. Some say that indigenous merely means that the church is made up of an indigenous linguistic group. Others claim that a local church becomes indigenous when the church has local leaders, even though the pastor might sprinkle English into his sermons, receive a subsidy from a church in North America, and sing Western translated songs in a thickly Asian context.

In the 1800s, missions strategists Rufus Anderson and Henry Venn developed the "three-self formula": self-governing, self-supporting, and self-propagating. Their formula carries weight to this day in defining the indigenous church.

John Nevius, who was a Presbyterian missionary to China and Korea in the mid-to-late 1800s, challenged the missionaries of his time to commit to and enhance the three-self formula of Anderson and Venn. Additionally, Nevius promoted and implemented the following principles:

- Christians should continue to live in their neighborhoods and pursue their occupations, being self-supporting and witnessing to their co-workers and neighbors.
- Missions should only develop programs and institutions that the national church desired and could support.
- The national churches should call out and support their own pastors.

- Churches should be built in the native style with money and materials given by the church members.
- Intensive biblical and doctrinal instruction should be provided for church leaders every year.[9]

Missionary Roland Allen (1868–1947) diligently promoted the three-self principles through a discourse on St. Paul's missionary methods. His classic book, *Missionary Methods: St Paul's or Ours?* is widely read in the twenty-first century. In *The Indigenous Church*, Melvin Hodges calls us to emphasize cultural relevancy along with the three-self formula. Hodges's book was one of the first that I read on the indigenous church. His missions experience was in Latin America and the West Indies, and he served as a professor in the Assemblies of God graduate school of theology and missions. Gailyn Van Rheenen quotes Melvin Hodges in his article, "Money and Mi$$ion$ (Revisited): Combating Paternalism":

> Melvin Hodges popularized indigenous perspectives in the 1950s with the publication of his book On the Mission Field: The Indigenous Church. He defined an indigenous church as "a native church …which shares the life of the country in which it is planted and finds itself ready to govern itself, support itself, and reproduce itself," (Hodges 1957, 7). This formative definition expanded the Three-Self Formula by saying that missions churches should be self-propagating, self-governing, and self-supporting while reflecting God's will in culturally appropriate ways. The church, according to Hodges, must be like a banana plant in Central America—so indigenous to its environment that it requires no special attention to thrive. Banana plants grow in this climate wherever there is adequate water. A banana plant in Canada, however, cannot survive without special care. Before winter it must be dug up and transported indoors and seldom, if ever, is able to bear fruit (Hodges 1953, 7-8). The fruit of paternalism, according to Hodges, is anemic mission churches that are not allowed to grow naturally in the soils in which they were planted.[10]

In my chapter on definitions in part 1, I included the six self-principles of Dr. Alan Tippett, a former missionary to the Fiji Islands who is presently an anthropologist and church-growth specialist. He advocates that indigenous principles should be established from the beginning and not transferred over at a later time. He expands the three-self formula by describing six marks of the indigenous church:

1) Does the church have a healthy self-image?
   Does it view itself as the Body of Christ in its own community?
2) Is the church self-functioning? *Autonomous*
   Does it contain all the parts necessary for caring for itself and its own outreaches?
3) Is it self-determining?
   Is the church autonomous—capable of making its own decisions?
4) Is it self-supporting?
   Does it carry its own financial responsibility? Does it finance its own service projects?
5) Is it self-propagating?
   Does the church have its own missionary outreach?
6) Is it self-giving?
   Does it manage its own service programs such as hospitals, seminaries, relief projects and so on?[11]

Anderson, Venn, Nevius, Allen, Hodges, and Tippett make us realize that the concept of the indigenous church has been well thought-out over the generations. Of course, as was said earlier, it's important to recognize that "self" in these contexts is not about independence from God or community. Wrapped up in the principle of self as it is used by these key missiologists is the idea that the desire and practice of depending on Christ rises up from within and is portrayed in conjunction with a community of believers. For example, a church that has a healthy self-image might say, "We have a responsibility for the neighbors around us. We will ask God to enable us to minister to our neighbors through the Holy Spirit. Our knees will be worn out in prayer for our surrounding community. Our sweat will be the evidence of our love in action. Missionaries, pray for us that God will make us a relevant voice to our community."

Another way to define "self" in this context is to say "motivated and flowing from within and extending outward." Charles Brock, a veteran church planter, suggests using the term "Christ-sustained ability,"[12] indicating that the self-ability to do something is motivated and sustained by Christ. Thus, if we say "Christ-sustained determining," we are expressing that a church has the vision and ability to make its own decisions with dependence on Christ.

PARTNERSHIPS

Many missions-oriented people have stated that globalization offers the unique opportunity to be a one-world, interdependent body of Christ, and North American Christians need to seize the opportunity be a part of the action. This action usually translates into forming partnerships with Christians, churches, and ministries in other parts of the world. The idea is that through partnerships, the Great Commission will be fulfilled more expediently.

A widely accepted definition of partnership is "an association of two or more autonomous bodies who have formed a trusting relationship and fulfill agreed-upon expectations by sharing complementary strengths and resources, to reach a mutual goal."[13] Ideally, this definition sounds awesome, but what I personally have experienced and seen in action is lopsided partnerships. The "outside" partners usually consider themselves as the powerful (more experienced, more resourced, more knowledgeable) Christians working with the weaker (less experienced, less resourced, less knowledgeable) "inside" Christians. If any degree of dominance exists in the partnership, local initiative becomes dormant. More often than not, partnerships end up being about one partner giving funds to the other partner. Solomon Aryeety states his concern about this manner of partnership:

> Some have chosen a simple equation: Western money dollars + African availability and zeal = missionary enterprise ...[This model] has the potential of killing the very same African initiative it purports to bring about. For us, it is of the utmost importance that this enterprise be truly indigenous.[14]

Partnership is supposed to work both ways, so I have to ask: in regard to North American church partnerships formed with Majority World church partners, how much have the North Americans allowed their cross-cultural partners to have influence in their propagation, support, and government within their own stateside ministry context? When the cross-cultural partners do come to North American churches or organizations, it is usually for the purpose of sharing testimonies of how valuable their North American partners are. Or they come to learn how to do church in the North American context, so they can take back what they have learned to their respective countries. Are partnerships without true interchange really interdependent and absent of paternalism? Is it possible, in many cases, that the relationship is more of a dependent-ship than a true partner-ship?

How many of these "partnerships" are actually formed between two or more autonomous (self-directed and self-sufficient) entities? I have received numerous e-mails from around the world requesting that I enter into a partnership with a particular ministry or church. Those general requests are always followed up by a plea for finances. To be honest, most requests for money are wrapped up in partnership rhetoric, but the bottom line is the desire for money. Can a dependent group truly enter into an interdependent relationship? Robert Reese shares his thoughts on this:

> A dependent person cannot simply jump into being interdependent without first moving out of dependency. If we simply try to ignore the issues surrounding dependency and form "partnerships" between independent and dependent groups, we will only perpetuate dependency because some of the "partners" will have little to offer of any perceived value. Therefore, many arrangements now called "partnerships" are actually the continuation of dependency.[15]

Some missions strategists have stated that partnership models should completely replace indigenous models. In answer to that, I must ask: if the partnership model replaces the three-self model, are we more likely to replace self-propagation, self-support, and self-government with partnership-propagation, partnership-support, and partnership-government, or with dependent-propagation, dependent-support, and dependent-government? I do believe many sincere people are working diligently to guide and provide healthy interdependent partnerships. But I "spy with my little eyes"[16] a whole lot of paternalism, and I am worried that massive access to the world is ushering in a type of postmodern colonialism.

I am not advocating that North Americans step out of the realm of missions, but I am encouraging us to carve out ways in which we intentionally work from a place of humility and as facilitators. According to S. Kaner, "The facilitator's job is to support everyone to do their best thinking and practice. To do this, the facilitator encourages full participation, promotes mutual understanding and cultivates shared responsibility. By supporting everyone to do their best thinking, a facilitator enables group members to search for inclusive solutions and build sustainable agreements."[17]

Terms aside, what is really important is that every house church movement, every people movement, every church planting movement, every apostolic movement, every church, every group of disciples within a community, every servant-leader must have psychological ownership of their own purpose and function. This heartfelt ownership cannot be dependent on outsiders. Outsiders must deliberately affirm and not undermine psychological ownership of a group's purpose and function as these respective peoples serve the Lord in their indigenous context.

LESSONS FROM THE CELTS

If you have the opportunity, I recommend you read *The Celtic Way of Evangelism* by George Hunter III. The gist of Hunter's book is to invite us to see how "the Celtic way" of doing church is a suitable model for the West today.

In the latter end of the fourth century, Celtic pirates made their way into Britain and captured a young man we now call Patrick, enslaving him in Ireland. During Patrick's six years in Ireland, he cultivated a profound relationship with the Creator, a profound understanding of Irish culture and language, and a profound love for the Irish people. The amazing part of the story is that Patrick—"St. Patrick," in fact—eventually returned to the place of his Irish captors as a missionary. And it is here that his story becomes relevant to us: while the religious influencers of Patrick's sending church assumed that he would plant churches in the Roman way, Patrick defied the norms and started an Irish movement for Christ.

Hunter asks the question, "What would a visitor from Rome have noticed about Celtic Christianity that was 'different'?"[18] He goes on to explain:

> The visitor would have observed more of a movement than an institution, with small provisional buildings of wood and mud, a movement featuring laity in ministry more than clergy. This movement, compared to the Roman wing of the One Church was more imaginative and less cerebral, closer to nature and its creatures, and emphasized the "immanence" and "providence" of the Triune God more than his "transcendence."
>
> Most of all, the Roman visitor would notice that Patrick's "remarkable achievement was to found a new kind of church, one which broke the Roman imperial mould and was both catholic and barbarian." That "new kind of church" gradually displaced the parish church as Irish Christianity's dominant form of Christian community."[19]

In actuality, visiting Romans would have been shocked when the so-called barbarians weren't civilized carbon copies of themselves. The Celtic movement for Christ was not about the barbarians becoming someone else; it was about them becoming Celts whose dedication to God permeated every aspect of their lives and communities. Hunter expounds on their indigenous and contextualized approach:

> We saw how their strategy of indigenizing the forms of expressing Christianity in the life and culture of each "barbarian" population helped the gospel's meaning to break through time and again. By the eleventh century their "culturally relevant" movement had adapted Christianity to the language and culture on many different Celtic and Germanic peoples; indeed, the number of cultural adaptations they managed was unprecedented.[20]

"Time and time again": such breakthroughs are the result of valuing and promoting indigenous movements for Christ. We have talked much about modeling in this chapter, and today, Patrick is a tremendous model for us. Let us emulate Patrick's passion for allowing people to know God, the Father of our Lord Jesus Christ, through their own culture. We have much to learn from the Celts.

LEAD THE COWS TO GRASS

In the balmy Cambodian mornings and evenings, I loved to watch the Cambodian boys leading their cows back and forth to the pasture. It was a familiar sight; thus, a comforting one. One of the main goals of a young farmer is to lead the cows to grass, while doing all he can to keep those cows from trampling the crops. As a missionary, I want to lead people to God's grass without trampling their culture. I want to plant the gospel and allow the church to grow out of its indigenous soil. It takes self-discipline on the part of missionaries to encourage the planting of indigenous churches and movements for Christ, but it is well worth the effort. May the Tibetans say, "He is our God." May the Cambodians say, "He is our God." May the Taiwanese say, "He is our God." May the Celts say, "He is our God." May the West of today say, "He is our God."

> "When you can put your church on the back of my camel then I will think Christianity is meant for us Somalis."
>
> CAMEL HERDER, NORTHERN KENYA

CHAPTER EIGHT

SERVE AS A LOW-PROFILE MISSIONARY:

CONDUCTING MISSIONS WITH QUESTIONS INSTEAD OF ANSWERS

"Pastor Veasna, I notice that the people in your church really respect your leadership. People in my church compare me to the missionary. I cannot preach like him, or play an instrument, or find jobs with organizations for those in my church. Why the difference in your church?"

"Our church did not operate full speed ahead from the beginning. The missionary who planted our first church remained low profile. He refrained from introducing public ministry activities until we could do it ourselves. He did not center the church plant around his economic advantages. The church grew up with our leadership, not his. There was-n't this day of transferring leadership from missionary to local leaders."

In North America, we have an old saying: "To understand a man, you need to walk a mile in his shoes." Another famous quote, spoken by Atticus Finch in the classic book *To Kill a Mocking Bird* by Harper Lee, is: "You never really understand a person until you consider things from his point of view—until you climb into his skin and walk around in it." Serving as a low-profile missionary involves climbing into another's skin and walking around in it.

A businessman from my home state of Minnesota went to Northwest Kenya on a trip with his pastor and friends. Ward Brehm could not help but commit his experience to writing. Ward's book was widely distributed, and a copy actually made it back to West Pokot, where Ward had spent two days. Well, the book landed in the hands of the wrong person—or should I say the right person. After reading the book, Pastor John Lodinyo, a Pokot warrior turned pastor, wrote a letter to Ward. In the letter, Lodinyo expressed his aggravation with Ward's description of his people. His basic sentiment was, how dare Ward give such an inferior account of his precious people?

After Ward recovered from the shocking letter, he wrote Lodinyo a sincere apology. This interaction between the two men formed a friendship. Ward visited Lodinyo numerous times, and eventually Lodinyo came to see Ward in Minnesota. During an outdoor picnic, an interesting conversation unfolded:

> My wife, Kris, then said to Lodinyo, "Well, it's wonderful that you have finally come to our home after Ward's many visits to your community." He responded, "Ward has never been to my community. And in fact, we have never been together." His comment raised the collective eyebrows of my entire family. Now I assumed Lodinyo was having some language difficulties, so I reminded him that I had been to West Pokot nine times, and five of those times I had indeed been with him. He turned his head slowly, and his eyes were piercing as he said to me, "No, we have never been together. When you come, you are always with your people you bring. You stay in a separate house on the hill. You eat with your group, sleep with your group, and only meet with us for a short time." …The ensuing silence confirmed the truth of his words.[1]

Lodinyo went on to explain that Ward's visits were more ceremonial in nature than a sincere experience of everyday life in the West Pokot community. In other words, the Pokot community treated Ward and his friends as they would any other visitor—with extra-special care and fanfare. Perhaps this type of care could be compared to what we experience when we sell a house in North America. Specialists come in and empty the house of the owner's personality and that lived-in feel. They remove personal items, redecorate, and create perfect, model-like surroundings. If potential buyers were to try to explain the house to the owners based on what the realtors did to the house, the owners would say, "That doesn't sound like our house." The potential buyers merely had an artificial encounter in the house.

Lodinyo gave Ward a challenge: "Spend five days with me in the real bush of West Pokot. Then we will know each other, and you will know West Pokot."[2] After days of agonizing thought, Ward agreed to walk with Lodinyo for five days in his world. Ward and Lodinyo walked together as real friends in the dust of West Pokot. Based on this friendship walk, Pastor John Lodinyo wrote the following about Ward:

In Africa, white men don't walk. The missionaries, the doctors, the donors, when they come, they come in vehicles. They always drive. Ward was different. Ward walked …So the message went out across the land: "A white man is walking to Mbaro." It was the first time many along the way had seen a white man. It was historic. Historic! Babies will be named after him! Ward is, to us, a legend. To this day, people are still talking about him, the white man who walked. At the end of our journey, the elders gave Ward the title Nyakan, meaning "a brave man who faces the unknown with only faith in God." Ward crossed not only mountain ranges, but also lines of convention. He broke barriers. He is no longer viewed as a donor. He walked and in the process became one of us. Ward is our friend, our brother, a warrior, a Pokot. If his accomplishment could be reflected in his skin color, he would have come home black.[3]

This time, Ward did not experience West Pokot and the people as a missionary or doctor or donor in a vehicle. Ward broke the stereotype. He set aside his high-profile position and walked with and among the Pokot people. Rare indeed! Lodinyo called it historic—never been done before. When you think of this experience in the light of missions, ask yourself: should a shedding of one's skin (setting aside your identity to experience someone else's identity) be rare or common? I think most of us would answer "common." But the actual process is easier said than done. A missionary couple who lived in Irian Jaya expressed their struggle to live a low-profile lifestyle:

> The greatest challenge we face in ministry in Irian is the day to day struggle against our far superior standard of living, the status of wealth we have, in comparison to the people God has given us to minister to. They clearly are aware of the "gulf between" and desire to attain to that standard of power and wealth they see in us. We sought to cut back, and live more simply than most missionaries in Irian Jaya. But the struggle remains. So opposite of the example of incarnation given us by Christ. But, also easy to justify. Missionaries do it everyday.[4]

I know the justifications. We will never really become like our hosts, so trying too hard looks like false humility. A healthy and live missionary is better than a sickly or dead missionary. Our families come first. We are after holistic transformation (spiritual, physical, societal, educational), and our material abundance contributes to that holistic development. But the honest truth is, when we flaunt and use our economic advantages as missionaries, we create barriers. We become conventional, and we are viewed as donors. Would it be better if we were called "a brave man who faces the unknown with only faith in God" or "a great white missionary who rode in his vehicle and met all our needs"?

I have learned a lot from John Lodinyo and Ward Brehm. Thank you, Ward, for apologizing to Lodinyo and taking up his challenge to walk through West Pokot. Thank you, Lodinyo, for having the courage to write a letter to Ward and inviting him to walk with you.

TWENTY-YEAR SETBACK

In 2008, I had the opportunity to meet Pastor Levy Moyo in England, through Glenn Schwartz, founder and director of World Mission Associates. Levy Moyo had written a book called *The Gloved Handshake*. In it, Moyo shares about a experience during his years as Secretary General of the Apostolic Church in Zimbabwe.

He and a committee met to plan for a national convention. They made a difficult but strategic decision that the mother church would not subsidize the convention. All participants were responsible for their own transportation and food. The committee desired to train themselves and the churches to steward their own ministries and to contribute to the cause of the church as a whole. They knew that if they did not introduce self-reliance, the national church would become steeped in unhealthy dependency.

The convention participants were clearly notified that each person was responsible to pay a fee for food and provide his own transportation; however, they were accustomed to someone else paying the bills, and the participants arrived without money. The leaders of the convention knew that if they solved the problem by instantly providing food and services, they would create a long-term problem of dependency. To stay true to their goal of developing a self-responsible national church, Pastor Moyo announced that those who did not pay the fees would have to find another source for their meals outside of the meals provided at the conference. Pastor Moyo and the other conference leaders made this decision with much pain, but for an extremely important reason. Pastor Moyo likened the process to that of African women putting hot pepper on the breast to wean babies. The leaders had to cause a degree of pain for the greater purpose of weaning the national church from the Western breast.

During the lunch break at the conference, Pastor Moyo was asked by another pastor to accompany him to the market. As they arrived at the market, Pastor

Moyo's friend bought a significant amount of meat and maize. Pastor Moyo assumed that his friend was buying food for those in his party or even for others at the convention. The action was praiseworthy, since this was an African sharing his local resources with his African brothers and sisters in Christ.

At the close of the afternoon session, the man who bought the food headed up to the platform. He announced that a good-hearted missionary had bought food, and everyone could eat freely.

Pastor Moyo's heart practically stopped as he lost face in front of six hundred people. This one seemingly generous action destabilized Pastor Moyo's relationship with his national church flock and pounded the African people into a deeper rut of dependency. He wrote, "That day I was embarrassed and isolated. I will never forget that day because it was the day I felt the impact of losing full leadership in the national church and the church going twenty years backward."[5]

There was a day when I would have intervened just like the missionary who attended the conference. These thoughts probably crossed his mind: "How great would it be if everyone could eat at the conference and not worry about problem-solving meal issues. I could really make a difference here today." Well, the missionary did make a difference, just not the one he intended. This interaction between missionary and host culture is a perfect example of functioning out of a high-profile role. The self-imposed high-profile role of the missionary sabotaged the local leader's opportunity to build trust and respect among the local people within his realm of responsibility.

COMPROMISING HEARTFELT OWNERSHIP

We do not have to look very far in many countries to see missionaries serving in high-profile roles; in fact, it's a popular way to plant churches. The missionary models how to "do church" until the responsibility of the church can be transferred to local leaders. This pattern seems logical, but it is loaded with long-term problems.

First, by the time the missionary transfers the responsibilities to the local believers, there is already an ingrained mindset that this is the missionary's church. Transferring leadership responsibility overlooks the development of heartfelt ownership of the ministry and causes the locals to feel as though they have inherited the ministry. Heartfelt ownership of a church or ministry is like the heart that pumps our blood; it is necessary for life. Take away or never produce heartfelt ownership, and you end up with apathy, indifference, and disloyalty. So many churches that are centered on a charismatic leader fall apart when that leader moves on. Instead of taking heartfelt ownership of the life of the church, the people ride on the wings of the leader's heartfelt ownership of the ministry. The leader moves on; the wings go with him.

When missionaries birth, develop, and then hand over ministries to local people, heartfelt ownership is put at serious risk. But there is a second issue as well. In cases where the missionaries initially fill high-profile ministry roles, the local leaders have difficulty filling the shoes of those missionaries. The majority of missionaries serve in ministry roles to their fullest capacity, leaning on years of experience, plenty of resources, and ample equipment. Additionally, they often provide fringe benefits such as English lessons, jobs, medical teams, musical instruments, and equipment. When it is the local leaders' turn to conduct ministry, they struggle to find acceptance because the church members miss the missionary's charity, expertise, and charismatic personality.

Lastly, there is the ever-present problem of failing to plant a truly indigenous church. Missionaries often conduct and model ministry based on church models from their own countries, albeit with some variation. Inevitably, the church develops a foreign personality, structure, and style.

These three long-term problems mean that local leaders, with no sense of heartfelt ownership, inherit a foreign-style church in which the members constantly require the missionary's presence. How do I know this? I learned the hard way—from experience. We cannot assume that the transfer of heartfelt ownership will simply accompany the transfer of responsibility from ourselves to local leaders. Thus, I suggest we allow Pastor Veasna's experience to guide our experience:

> "Our church did not operate full speed ahead from the beginning. The missionary who planted our first church remained low profile. He refrained from introducing public ministry activities until we could do it ourselves. The church grew up with our leadership, not his. There wasn't this day of transferring leadership from missionary to local leaders."

I wonder why God created women in such a way that they carry their babies for nine months in the womb. Why not one month or two months? God could have arranged it so babies develop faster. Perhaps one of the reasons is so that the mother will develop a deep-seated ownership of her baby's well-being—an unrelenting sense of responsibility, love, and concern. Upon going through the struggle to both carry the baby and give birth, the mother develops a profound connection and conscientiousness for her child.

A mother's unwavering sense of responsibility for her child is not something handed to her, but is part of her innate nature and is strengthened through the birthing process, which includes nine months of pregnancy. Likewise, a missionary cannot merely hand over a sense of heartfelt ownership to locals after the church already has a full life of its own due to the missionary's effort. It is the process of birthing and nurturing a church that develops true ownership.

Local leaders who lead without an intense sense of heartfelt ownership will lack motivation and may easily abandon the church in times of testing. So how does a missionary lead differently? Steve Saint, a missionary who teaches on unhealthy dependency—something he experienced in a big way among the Huaorani of Ecuador—gives us practical advice:

> Missions is not to go in and create and control church for other people nor be the church for them. It is not our job to insure that it functions. It is simply and only to plant the church in every people group and nurture it until it is able to propagate, govern and support itself. When missions go beyond that, then they are imposing themselves in the area of responsibility that belongs to the indigenous people and then everything gets out of whack.[6]

"Nurture" is an important word here, because some may think that nurture means to fulfill high-profile roles for the sake of modeling—but that almost always turns into doing the job for the locals. Steve Saint states that missionaries should not even "create church" for other people. How do you *plant* a church if you do not *create* church for a particular people group? Well, how about making disciples and facilitating them to "create church" (however they see fit) by pointing them to God's Word? Can you imagine what could happen if a group of people had no preconceived ideas of what church should be like other than the Word of God? How different would church be from how we know it?

Serving as a low-profile missionary—encouraging and training from behind the scenes as much as possible—opens the way for dedicated local leaders to feel heartfelt ownership and connect well with those in their realm of ministry. This is a church worthy of being the first link in a chain of churches planting churches.

Hudson Taylor, who served as a missionary in China, went to great lengths to become low profile by his humble approach of becoming like the Chinese as much as possible, even at the ridicule of his colleagues. We need the Hudson Taylors of today.

CONSCIOUS AND UNCONSCIOUS PATERNALISM

Recently, I attended a forum in Kenya where a Kenyan pastor shared that there was once actually a slave ship called Jesus. Based on his statement, I did a little research on names of slave ships. Sir John Hawkins was the first English captain to bring Africans to the Americas on a ship—a seven-hundred-ton ship that sailed in 1562. Being a religious man, he called his ship *The Good Ship Jesus*. He commanded a truly tight ship in which the crew were expected to respect and to love one another, while kidnapped Africans were chained in the bows of the ship. When missionaries eventually arrived in Africa proclaiming Jesus, you can imagine the confusion and suspicion they aroused!

During this Kenyan pastor's presentation, he revealed how the Africans systematically faced slavery by foreign slave traders, colonialism by European colonizers, and paternalism by Western missionaries. Slavery, colonialism,[7] and paternalism[8] figuratively and literally broke the backs of African people and ingrained within them the message that someone else would think and act for them. The effects of this terrible trio still have a negative influence within the churches in Africa today.

One of the purposes of the forum was to discover how African leaders could reverse the mentality of inferiority which keeps the churches from growing. I believe that missionaries need to join the African leaders by acknowledging paternalism and refraining from it.

Gailyn Van Rheenen, who writes monthly missiological reflections for "Missions Alive", gives us insight into what paternalism is:

> Generations of missions scholars have sought to determine how to overcome or eliminate paternalism, or "the dominance of the sending culture over the mission process" (Van Rheenen). Paternalism occurs when missionaries and their sending churches and agencies consciously or unconsciously assume that they possess superior knowledge, experience, and skills and, consequently, exert control over local Christians and their leaders. This control is almost always exerted through financial arrangements and the implicit authority of money. New Christians are reluctant to "bite the hand" of those helping them—even if that hand is manipulative.[9]

A low-profile missionary avoids the conscious and unconscious paternalism that is described by Van Rheenen. In their book *When Helping Hurts*, Steve Corbett and Brain Fikkert describe the various forms of paternalism: resource, spiritual, knowledge, labor, and managerial. Using their terms, let's look at each form:

> *Resource paternalism* is when we (missionaries) give financial and material resources while diminishing the recipients' motivation, willingness, and obedience to mobilize, sustain, and steward the work within their realm of responsibility.
>
> *Spiritual paternalism* is operating out of a sense that we (missionaries) have superior spiritual experience and understanding. For example, have you ever seen a room full of local believers praying for a sick person, and at the center of the activity is the missionary laying his hands on the ill person? This scene is common and sends the message that the local believers are spiritually inferior.
>
> *Knowledge paternalism* is conducting ministry with the premise that we (missionaries) know how to best conduct ministry in that setting. If a local church looks like a carbon copy of a church from another cultural context, evidence indicates that someone with knowledge paternalism influenced that church.
>
> *Labor paternalism* manifests itself when we (missionaries) do the work for others or fulfill roles in a cross-cultural context. Visitors painting orphanages, refurbishing church structures, or serving as chairmen in place of natural constituencies—people who are benefited by that ministry and who are capable of doing those very tasks—are examples of labor paternalism. I read an article in my hometown's newspaper about a church in Mexico that was painted six times in one summer by six different visiting teams!
>
> *Managerial paternalism* is planning and directing affairs for others to ensure our (the missionaries') desire for efficiency and productivity. Sometimes we hide behind the proclamation that we are merely modeling. Prolonged modeling is often an excuse for not wanting to step aside and allow others to plan and manage.

These five types of paternalism rob local people of the privilege of being faithful stewards of their own *resources*, *Spirit-led* ministers, *knowledgeable* leaders, capable *laborers*, and successful *managers*. Paternalism freezes people in a place of complacency and apathy. Those who perpetuate paternalism think that they must take charge if they want anything to be accomplished—but this is a myth.

Corbett and Fikkert share a list of reasons why locals may not take charge, one that applies to many missions settings:

- They do not need to take charge because they know that we will take charge if they wait long enough.
- They lack the confidence to take charge, particularly when the "superior," middle-to-upper-class North Americans are involved.
- They, like we, have internalized the messages of centuries of colonialism, slavery, and racism: Caucasians run things and everyone else follows.
- They do not want the project to happen as much as we do. For example, they might know the project will accomplish little in their context but are afraid to tell us for fear of offending us.
- They know that by letting us run the show it is more likely that we will bring in money and other material resources to give them.[10]

Paternalism is not reflective of a fatherly figure bestowing benevolence upon a child. Rather, it is intrusive and feeds the ego of the paternalistic partner. A degree of paternalism is unconscious; however, low-profile missionaries consciously and consistently steer away from it. William Smallman, who wrote about nationalizing global ministry training, made this insightful statement in his book *Able to Teach Others Also*: "The incipient church can flounder and stagnate in its first generation if it has no leaders who think their own thoughts within the framework of the universally applicable Word of God."[11]

I believe we are able to—and need to—encourage local leaders to think and do within "the framework of the universally applicable Word of God." Let's bury slavery, colonialism, and paternalism and never hope for their resurrection!

If we shape our own thoughts by the Word of God, the wrongness of paternalism should be evident. God is the only one who has the right to be paternalistic, and even he does not exercise that right! The fact that God gave us free will reveals his distaste for paternalism. Jesus did not stagnate the first generation of disciples by paternalistically keeping them in a forever state of childlikeness. The first-generation disciples, working in conjunction with the Holy Spirit, were capable, self-reliant men who impacted the world for all generations.

We do, however, see paternalism happening in Scripture. Joseph and Mary struggled with a degree of it. Luke describes Jesus as someone who grew in wisdom and stature and in favor with God and men (Luke 2:52). This description was revealed after the event of Jesus's separation from his parents. During their family travels, Jesus, who was twelve years of age at the time, stayed behind to do his work in the temple. His parents became frantic and searched for three days until they found him playing with marbles in the alleyway. No! They found young Jesus answering questions for the teachers at the temple. Everyone who heard him was utterly amazed by the profoundness of his words. Jesus's mother was frustrated and felt mistreated. Jesus responded firmly, "Didn't you know I had to be in my Father's house?"

Somehow, I cannot help but feel my pulse quicken as I reflect upon Jesus's experience. As missionaries, we desire to see churches within our host countries grow in wisdom and stature, and in favor with God and men. What a beautiful description of a movement for Christ!

Jesus had psychological ownership of his role, and he knew how to navigate his life in order to fulfill it. Not even Jesus's parents could prevent his fulfillment and growth through paternalism. And ultimately, they responded well to his rebuke. Joseph and Mary knew they had to let Jesus psychologically own and fulfill his role. Instead of forcing their "parenthood" upon Jesus, they stepped back and treasured all things in their hearts.

As missionaries, we long to be like Joseph and Mary and restrain from imposing paternalism among those to whom we minister. We know that our role is to release and allow local churches and leaders to fulfill their God-given roles. We serve by staying in the background and treasuring their growth as their ministries gain the favor of both God and men.

John and Helen Dekker spent twenty-one years in Irian Jaya as missionaries. They invested their lives among the Dani, planting churches and equipping the Dani to serve as missionaries to the many tribes of Irian Jaya. John and Helen regularly visited the seventy-nine Toli Valley churches and the sixty-five Dani missionaries. Upon John and Helen's visits, the Dani often asked John to preach. John responded in the following manner, "We come, and we go. But you have God's Word in your hands, and it will stay. That is what is important."[12]

PLANTING CHURCHES USING QUESTIONS

At first glance, using questions as a method to plant churches seems nonsensical—but I think it is a perfect way to plant an indigenous church. The missionary uses questions, progressing through various stages, to facilitate believers to conduct themselves as a community of believers.

For example, let us say that a group of believers within Cambodia has read some Bible stories and verses relating to worship. Through conversation, the missionary discerns that the local believers are ready to begin intentional worship as a community. At this point, the missionary does not instantly introduce worship content, style, or forms from his or her culture. Rather, he or she asks the following questions to facilitate this local community of believers to form themselves according to principles in the Bible and their own cultural expressions:

- According to biblical examples, in what ways did faith communities or people worship God?
- According to biblical examples, what attitudes did worshipers exemplify?
- According to biblical examples, how did worshipers displease God?
- According to Cambodian culture, how do you show respect and adoration?
- According to the Bible and Cambodian culture, how do you want to worship?
- What gifts and resources do you have within you and around you that you could use to worship?

Through such questions, asked at foundational stages, at least two powerful ingredients of a healthy church will take root: psychological ownership—local believers will be stewards of their worship—and indigeneity—the worship will be conducted and expressed according to the local culture. The goal is to use facilitating questions for all stages of church planting and development. This coaching technique enables the missionary to remain low profile and allows the local churches to plant, grow, and multiply ministry by depending on the Holy Spirit, being in tune with their own culture, and serving as stewards of their own human and local resources.

Patrick Lai, who has served as a tentmaker for twenty-three years in the 10/40 window (the part of the world that is least reached, located between 10 and 40 degrees north of the equator), talks about allowing the church to be tried versus formed by outsiders:

Cultural expectations concerning "what is a church" should be tried, not formed. Believers need to be discipled in the principles but not the forms of "church." Believers need to discover in the Holy Spirit and within their own culture, ways to feel comfortable practicing their faith and ecclesiology. There is a danger of new believers uncritically embracing western thinking and models. We should go to great lengths to ensure that the emerging church meetings can be readily reproduced by those who attend. This means even with the first gatherings of believers, the potential national leaders should be involved in leading. Time and effort is to be taken to teach leadership principles and allow believers to work out these principles within the parameters of their own culture.[13]

Planting churches by asking questions instead of giving answers takes discipline, creativity, and practice. In my experience, when a local pastor sought my advice, I was tempted to blurt out my answers. Yet patience and facilitation through asking questions allowed the local pastor to walk away with confidence, culturally relevant solutions, and psychological ownership of those solutions. Facilitation questions cause contemplation, contemplation causes reliance on the Holy Spirit, reliance on the Holy Spirit results in discernment, discernment leads to effective practice, and effective practice produces capable indigenous leaders.

GIVE ME BACKUP!

One day, as I was running along a path around the lake in Minneapolis, I saw a boy who was climbing down a tree from branch to branch. He called out to his dad, "Give me backup!"

His dad replied, "Do you need help?" The boy responded, "No! I just need backup!" The father smiled, most likely thinking, "What is the difference?" However, in the boy's mind, there was a difference. The boy did not want his father to do anything, but rather, to stand by and provide moral support. This isn't a bad model—and it's very biblical. The apostle Paul "gave backup" to Timothy:

> I remind you to fan into flame the gift of God, which was in you through
> the laying on of hands. For God did not give us the spirit of timidity, but
> a spirit of power, of love and of self-discipline. (2 Timothy 1:6–7)

Paul wrote many letters, and his second letter to Timothy was most likely his last. In a low-profile manner, Paul offered Timothy encouragement, affirmation, and exhortation. As missionaries, we need to learn to lend our moral support, rather than doing for others. Those within our host cultures want backup, not help. Let us be instead of always doing.

Suzanne Worley, who helped me make some initial edits in this book, brought it to my attention that Jesus required his disciples to implement a low-profile approach when he sent them out. Luke 9:1–6 reveals that Jesus sent the disciples out empty-handed and instructed them to stay in homes. How did this develop psychological ownership of the kingdom message among those who heard it? Because the disciples stayed in homes and didn't bring material goods to the relationship, the hosts were allowed to immediately participate in ministry through sharing and giving, rather than becoming recipients of high-profile leaders.

In gymnastics they have what is called a spotter. A spotter is not the gymnast, but rather one who offers facilitation of the gymnast's movements. Spotters can spot by merely tapping a leg to facilitate accurate movement or by physically guiding the gymnast through the athletic motion. I think we need a lot more "leg tappers" among our missionary constituency—people who will administer a slight tap to reorient someone whom we are training rather than taking over.

As humans, we are driven to achieve and to prove ourselves, which often means we are more geared toward high-profile roles. It takes discipline and humility to serve others by being low profile. Jesus understood this discipline and practiced it as he refused to prove himself to his mockers throughout his journey on earth.

High-profile missionaries leave defeated people in their trail. Low-profile missionaries humbly empower the indigenous man and woman to be God's instruments of noble purposes. "Being in someone's shadow" is a common English idiom that says there is no room for us to be passive. But I suggest that a missionary leader who intentionally positions himself in someone's shadow, with the goal to empower that person, is a great leader.

> "No coach has ever won a game by what he knows; it's what
> his players know that counts."
>
> LEGENDARY FOOTBALL COACH, PAUL "BEAR" BRYANT

CHAPTER NINE

PLAN FOR SUSTAINABILITY:

AVOIDING UNHEALTHY DEPENDENCY BY MOBILIZING LOCAL RESOURCES

"Pastor Veasna, our church members crumple their money up in a wad and put it in the offering. We have very few resources to conduct ministry, let alone think about expanding in other villages. They give so little and yet come to church to ask for money, medicine, or other assistance. The mission organization wants me to urge the church members to give more, so they can wean away my support. I try, but it is difficult because it looks like I am promoting them to give for my sake."

"That is a difficult problem to overcome, brother. The fatalistic mentality that says they are too poor and have nothing significant to contribute is deeply rooted in their psyche. They view the mission organization as the founder and the provider. You can teach on tithing and giving until the cows come home, but the message will fall on deaf ears. You may have to become bi-vocational for a season until the church views themselves as stewards of their resources and gain a sense of responsibility to support their leaders versus depending on mission organizations and churches abroad."

The sounds of tanks and weapons being discharged were way too familiar for Cambodians to ignore. They knew something big was happening, and all those old feelings from the genocide came surging through their emotional bloodstreams. In 1996, the partner of a coalition government in Cambodia committed a bloody coup d'état in the capital city. The coup was brutal, and a large percentage of the foreigners were evacuated, including missionaries.

For the Cambodian church, the mass exit of missionaries presented a problem. The majority of Cambodian churches and ministries were on life support—dependent on outside funding. When the missionaries unexpectedly evacuated, that life support was cut off, and the church started to kick and fling to catch its breath. Local pastors, teachers, translators, directors, and so forth went to their respective missions organizations for their salaries and funds, but there was no one to collect the money from.

I heard many missionaries saying that this was a wake-up call to them, and that they were forced to realize that they needed to implement missions in a way that did not make local people and ministries dependent on missions funding. But the evacuation was short-lived, and for the most part, missionaries made few adaptations. They reconnected the life support. The crisis indeed made us aware of a flaw in our missions paradigms, but perhaps the effort to make a paradigm shift was too complicated, too much work, or too emotionally expensive. Personally, I increasingly developed a discomfort with how our missions approaches caused unhealthy dependency—a term which certainly describes what happened among the Cambodian local believers, leaders, churches, and ministries when the foreign resources were suddenly gone.

Unhealthy dependency in a missions context is not an isolated issue related to a coup in Cambodia. It is a worldwide missions dilemma that each and every person who is involved in missions needs to take seriously.

Before we journey through this chapter, it's important to establish one crucial reality: those who promote the overcoming of unhealthy dependency are intently aware of and concerned for the poor and the immediacy of spreading the gospel. But it is our belief that the very methods we use to relieve poverty and expedite the Great Commission often undermine those outcomes. Thus, in this chapter we will look at the reality, meaning, unintended consequences, and root causes of unhealthy dependency, as well as some examples of ways to overcome and/or avoid it.

One day in Cambodia, I could not tolerate the pain on the bottom of my foot any longer. I rested on the ground and refused to walk another step. I had trouble believing that a tiny black dot on my foot could do so much harm. Two of my friends retrieved a razor blade and lanced the black spot on my foot. They had fun; I did not! Suddenly, a yellowish-brown pus shot straight into the air. The poking and cutting hurt, but the end result was welcomed—my foot quickly healed from the infection. Unhealthy dependency is not a cheery topic, and it involves a degree of lancing and cutting. But it's time we are willing to dig deep and cause some pain to impart health where it is desperately needed.

Dealing with unhealthy dependency, wide and deep, may make you feel overwhelmed and unsure of yourself, maybe even reticent to help at all. Don't be afraid; your compassion will bounce back. The Holy Spirit within you cannot help but be compassionate! My hope is that your compassion will be bathed in Proverbs-like wisdom. Looking back, I wish someone had told me about the dangers involved in helping others without examination of the deeper issues.

There is no shortage of books on compassion, but few that address "unexamined generosity"—a term coined by Bob Lupton in his article "Vacationaries."[1] Do not allow this chapter to squash your compassion. Instead, allow it to shape your compassion for the sake of the helper and the helped. I pray you will come out of this chapter passionate about being compassionate, but equally passionate about avoiding unhealthy dependency.

Two Bicycles Cause a Church Split

Christopher Little, who served as a missionary in parts of Africa, tells of a story in which he discovered the reality and effects of unhealthy dependency. Chris was teaching at a Bible school in Mozambique that was administered by the local church. Chris arrived every day to the Bible school in a vehicle, while his Mozambican colleagues arrived on foot. Then Chris had a grand idea: "I should buy my two fellow professors bicycles; it will ease their travel." Chris excitedly supplied his coworkers with bicycles for their convenience.

Several days later, Chris received some unexpected visitors: the provincial pastor and the church treasurer. These two men gently shared with Chris that his benevolent act was a problem. In the past, missionaries had arbitrarily handed out gifts, bypassing the local leadership. These handouts had caused major issues, so the local leadership in charge of the Bible school had developed strategies to avoid such problems.

Chris apologized and was pleased that they had confronted him, but the fallout was already in motion. The local pastoral leaders who were striving to be consistent with everyone requested that the two professors give the bikes back to Chris. The two professors did not want to comply, which led to confusion and discord. Eventually, one of the professors gathered a few other disgruntled members of the church and left to start his own denomination.

Chris summarizes his experience in this manner:

> It is said that the road to hell is paved with good intentions; I can testify from first-hand experience that the road to church splits is sometimes paved with the good intentions of missionaries! Out of my desire to be compassionate and unselfish, I had done more harm than good.[2]

Chris eventually moved to work in a northern city called Nampula. Within days of Chris's arrival, the pastor gave Chris an orientation. He told Chris not to bring any outside resources into the church. Even after Chris's experience with the two bicycles, Chris still struggled with grasping the danger in giving stuff away to the local people. Chris actually quoted Luke 6:29–30 to the pastor: "If someone takes your cloak, do not stop him from taking your tunic." The pastor firmly responded: "Those verses don't apply here!"[3]

This seems like a harsh and extreme answer, but the pastor had seen, again and again, jealousy, corruption, and apathy taking root in his church due to missionaries introducing outside resources. One of the local pastors, by the name of Bolacha, explained their convictions as a church in more depth:

> One day Bolacha explained to me that there are two kinds of gospels in this world. The first one, the Gospel of Christ, provides for forgiveness of sin, eternal life, and sets people free from the power of the devil. This Gospel involves suffering since Christ commanded us to take up our cross and follow Him (Matt. 16:24). The second gospel, the gospel of goods ("o evangelho dos bens" in Portuguese), is the counterfeit gospel which offers material wealth alongside the true Gospel, enticing people to become Christians. In his opinion, the fundamental problem with the gospel of goods is that when the goods run out the people run away. He said he had seen denomination after denomination import shipping containers of food, clothes, etc., during times of drought and famine, attracting thousands of people. But when the shipping containers stopped coming the people were nowhere to be found. He felt our church was presenting the true Gospel of Christ so that people would not be confused about the way of salvation and what it means to be a committed disciple of Christ.[4]

In due time, Chris had an opportunity to practice what he had learned from these indigenous leaders. During one of the rainy seasons, the church was damaged and the local leaders began to discuss how to rebuild it. One of the pastors asked Chris to find money from the West so they could build a cement church. Chris immediately remembered the bike incident and the lead pastor's words during his orientation upon arrival to the area. Instead of complying with the request, Chris committed to help mobilize the creativity and motivation of the local church people. Indeed, they built their own church. How? With all-night prayer meetings, bags of cement that were sacrificially given slowly but surely, and dedicated labor.

Whether Chris could define his experience as one of "unhealthy dependency" at the time or not, he understood the reality of it. I thoroughly relate to Chris's process of reaction, acceptance, and transformation as he discovered his participation in creating unhealthy dependency and cultivating sustainability. As I read his account, I sense his elation in transitioning from an instigator to a mobilizer.

UNHEALTHY DEPENDENCY AND SUSTAINABILITY

Unhealthy dependency is something we want to intentionally avoid—but what do we promote in its place? The answer is *sustainability*. Other interchangeable terms are *self-reliance, self-sustaining,* and *self-supporting.*

In the twenty-first century, sustainability means different things to different people. The term is most often used in human-environmental realms. In this sense, sustainability charges humans with learning how to meet present needs without destroying the environment, especially for future generations. Sustainability is a key term in community development, where it refers to identifying and mobilizing human and natural resources in the local context. In other words, the local people and local resources become the integral ingredients to their own development.

In the context of missions, how do we best define unhealthy dependency and sustainability? Understanding these concepts properly will go a long way toward helping us build a new paradigm:

UNHEALTHY DEPENDENCY = FAULTY SELF-PERCEPTION

Glenn Schwartz, who has donated twenty-five years to overcoming unhealthy dependency in Christian movements, coined the phrase "other-induced dependency." Other-induced dependency is a condition of becoming dependent upon the money and resources brought to a particular group from the outside. Robert Reese defines dependency as "The unhealthy reliance on foreign resources that accompanies the feeling that churches and institutions are unable to function without outside assistance."[5]

Unhealthy dependency includes a material, psychological, and spiritual component. All together, it creates a faulty self-perception that is death to effective indigenous church growth.

SUSTAINABILITY = HEALTHY SELF-PERCEPTION

Sustainability means that persons and groups have the desire and capacity to mobilize local resources (resources God has put close at hand) in order to own, sustain, and operate the work locally as well as multiply beyond the local context.[6]

Another simple way to describe sustainability is to say that the people who are most associated with a particular ministry, church, or organization have the ability to sustain and develop it.

Like Christopher Little in Mozambique, we have the opportunity to promote sustainability. In other words, we have the opportunity to give fair opportunity for communities in Christ around the world to use their God-given gifts and personhood, to rely on God's sovereignty, and to be locally dependent on one another instead of bypassing self, local believers, and God to depend on foreigners.

Those who are steeped in unhealthy dependency have a faulty self-perception. A faulty self-perception is exposed through how a people perceive themselves: "We can't do it ourselves. We don't have anything to contribute. Let's ask the people abroad to help us. They seem to have a way with God. Everything we do is inferior."

When a group of people nurse such defeated thoughts within their hearts, the only place to go is down—a downward spiral toward self-defeat. Such a person or group of people does not see himself or themselves in the light of truth and real potential in God. Something has happened to them in their upbringing as a church or ministry to cause them to focus on their weaknesses.

On the other hand, those who practice sustainability have a healthy self-perception, which causes them to cheer: "We are responsible stewards. Our sweat needs to be a sign of our contribution. Our tears need to reflect our prayers. We ask and seek God. We mobilize the resources God has put around us. We do our share of giving and sacrificing. The brothers and sisters of our church meet one another's needs."

On our part, it takes prayer and intentionality to build a healthy self-perception in others. As missionaries, we have such a blessed opportunity to encourage people of other nations to perceive themselves as "more than conquerors" through Jesus Christ in their everyday context.

TREATING ROOT CAUSES, NOT SYMPTOMS

It was a typical steamy day in tropical Cambodia, so standing in the river was a treat, not only because it gave me some relief from the heat, but because people were being baptized as a testimony to their faith in Jesus Christ. While I was standing in waist-deep water, I felt something bite my ankle, but I remained in the water for another thirty minutes. As I stepped out, I looked at my throbbing ankle and noticed fang marks: one hole on each side of my ankle bone. I put an ice pack on my ankle to reduce the swelling, but with every few minutes, the swelling moved up my leg. I realized that ice would no longer help and that I needed to go immediately to the doctor. The doctor treated the root cause—poison—and I slowly recovered from the water-snake bite.

Snakebites, disease, and illness will eventually kill a person if the root cause is ignored and only the symptoms are treated. In missions, we often see symptoms of unhealthy dependency, but ignore its root causes.

One day, some of us missionaries were chatting about how the Cambodian churches lacked the motivation to give and sustain their work and pastors. Some missionaries suggested that a strong emphasis on giving and tithing needed to be spread throughout the local Cambodian churches. We concluded, "If pastors taught more assertively about giving and tithing, local churches would take their stewardship responsibilities more seriously." But as I gave the issue more thought, I sensed that we needed to look deeper and identify the root causes rather than merely addressing the symptoms. A lack of sharing and giving—a key biblical principle—was a symptom of something deeper. I came to believe that we wanted the local Cambodian pastors to deal with a weakness we had created. We needed to ask ourselves what had led to this problem in the first place. How did our methods of planting and developing local churches contribute to the symptoms of anemic stewardship within them?

Had we dug deep enough, I believe we would have identified this truth: the seemingly unlimited resources we used to plant and accelerate the growth of the church had created a "we can't and we don't need to" mentality among the Cambodian churches. Cambodians who experienced the mission-established church absorbed just as much from observation as they did from hearing sermons on giving and tithing. And this is what they saw: mission money used to pay their pastors' salaries, subsidize outreaches to their communities, purchase land, construct their buildings, provide their equipment, and the list goes on. Surely, the Cambodian new believers developed a mindset that the missionaries or Western church were the ones to foot the bill!

If we ignore the usage of missionary money as a root cause of anemic giving, lack of self-support, and unhealthy dependency among the Cambodian churches, opting instead to preach more sermons on giving and tithing, we are guilty of merely treating the symptoms.

At one point, I was working in conjunction with a local Cambodian pastor to train some of his members to plant daughter churches. The soon-to-be church planters sat in a circle, and I asked them to share their experiences of why and how they came into a faith journey with Jesus. Their testimonies revealed that most of them began their faith journey because they received glasses, rice, land plots, or employment from Christian organizations. Upon hearing their stories, I knew that their experiences of how they came to know Christ would greatly affect their church planting approaches. As the church planters launched into various areas to plant churches, they began to ask the pastor and me for glasses, rice, land, and jobs for other people as a means to share their faith. The pastor did not have these types of resources readily available. I considered my options and realized that the only way I could keep this church planting process alive was to feed into the chain of unhealthy dependency. I was not willing to create a spirit of dependency around myself. So I declined their requests as well. One by one, the church planters quit when they realized they would not personally receive ongoing hand-outs and salaries or goods to pass on to potential believers within their realm of ministry.

Despite the majority withdrawal, several of these Cambodian church planters stayed the course. As they visited people and shared about Jesus, a question was repeatedly posed to them: "How much money do you make, and can you get me a job too?" Folk Buddhists among their community perceived the Cambodian church planters as paid hirelings of a foreign organization. Even worse, many Cambodians perceived those who joined the "Jesus religion" as traitors who were lured by opportunity for handouts, money, and jobs.

In both of the above examples, the following symptoms of unhealthy dependency were evident: 1) the expectation of ongoing subsidies and material benefits in order to serve God; 2) the false assumption that spreading the gospel requires a surplus of money and handouts; 3) the perception that Cambodians are willing to forsake their own culture to become Christians for material gain; 4) the destruction of the testimony of Jesus Christ and the credibility of the testifier; and 5) the lack of ability or willingness among the Cambodian believers to share, give, support, and sustain their own local churches, ministries, and leaders. The root cause was equally evident: the unwise usage of missionary money in the stages of evangelism and church planting.

If we are going to treat the root causes, we need to pray, observe, research, and identify those root causes. Some root causes are more obvious than others. Some root causes can be treated with a mere tweak here and there (antibiotics), others need crucial transformation (surgery), and others need a paradigm shift (heart transplant).

If I were a medical student, would I want to know the symptoms to a disease or the root cause first? I am afraid to get vaccinations and faint when I do, so I am not even close to being a medical student—but I would need to learn the symptoms of any particular disease before I could understand the root causes.

GOING IN CIRCLES: SYMPTOMS OF UNHEALTHY DEPENDENCY

One day I was riding my motorcycle on a narrow path between two rice paddies. Eventually, I needed to turn around and go the other direction. When I was halfway into a U-turn, the cycle headed straight for one of the rice paddies. Fear caused me to grip the handles of the cycle so tightly that my fingers froze in such a way as to keep giving the cycle more gas. I kept driving in tight circles in the rice paddy, but could not get my hands to loosen up! Finally, I ended up flat on my face. As I stood up, I was covered in mud and soon-to-be bruises. The kids walking along the rice paddies had received their entertainment for the day, and I had illustrated my own point very well: creating unhealthy dependency is like trying to accelerate for the purpose of going forward, but you end up going in circles instead.

David Garrison, author of Church Planting Movements, words it this way:

> One of the surest ways to cripple a Church Planting Movement is to link church reproduction to foreign resources. Whenever pastors look beyond their own membership and local resources for salaries or buildings, they bleed the life out of their movement.[7]

The real sadness is that unhealthy dependency is a guarantee that authentic movements for Christ will not transpire. I had the opportunity to meet and converse with the Reverend Hanok Tamang, a pastor and church planter in Nepal. As president of a fellowship of churches, Pastor Hanok often visited the churches within his network. At one such church, the local pastor informed Pastor Hanok that the members of his good-sized church were too poor and were not giving on a regular basis. The pastor proceeded to tell Hanok that they needed financial support.

After sharing a meal and prayer, Hanok and the local pastor dialogued about ministry. The local pastor told Hanok that their church had a total of seven full-time ministers. Hanok was amazed and complimented the local pastor by defining his church as a role model to others. Oddly, the local pastor dropped his head at this; Hanok saw that something was amiss. Through further dialogue, the local pastor revealed that all seven of these full-time ministers received a salary from the out-side—and they had done so for at least eight years. Pastor Hanok suddenly under-stood the mystery behind the church's struggle with poverty and lack of giving.

Pastor Hanok summarizes his thoughts on this experience:

Here I could see an indigenous church totally faltering, crippled and paralyzed with the disease of dependency. Here is an example of how the pastor and leaders totally failed to motivate the members of their church in giving—and how endless financial support from the outside crippled giving from the inside. It had also dulled their zeal for evangelism beyond their own little church boundary. Dependency had destroyed their passion for lost souls.[8]

The consequences of unhealthy dependency bleed, cripple, paralyze, and dull the indigenous vitality of local disciples to serve as empowered participants in the Great Commission.

Robertson McQuilkin spent twelve years as a missionary in Japan and served as president of Columbia International University from 1968–1990. Presently, Dr. McQuilkin writes and speaks worldwide. He describes in detail the destructive consequences of the "financial pipeline" that runs from the USA to the church in other countries:

The church or church leaders that secure a financial pipeline to the USA soon become mired in an ecclesiastical welfare state, because the send-money approach, rather than strengthening the souls of national churches, keeps congregations from becoming "self-governing" and "self-supporting." The recipients of these funds often suffer the following maladies.

Believers learn to depend neither on God nor on themselves. Because they have no need to give sacrificially of their own resources (however meager they may be), they never gain a sense of ownership. This postpones the day of true indigenization.

Leaders become preoccupied with raising North American funds. On a trip I took to India I was overwhelmed by the many who "worked" me for a dollar connection. Such a ministry orientation inevitably weakens faith, corrupts pure motives and compromises leadership integrity.

Those leaders who can't get to the "pipeline" become demoralized. They come to believe that the work can't be done without outside assistance, so why try?

Believers sue believers. In India, I was astounded to find few churches or ministries that weren't in the courts at war over property purchased using American dollars.

An independent and unaccountable higher class of Christian workers arises whose stylish life-styles are envied by "unconnected believers." It is little surprise that the motivation for "spiritual growth" is soon driven by something less than a hunger after righteousness. Should the donor seek to hold the recipient accountable for the use of funds to prevent such problems, the donor would be accused of reverting to the old paternalistic pattern and roundly condemned.[9]

Beyond Dr. McQuilkin's noted maladies, there are more: low self-dignity, stifled creativity, token giving, unwillingness to support local leaders and ministries, misplaced accountability (given to donors instead of the local church body), political alignment with the most well-funded missionaries, competition, superficial conversions, the undermining of local market systems, deficiency of lay leaders and volunteers, local believers perceived as hirelings of foreigners, and suspicion toward leaders due to hidden income. I have seen every one of these maladies in action in Cambodia. All are the result of unhealthy dependency.

According to Acts 2:42–47, the church enjoyed the favor of all people, and God added to their number on a daily basis. Luke's account sounds like a movement for Christ. There was something going on that attracted people to the fellowship of Jesus Christ and to the Lord himself. When the community observed the believers in action, they saw love, unity, sincerity, commitment, and generosity. They witnessed God working miracles among them. To the passerby and to the newcomer, there was something very admirable about what they heard, saw, and experienced:

They devoted themselves to the apostles' teaching and to the fellowship, to the breaking of bread and to prayer. Everyone was filled with awe, and many wonders and miraculous signs were done by the apostles. All the believers were together and had everything in common. Selling their possessions and goods, they gave to anyone as he had need. Every day they continued to meet together in the temple courts. They broke bread in their homes and ate together with glad and sincere hearts, praising God and enjoying the favor of all the people. And the Lord added to their number daily those who were being saved. (Acts 2:42–47)

In sharp contrast, unhealthy dependency creates something very unadmirable. The unbelieving community sees their fellow man maneuvering to obtain a better life (jobs, assistance, and free English lessons) from the foreigners. The community observes their neighbors going through the Christian motions at church, but living lives of disharmony at home. This is certainly not a replication of the church described in Acts, nor is it the ingredients of an effective church planting movement. A Kenyan pastor recently told me that there are Kenyan individuals who want easy money, so they go house to house with a Bible until they meet a foreigner who wants to support them and their newfound "ministry." A Ugandan leader declared that easy money has turned many of their leaders into liars. Dr. Bob Brenneman, a professor at North Central University and former missionary to the Middle East, told me that those who live in Turkey believe that their fellow citizens who have become Christians are paid to join the church. Something is wrong with this picture! I believe that we, as missionaries, are responsible to help dissolve this impression and do missions in such a way as to avoid creating this confusion.

From my observation, missions organizations have been able to establish churches using handouts, community services, financial assistance, grants, and building projects, and by using missions funds to pay salaries to local evangelists, church planters, and leaders. These local churches do grow, but most grow in the midst of all the ill effects of unhealthy dependency. I call this "dysfunctional growth" because when all the goodies are gone, the churches struggle to grow, let alone reproduce. There are so many fires to put out that the local churches barely have the energy to strategize. The local churches lack the motivation, God-given authority, and capability to multiply within their own indigenous context and beyond. Unhealthy dependency kills indigenous church movements, leaving local churches anemic instead of serving as healers to their own communities.

Now that we have a sense of the symptoms of unhealthy dependency, let us discover some of its root causes.

POVERTY ALLEVIATION STRATEGIES: MORE HARM THAN GOOD?

I am deeply aware of the Scriptures that mandate that justice and mercy be shown to the poor and neglected of society. I am just as deeply aware that the pressing needs of others are heart-wrenching. Cambodia is no stranger to genocide and poverty. I see. I care. I hurt. I weep. As a missionary in Cambodia for well over a decade, I did not see poverty for a few days and then leave on a plane. It rubbed up against me every day.

One particular day in Cambodia, I saw nets hanging everywhere in a fishing village along the Mekong. The smell of fish permeated the air. There were rows of similar boats, yet each one was unique, according to the maker's design. We heard the roar of small motors as boats came and went. Some children yelled and seemed to be calling to us. Inquisitively, we walked toward them. As I looked down, my stomach felt as though someone was shoving a fist into it. I saw an infant floating in the shallow part of the water. Her lips were blue and her body shriveled. I noticed a petite bracelet around her tiny wrist.

Fish and seaweed are supposed to float to shore, not babies. My heart was not made for such an agonizing encounter. I knew there was a tragic story behind how this baby ended up here. Did she fall off a boat or a makeshift house over the water? Did some mother lose her mind and toss her baby away? Did a drunken father neglect his child? How far had she floated downstream? What were her parents doing when it happened? Could they not feed another mouth?

As a missionary, I ask all the plaguing questions: How do I serve the poor? When planting churches, what is my role as it relates to helping others? The questions are simpler than the answers.

Authors Peter Greer and Phil Smith, who provide employment-based solutions to poverty, share this example:

Rebecca Loveless, who works with international ministries at Discovery Church in Orlando, describes the human dilemma she faces: "I felt guilty when I wasn't doing anything to help the poor internationally, but after trying a few projects, I now feel guilty as I see our actions might have actually harmed the people we are trying to help."[10]

Rebecca Loveless experienced what I refer to as the "guilt of a dichotomy." She felt guilty when she did not help the poor, and she felt guilty when she did help the poor. How could anyone possibly feel guilty for helping the poor? Rebecca discovered that her help actually did more harm than good.

Help that harms: is there such a thing? I did not used to think so. However, like Rebecca, I have learned that my help and my methods can actually make things more problematic—even if momentarily things seem better than before I entered the picture.

There is a book called *When Helping Hurts*, by Steve Corbett and Brian Fikkert, who serve with the Chalmers Center for Economic Development. The very title of the book indicates that what we sometimes consider help can actually hurt. Corbett and Fikkert wrote their book so as to applaud compassion ministry to the poor while at the same time urging North Americans to evaluate their alleviation strategies. Fikkert writes:

> Many observers, including Steve and I, believe that when North American Christians do attempt to alleviate poverty, the methods used often do considerable harm to both the materially poor and the materially nonpoor. Our concern is not just that these methods are wasting human, spiritual, financial, and organizational resources but that these methods are actually exacerbating the very problems they are trying to solve.[11]

None of us set out to do harm, but the reality is that we unknowingly do more harm than we think.

This problem is not unique to the church. These days, well-versed development economists are expressing regret and exposing the downfall of Western aid development in other countries. The claim is that Hollywood stardom and policy-making aid have not helped, and in many cases, these things have made poverty worse.

Dambisa Moyo was born, raised, and educated in Zambia and has a PhD from Oxford University in economics and vast experience in consultant roles. Moyo, who is an African woman, rightfully shares her view about unhealthy dependency in Africa due to aid efforts. Niall Ferguson summarizes Moyo's thoughts in his foreword to Moyo's book, *Dead Aid*:

> Why, asks Moyo, do the majority of sub-Saharan countries 'flounder in a seemingly never-ending cycle of corruption, disease, poverty, and aid-dependency', despite the fact that their countries have received more than US$300 billion in development assistance since 1970. The answer she gives is that African countries are poor precisely because of all the aid. Despite the widespread Western belief that 'the rich should help the poor, and the form of this help should be aid', the reality is that aid helped make the poor poorer, and growth slower.[12]

Moyo asks the hard questions—and she is not alone. Bookstore shelves are increasingly being filled with books by authors who dare to ask and search for answers along with Moyo. To cover in detail poverty alleviation strategies that cause more harm than good (or vice versa) is beyond the scope of this book. Steve

Corbett and Brian Fikkert do an excellent job of this in *When Helping Hurts*. If you have not already read their book, I highly recommend that you do. My goal here is to bring to the forefront the reality that many of our present-day "solutions" to poverty are causing unhealthy dependency and making conditions worse.

Helping and giving are our God-given duties, and they have a place in our missions endeavors. Helping is not the concern, but how much we help, the manner in which we help, what we do not understand about those we help, and the effects of our help on the recipients are matters worth intentional reflection and advance planning.

This is a hard topic, but it must be addressed. I did not watch helping that hurts like a play unfolding before my eyes; rather, I was in the cast, participating in it. In the early days, nobody told me that helping could hurt; it never crossed my mind. I often judged my help by the first reactions to it, in many cases misreading deeper issues. I grew into my understanding of helping that hurts the hard way.

On one particular Sunday in Cambodia, two ladies from a local church asked to borrow money from me to help them through a hard time. Without a second thought, I loaned them the money. These women meant well, but they had no workable plan to pay me back. They stopped coming to church to avoid embarrassment. I quickly learned that as a missionary attending a Cambodian church, I needed to stay clear of loaning and giving out money. Both actions became helping that hurts. This is merely one example in many.

Somewhere, compassion and discernment need to meet. Compassion coupled with ignorance leads to divorce—some kind of inevitable breakdown. Emotional responses need to be tamed by wisdom. Those individuals, churches, short-term teams, agencies, missions organizations, and missionaries who are moved by the poor, let it be so—it is our God-given design! However, we cannot blindly toss doses of our abundance upon others at their expense. If we had to do surgery on someone for the first time, would we not do everything in our power to research and understand the intricate details before applying that scalpel? Let us take the same delicate and strategic approach before applying our hands to someone else's country, oceans away from us. I know we would desire the same if outsiders came into our country and helped in ways they deemed necessary.

MONEY-INTENSIVE AND POWER-BASED PARADIGMS

These days, the terms missions and poverty seem like a married couple. I rarely hear a North American talk about missions without mentioning poverty. We have all heard the testimonies about missions trips, with phrases like, "They are so poor there. They live in crowded conditions and in tin shacks. The children run barefoot! All I could think about were my own children." Those who minister cross-culturally share pictures, words, and experiences that move everyone's heart to the vast needs around the world.

Globalization—the feasibility of our actually influencing the world—and repetitive, charismatic pleas to share our excess with the majority world through donations and service are before us like never before. Numerous American Christian authors today are calling North Americans to forsake lifestyles of "want-more-get-more" for the sake of radical living and giving. Wrapped up within that call is a motivational appeal to cultivate a heart of compassion and share resources. The authors usually refer to a missions trip as "the event" that changed their lives and giving habits: "The poverty and brokenness was intense. I wanted to give everything I own to those people who face such harsh realities."

As such writers share their missions experiences with their readers, they naturally challenge affluent North Americans to take on a lifestyle of generosity by giving to the less fortunate. Their passionate appeals lead people to look for somewhere to give, and they soon find avenues to share money, gifts, free services, and resources to those deemed "poor" in other countries via missions efforts.

These endless messages and images of the poor have caused the majority of North Americans to adopt and practice money-intensive and power-based strategies in the missions endeavor. A popular song on the radio has wrapped within its lyrics the following phrase: "From cathedrals to third-world missions."[13] Although the songwriter designed the lyrics to elevate foreign missions, I believe that the writer unknowingly describes, for the most part, the reality and pitfalls of North American missions in the twenty-first century. "Third World" was a term used during the Cold War to signify those countries which did not align themselves with capitalism or the North Atlantic Treaty Organization (NATO). Nowadays, people use the term to refer to the poor and underdeveloped countries.

But think about these words for a moment. What kind of image would a child grow up with if his parents called him "a third-family child" amongst the other siblings? Expanding further, the words "from cathedrals to third-world missions" give the impression that those who have a superior life are ministering to those who have an inferior life. Whatever the case, the song indeed reveals a truth: Western missionaries and Western churches operate out of material and economic advantages (from cathedrals) that the majority of the world (third-world missions) does not have. As the song reveals to us the attitude and reality of twenty-first century missions, Jonathan Bonk gives us a broader picture:

Material and economic abundance has been a hallmark of the modus operandi of Western missionaries throughout the past two centuries…

The sacrifices made by missionaries going abroad from the shores of the wealthy nations have been real. But here we have a paradox. Missionaries who bid farewell to the good life in North America and Europe have frequently, upon arrival in the country of their destination, found themselves regarded as rich…

In an economic variation of the David and Goliath theme so dear to the Christian heart, the last two hundred years have witnessed David (Western missionaries) wearing Saul's armor and caring Saul's weapons, marching against a Goliath (the mission field) clad in skin and armed with only a few stones and a sling. The economic might has been on the side of missionaries from the West—in some instances representing multinational mission agencies whose annual budgets exceed those of the host governments themselves and constituting those countries' most significant source of foreign exchange.[14]

So, what is the problem if those of us who have cathedrals use our material resources to every advantage amidst the so-called "Third World"? Why not use our vast armor and power to help those who are merely armed with a few stones and a sling? I know it seems straightforward—our blessings should be a blessing to the recipients, end of story. But it is not that simple.

These are merely three of the issues that surround the usage of money and status in North American missions efforts: 1) recipients become victims and patients; 2) we fulfill our own claims that people are too poor; and 3) we create an ecclesiastical welfare surrounding our missions work.

RECIPIENTS AS VICTIMS AND PATIENTS

When the person who "has way more" enters into the life of someone who "has way less," the relationship becomes like a fragile package—easily broken. The reason? The one who has way more often slips into the role of savior and healer, while the one who has way less becomes a victim and patient. Joel Wickre describes this tenuous relationship:

People who are treated as helpless come to hold a lesser view of themselves. People who believe they are "blessed to be a blessing" and not in need themselves come to a lesser view of the people they serve.

These victim and savior complexes create co-dependency that perpetuates the problems of poverty and far outweighs any temporary relief such missions provide …Poor people understand that getting help requires appearing helpless, and rich people unwittingly advance the helplessness of those they serve by seeing them as objects of charity, not equals.[15]

The picture below illustrates how the outside helper and the beneficiary behave in the midst of dependency syndrome:[16]

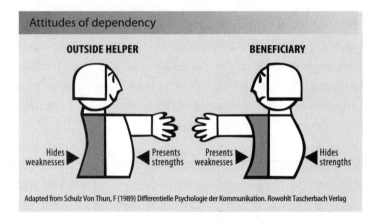

Adapted from Schulz Von Thun, F (1989) Differentielle Psychologie der Kommunikation. Rowohlt Tascherbach Verlag

The Bible inspires us to be givers, but not to slide into codependent relationships in which the giver receives some kind of guilt-free, hero-like inner satisfaction while the recipient becomes more needy and expectant. There is a Kenyan proverb that says nobody can use another person's teeth to smile. We need to steer far away from misleading people to think that they can or should use our teeth, but rather take pride in their own teeth.

While reading a one-page missions update report, I became very excited when I came upon these words: "Don't assume that we are poor and have nothing to give. When you do that, you insult God and diminish our ability to participate."[17] These words were spoken by a key Christian leader in the Democratic Republic of the Congo (DRC). The article goes on to describe how every DRC pastor of a self-sustaining church is mobilizing ongoing church planting through evangelism, praying for the sick, and showing compassion. After reading this portion of the report, I glanced down to a section called "Mission News." A short paragraph explained how missionaries presented the gospel within a community located in Europe: "Besides free haircuts, medical help, food distribution, and activities for children, workers handed out eight hundred Bibles for adults and four hundred Bibles for children."[18]

Do you see the irony in these side-by-side excerpts? What you do on day 1 affects day 100! If we start out church planting with free services, distribution, and handouts, we will end up with churches full of patients and victims.

SELF-FULFILLING PROPHECIES

One day, I was telling someone in North America about the desire of a particular pastoral leader in Nepal to challenge the churches within his country to support their own pastors. The first response from her mouth was, "Aren't they too poor to support their own pastors?"

I hear these words from Westerners again and again: "They are too poor to support their pastors. They are too poor to evangelize their own country. They are too poor to build their own buildings. They are too poor to minister to the needs of those around them." As soon as these words are thought or spoken about a people, a message is internalized, and that message drives our methods. The result is that the recipients of our message sense that they are too poor. I once heard an African pastor say that Africans did not know they were poor until someone told them so. Glenn Schwartz refers to the outcome of this kind of thinking and talking as self-fulfilling prophecies.

Of course, if we organize the church in other countries based on our economic level—misleading people to think that they must do Christianity in a Western manner—they will be too poor to reach our unrealistic demands. According to Luke 9:3, Jesus told the disciples, "Take nothing for your journey—no staff, no bag, no bread, no money, no tunic." Yet I have never heard anyone say, "The disciples were too poor for the task." On no account have I ever heard anyone preach a sermon to the effect that the Macedonian church should not have prepared an offering to help their mother church because they themselves were too poor.

If the premise that people are "too poor" drives our church planting strategies and missions paradigms, we will end up with followers of Christ and churches that think they are too poor.

ECCLESIASTICAL WELFARE

Many North Americans are aware that the welfare system in North America has caused more problems than it has solved. We could instantly make a list of the unintended consequences of welfare, but we often overlook the very same issues as we pour money into other struggling countries for the cause of missions.

"They're turning my people into beggars," exclaimed Juan Uloa. Uloa was a dedicated Christian and executive director of a microfinance ministry in Nicaragua. He motivated his people to overcome poverty through training, entrepreneurship, saving, and hard work—a combination any of us would applaud. As Juan worked throughout his country, he encountered particular areas in which the locals shunned the opportunity for training in entrepreneurship, small business loans, and savings plans. The people who most readily rejected Juan's team and their opportunities for self-development were in areas that churches from North America frequented. They had no motivation to build their capacity, work hard, or sustain themselves because of the "easy charity ...creating a new kind of welfare state."[19]

Bob Lupton, who wrote the account of Juan's experience, asks the hard questions:

> What peasant scratching out a bare existence could refuse suitcases bulging with new clothing for his family? What struggling pastor could resist the temptation to accept a steady salary and generous church income for hosting visitors, organizing volunteer work and staffing funded programs? What village would borrow money to dig a well or buy books for their school library or save money to build a church if these things were provided for them free of charge? If all they had to do was make their wish lists, show up for the schedule arranged by the donors and smile graciously until benefactors head back home, who would blame them for accepting this easy charity?[20]

If our missions paradigms revolve around the premise that people are too poor and therefore we must use money and power to minister cross-culturally, inevitably we will create an ecclesiastical welfare condition in the areas where we minister. Merely combining the words welfare and ecclesiastical—having to do with the church and Christianity—makes me sad. God created humankind with a work ethic evidenced by his command to care for his creation. I have seen and can imagine the ill affects of the ecclesiastical welfare syndrome on the credibility and power of the gospel.

I am thoroughly convinced that not one of us wants to do harm through our help. I just think that many are not aware of the issues that often hide beneath the superficial layers.

Typically, our first thought is that our surplus can fill a vacuum in the lives of others. But pay attention to the underlying assumption in that thought—that money is the real answer to people's problems. Benjamin Franklin once stated, "Money never made a man happy yet, nor will it. The more a man has, the more he wants. Instead of filling a vacuum, it makes one." Based on the wisdom of Benjamin Franklin—and of Jesus, who told us that a man's life does not consist of his possessions—is it possible that while we hope to fill a vacuum in the lives of those less fortunate overseas, we actually deepen a psychological, emotional, and spiritual vacuum?

Why do we, as North American Christians, give? Assuming that guilt over "having too much" is not part of the equation—and it often is—some of the incentives that motivate us to give are thankfulness, obedience, faith, empathy, compassion, and a sense of responsibility for God's kingdom on earth and in our communities. Yet our giving, which is compelled by healthy incentives, often undoes those same incentives in the recipients. Our one-way, bountiful giving often diminishes thankfulness, obedience, faith, empathy, compassion, and a sense of responsibility in the lives of those who receive from us. In other words, we may be unintentionally turning much of the world into victims, lifelong recipients who will not make the transition into giving themselves. While we develop our capacity for helping, we destroy their capacity for self-development.

Occasionally, people of these countries are spurred on by our giving for a season. But they eventually conclude that we can give because we have so much. Is it possible that the materially poor see us as being like the rich putting their gifts into the temple treasury in the story of the widow's offering in Luke 21:1–4?

As Christians who want to be obedient in our own lives, this is not an easy issue to figure out. If we hold back on our giving, is it possible that we will become mere recipients? Absolutely. The apostle Paul said, "It is better to give than receive" (Acts 20:35). Paul told the Corinthian believers to excel in the grace of giving just as abundantly as they excelled in other areas of life (2 Corinthians 8:7). But Paul goes on to explain that everyone should be both a giver and a recipient. "At the present time your plenty will supply what they need so that in turn their plenty will supply your need. Then there will be equality" (2 Corinthians 8:14).

The key words are "in turn." Remember Joel Wickre's words: "People who believe they are 'blessed to be a blessing' and not in need themselves come to a lesser view of the people they serve."[21]

Perhaps we need to find a way to implement missions so we too become vulnerable, so that we truly do life in community—supplying and being supplied as equals. Personally, I prefer the word *sharing*, as it indicates mutual giving—and no one stays a recipient for very long. My colleague Glenn Schwartz states frequently that we are very near to turning the majority of the world into recipients.

With Scripture in mind, we should all strive to be givers and expect to be receivers. Those of us who live in North America need to redefine giving. When we think of giving in our culture, we almost immediately think of money. Honestly, giving money is actually easier than other forms of giving—it's quick and does not require sweat and blood. How about giving tears, listening for hours when you are tired, making someone laugh at just the right time, working side by side in a field, unlocking entrepreneurship, praying with someone through the night, speaking comfort in another's heart language, allowing others to meet your needs, teaching someone a skill, riding squished together in a public taxi, or cheering on a student for his upcoming exam? A woman cleaned Jesus's feet with pure nard, Mary sat at Jesus's feet, Jesus washed the feet of his disciples, Dorcas made clothing for the poor in her community, Lydia offered her home to Paul and his companions, and Paul labored side by side with Priscilla and Aquila. Jonathan Bonk cautions us to not stray so far from Jesus's model for apostolic life and ministry:

> The money-and-power-based strategies and statuses generated by the institutional and personal affluence of Western missionaries contradict principles that are at the very heart of Christian mission as prescribed in the New Testament. The incarnation and the cross of our Savior are models for apostolic life and ministry. For those of us who insist on clinging to our prerogatives as privileged Westerners, the missiological implications of the incarnation are clear.[22]

I am thoroughly convinced that we can and will find creative ways to help without hurting, to serve without creating dependency. Let's put our heads together to create new paradigms—or rather, to revisit old ones, models that do not operate out of Western institutional and personal affluence, but rather follow the patterns of the apostolic life and ministry of Jesus, the disciples, and Paul (the church planter among the Gentiles—the unreached people groups of his time). Let's set aside strategies that override the mobilization of local resources or spread a form of Western Christianity that is too expensive and complicated to reproduce. Let's start telling an alternative story.

A RECIPE FOR DEPENDENCY: BEGINNING, ACCELERATION, AND ALLEVIATION

Helping that hurts most often transpires when outsiders unwisely use external resources to begin ministries, accelerate growth, and alleviate poverty in cross-cultural settings. In my case, I fostered unhealthy dependency by beginning a form of church in Cambodia that was partially suited for my North American context and access to resources from my homeland. In my early years, I modeled a form of church that was impossible for local Cambodian believers to emulate. I concluded that the believers' inability to emulate a Western form of church was not an issue. I surmised that I could temporarily provide the finances needed for rent, evangelism, and worship, and then someday in the future the local church would assume those responsibilities.

That "someday in the future" remained in the future. The church members grew accustomed to missions subsidies to maintain and grow their church. They viewed me, as a missionary, and the missions organization as responsible for the church that supposedly existed to benefit them. In the church's growing-pain years, they did not develop a sense of ownership or stewardship of their church. When I decided to wean away subsidies (or deny new appeals for funds) for the sake of cultivating a self-sustaining church, they perceived me as wanting them to fail. Using missions funds to plant a church at the beginning hampered the creativity, motivation, sense of responsibility, and sacrificial mentality of the people in that very church. *All this fallout because I thought the Cambodians were too poor to do church in the way I deemed necessary!*

I once heard a Cambodian pastor tell a story about an elephant. While the elephant was young, the master chained the elephant's leg to the base of a large tree. As the elephant matured, he walked back and forth around the tree, limited by the chain. Eventually the owner unchained the adult elephant, but the elephant continued to pace the same route, never venturing beyond the allowance of the phantom chain. The elephant had no physical chain, but he conducted himself as if he were still chained.

Mentalities are formed deep within the psyche. Our formative years with our parents and siblings greatly influence how we as adults function and interpret life. Psychologists and counselors spend ample time helping people see how life while "growing up" has impacted their thoughts, attitudes, and behaviors in adult life. As missionaries, we cannot create a welfare dependency mentality in the formative stages and somehow expect that a few strategic changes here and there will instill the vision and practice of sustainability. Rather, we should endeavor to conceptualize and plant with sustainability in mind from the beginning. We must stop putting phantom chains around the psyches of those to whom we minister.

Acceleration is another common motive for giving that leads to dependency. Peter Greer and Phil Smith, authors of *The Poor Will Be Glad*, share an example of a church in Pennsylvania that formed a partnership with a church in the Ukraine in order to accelerate the growth of the Ukrainian church.[23] The church in Pennsylvania sent a team to the Ukraine to conduct a needs assessment. After reporting the needs of the Ukrainian church to their home church in the USA, the members systematically shipped over food, clothes, and medicine. Eventually, the church in Pennsylvania provided funds for the church in the Ukraine to buy land and expand their church building. The North American church members gave each and every resource with loving concern. The church in the Ukraine felt deeply blessed, and they used the money to advance their ministry.

Unfortunately, something started to happen. What initially seemed like a blessing began to morph into a curse for the receiving church. The pastor watched as his Ukrainian church family slowly but surely changed. The ample gifts paralyzed the motivation of the church members. Their own spirit of giving and service shriveled because they knew someone else would provide for their needs. The pastor realized that the church's ability to sustain itself was being undone. Making matters worse, the unbelieving community viewed the church as competition because the handouts undermined their local market system, which sold the same products that were being shipped from the USA. I imagine it was almost impossible for the Ukrainian pastor to reverse the consequences. *All this fallout because a church in North America thought the Ukrainians were too poor to do church in the manner the North Americans deemed necessary!*

In 2008, I attended a forum on unhealthy dependency. A president of a university in Russia was one of the participants. He shared one personal story to illustrate how a gesture from the outside to accelerate evangelism quickly stifled local initiative and actually "un-grew" a church. I will retell his story to the best of my recollection: Those who were participants of the church rode their bicycles to and from the church. Likewise, the pastor rode a bicycle to several villages to visit and encourage those from the church and others in the community. One day, a visiting team from America sat with the pastor and informed him that his method was not effective. They explained, "If you had a car you could visit more people in a shorter amount of time."

The visiting team committed to raise money for the pastor and send it to him so he could buy a car as soon as possible. After the team departed, the pastor stopped riding his bicycle to visit people and immediately applied his energies to building a garage for the car. It could not be a modest garage, but needed to have thick security walls and an expensive iron gate to ensure the car would remain safe from robbers and vandals.

The money for the car eventually arrived. But there was one major problem, the pastor did not have a license and did not know how to drive. The church had to find someone outside of the church who knew how to drive and could chauffeur the pastor. Eventually they found a driver, but he only had free time during odd hours, and he expected a salary. The church could not afford the petrol, and eventually the car broke down—no one knew how to fix it. The car was eventually stored in the garage. By this time, relational bike evangelism had become a thing of the past. The church suffered as a result. *All this fallout because a church in North America thought a church in Eurasia was too poor and incompetent to do evangelism in a manner the North Americans deemed necessary.*

The Southern Baptist Convention is the largest Protestant denomination in the United States of America. Jerry Rankin, the president of the International Mission Board of the Southern Baptist Convention (IMB), shares what happens when missionaries and missions organizations try to accelerate growth in other parts of the world:

> Throughout most of the history of the International Mission Board missionaries went out to win the lost and plant churches. As results emerged they worked diligently to organize these new churches into associations and conventions with a vision toward their cooperation and eventually assuming responsibility for the work. Such action was well-intended but probably premature in most situations as the initiative did not come from the churches but from missionaries seeking to replicate a model of denominational life in the U.S.
>
> It was necessary for the missionaries to serve in roles of denominational leadership. Because seminaries would be needed to train the pastors, these institutions were established based on the familiar western educational programs at home. Hospitals, publishing houses, student centers and a plethora of other ministries were quickly built because of the needs of the people on the mission field and to serve the churches. Of course these institutions required massive budget resources to be established and maintained "on behalf of the churches." It was all envisioned on the conviction that the local churches would quickly grow to assume responsibility for these vital ministries, but it never happened.
>
> There was little initiative for them to assume that responsibility,

especially when the missionaries from abroad were willing to provide the resources and leadership. The context of impoverished economies actually made it impossible for nationalization to displace dependency in maintaining sophisticated, high cost western-type institutions and organizations. Seldom would church growth rates exceed 2 to 4 percent because missionary time and budget was consumed in maintaining conventions and institutions. Building church buildings and supporting national pastors inhibited growth because of budget limitations.[24]

Missionaries and churches abroad often force growth by running out ahead of the national church. They create and fund structures on behalf of the national church with the intention to expedite the emergence of what they would call a legitimate "church."

IMB recognized unhealthy dependency in their missions efforts and did something about it. They worked diligently to encourage national ministries to function without depending on missionary leadership and finances. Ministries were reshaped to match the capabilities and resources of the local churches. Some ministries were stopped due to lack of relevance in the local context. This adaptation caused the national church to grow and multiply, even extending themselves to unengaged people groups. Jerry Rankin tells us some of the details:

> As we trained the leaders and evangelists to understand the spiritual and biblical nature of the church as a fellowship of believers worshipping, teaching, witnessing and ministering, superfluous elements of forms, facilities and paid leadership were eliminated, and the churches began to multiply. After three years churches reproducing started more new churches than the national church planters and missionaries. After another 10 years they had grown to 440 churches.[25]

Our tendency to try to accelerate the growth of the church in other people's countries creates unhealthy dependency. If we concentrate on making disciples and leave our imposed forms and structure out of the process, healthy indigenous churches will be the result.

Our attempts to alleviate poverty are a final ingredient in the creation of unhealthy dependency. A simple story illustrates the problem:

How could compassionately giving eggs to a community cause harm? Peter Greer and Phil Smith, authors of The Poor Will Be Glad, share about a church in

North America that extended a hand to help alleviate poverty in Rwanda after the genocide of 1994.[26] Within a particular village in Rwanda, a local man was running a small poultry business which supplied his community members with eggs. Then a North American church adopted this village—a practice in which a church from one country provides assistance to a village or church in another country. As one of their poverty alleviation strategies, the church in North America distributed free eggs in the village. The imported eggs ruined the local business-man's poultry livelihood. Eventually, the North American church moved on to other places that they deemed needed their help. The end result? The village in Rwanda had no local access to eggs. They had to import eggs from other towns and pay higher prices than they had back when there was a local poultry business. *All this fallout because a church in North America thought the village in Rwanda was too poor to mobilize their own local assets.*

Using substantial outside resources to begin ministries, accelerate growth, and alleviate poverty has led to churches that expect help instead of giving help, bicycle evangelism replaced by broken cars and broken spirits, national churches that are too incompetent to carry out their biblical responsibilities, and crushed livelihoods and depleted work ethic. Let us reverse the unhealthy dependency that often happens by working toward a goal of responsible self-help—right from the start.

Toward Responsible Self-Help

One day I sat among Christian leaders from Uganda, Zambia, Kenya, and Nepal. Each one expressed their appreciation for missionaries and their help. However, these leaders were intentionally gathered to solve significant problems caused by that very help! Each participant shared how relying on assistance from abroad had stripped their local people of dignity, motivation, vision, stewardship, accountability, and much more.

These contemporary testimonies confirm that there are harmful ways to help, methods which put people in deeper holes and create a black cloud around the credibility of the gospel. These pastoral leaders of great nations were basically saying, "We do not want to be treated as though we are poor and incapable. We want the believers and churches within our countries to rise up and take respon-sibility, to believe more and do more than ever before with the resources God has placed around us. We want to move away from unhealthy dependency, which cripples us, and move toward self-responsibility." What I heard these men say is that they wanted to be a part of the healing process of unhealthy dependency.

One of the leaders from Kenya, Pastor J. Charagu, expressed it this way:

An animal does not hate that person who just sees it and keeps quiet but he hates him who sees it and shouts out about it. And the same case applies to an enemy, an enemy will never have a problem with you even when you see him and keep quiet. But the minute you identify an enemy and shout about it, that is when he decides to face you. So, this enemy called "unhealthy dependency" has been there a very long time. I want to believe that very many people have seen it, but it is only this group here, plus maybe a few other people out there, who have decided to shout about it. My appeal to all of us is that we should not keep quiet but continue shouting and shouting and shouting.[27]

Shah Ali (a pseudonym) is a man who discerned the existence of unhealthy dependency in his context and worked toward a solution. A follower of Jesus Christ, Shah Ali had shared his faith with his Muslim father. The father viewed Shah Ali's faith as a rejection of his own identity: religion, family, and culture. The grief-stricken father tried to kill his son with a sword.

Shah Ali's gut-wrenching experience with his father prompted him to evaluate the approaches being used to share the gospel and plant churches in his context. In an article written with Dudley Woodberry, he revealed two key issues related to the methods being used and how he and his team reshaped their approaches based on those issues.

The first problem was that the gospel and all that it entails was perceived as foreign. By the time the gospel came to the Muslims in this area, the message was loaded with Western and Hindu culture. Shah Ali's people called Christianity "a foreign religion of infidels." Secondly, the Muslims viewed humanitarian services as a way to manipulate people into the Christian faith. They were not entirely wrong: some Muslims did comply with the Christian faith, to some degree, in order to receive help. Onlooking Muslims saw through this facade, which watered down the credibility of the gospel. Ali noticed that the donor-recipient way of doing things was eerily similar to the colonizer-colonized way of doing things. Donated food from abroad often negatively influenced the market system by taking away business from local farmers.

Technology introduced through humanitarian work helped those with skills and finances while increasing the gap between the poor and the wealthy.

The conclusion of many that Christians were foreign religious infidels manipulating people through humanitarian work was not the outcome Ali and other faithful followers of Christ desired! Shah Ali knew he needed to be proactive in developing sustainable ministry patterns for the health of the church and the image of the church. Thus, Shah Ali and friends adapted their ministry approaches by addressing the foreignness of the gospel and the foreignness of humanitarian efforts.

Shah Ali and his co-laborers implemented several changes to address the foreignness of the gospel. Shah Ali translated the New Testament using vocabulary suited for Muslims rather than Hindus. His team replaced Hindu-background believers with Muslim-background believers to share the gospel among the Muslims. They used local expressions of worship to God that were relevant to the Muslims. Instead of calling themselves *Christians*, which had a derogatory meaning to Muslims ("a foreign religion of infidels"), they referred to themselves as *Submitters to God*. Shah Ali learned to use the Qur'an as a bridge to discussion instead of ignoring a key holy source in the lives of Muslims. He and his team opened opportunities for God to reveal his power through signs and wonders. They intentionally moved away from a paradigm of personal decisions and extraction (kids groups, youth groups, women's groups, etc.) that is popular in North America to minister through heads of households and to intact groups. Finally, they developed mediums to minister to and train oral learners, who were the majority in their area.

Beyond adapting to the local context, Shah Ali and his counterparts worked toward what they call "responsible self-help." First of all, they refrained from giving financial help to "Jesus mosques" (what others may call churches) and imams (what others may call pastors). Secondly, Shah Ali's group adapted the methods of serving human needs to ensure that no one was excluded based on religion or belief. Finally, any help offered led to responsible self-help. These actions helped remove the suspicion that people, churches, and pastors sided with Christianity to gain access to foreign help and money.

Shah Ali and his coworkers started a national church planting program. They taught national workers to de-Westernize the gospel and taught them sustainable methods of producing food. One of the main projects the church planters implemented was teaching local farmers to develop an integrated fish and vegetable cultivation system. To encourage the sustainability of the systems, the church planters used reproducible and local technology. The fishponds and vegetable gardens empowered each other: the fishponds were dug and the dirt was used for the gardens. The leaves and stems from the vegetables fed the fish, and the fishes' excrement provided fertilizer for the gardens.

Shah Ali and J. D. Woodberry express their thoughts about this "responsible self-help" approach to church planting:

The models we are developing have been used by God in raising up many new disciples and expressing His concern for total persons with physical and spiritual needs. Likewise the Messianic Muslim movement has spilled over into a neighboring country through the normal visiting of relatives; when colleagues and I visited a South Asian country recently, a whole Muslim village began to follow Jesus.[28]

Shah Ali strategized a way to depart from unhealthy dependency and work toward responsible self-help. He worked creatively to reverse the misconceptions among his Muslim neighbors that missionaries are foreign religious infidels who manipulate people. Through the discernment of the Holy Spirit, we can combine our minds and energy with people like Shah Ali in order to work toward the same goals.

EXTERNAL SAVIORS AND LOCAL CHAMPIONS

I view Shah Ali as a local champion, someone from the inside who rallied those around him toward responsible self-help. When I initially went to Cambodia, I really wanted to make life better for genocide-weary people. Yes, I meant well, but to some degree, I had an external savior complex. Peter Greer, who has a wealth of experience with income-generation strategies, wrote something that will forever stick in my mind and shape my missions strategy:

> The [income-generation] movement is radically different from traditional charity. It focuses on long-term systemic change and lasting employment patterns, not short-term quick fixes. It emphasizes the importance of partnerships and local champions, not external "saviors" descending to solve the problems of the poor.[29]

I believe my drive to solve the problems of Cambodians often caused me to overlook and miss opportunities to promote local champions. So-called external saviors come and go, but local champions are there for the long haul. God raised up David as a local champion (1 Samuel 17). Everyone who was concerned with the desperate task of defeating Goliath overlooked David as a potential champion. Saul and David's brothers tried to convince the shepherd boy to return to his substandard responsibilities. Eventually, Saul relented and allowed David an opportunity to face the giant. Of course, Saul assumed David could only succeed with his imposed armor. David informed Saul that he indeed was not used to such fancy and cumbersome armor. Instead, David gathered up his own local resources: a sling and five smooth stones. Unbelievably to bystanders, David triumphed over the giant. But David did not become a champion that day; he was a champion waiting for someone to believe in him.

How we think about the poor and the conclusions we form about them will shape our efforts. Robert Lupton gives us a picture of how we should view people from all walks of life.

> Scripture describes a Kingdom comprised of diverse people with all manner of gifts and talents. Each citizen of this heaven-based Kingdom has been given an important work to do …It is disquieting to realize how little value I attribute to "the least of these" the ones deemed by our Lord to be great in the kingdom (Matt. 5:19, NIV). I have viewed them as weak ones waiting to be rescued, not bearers of divine treasures. The dominance of my giving overshadows and stifles the rich endowments that the Creator has invested in those I have considered destitute. I selectively ignore that the moneyed, empowered learned ones will enter the Kingdom with enormous difficulty.[30]

Imagine if we viewed every person within each segment of society as a contributor—if we saw all people as possessing all manner of gifts and talents. Let's approach missions with the premise that we are not meant to be external saviors, with the firm belief that there are local champions everywhere, needing a word of encouragement to mobilize their local skills and resources.

A SOUTH AFRICAN PASTOR AND A BUFFALO

Is God concerned about unhealthy dependency? Glenn Schwartz has shared a story told to him by a South African pastor. A South African pastor was speaking in various churches throughout America to raise funds for his ministry back home. One evening, the South African pastor called home to talk to his family. His wife was not there, so he talked to his sister-in-law. She told her brother-in-law that God had given her a message for him through a dream: "When you are in America, don't chase buffaloes."[31] The pastor had absolutely no idea what the dream meant.

One particular Sunday, the South African pastor received an offering from a church in America. The treasurer did not write a check for the lump sum, but rather gave the South African pastor the exact cash and coins given in the offering. When he counted the money, he discovered an unusual nickel: it had an image of a buffalo. Immediately, the pastor remembered his sister-in-law's dream and realized

God did not want him to chase money in America. The following day, the pastor had breakfast with a businessman who owned four planes. The well-off business-man offered the South African pastor money for his ministry. Remembering his sister-in-law's dream, the pastor declined the financial gift from the businessman.

While on a plane headed to Johannesburg, the pastor had another opportunity to receive funds from a businessman. The pastor informed his flight companion that God would take care of his people. The pastor returned to his church and motivated the members to build their own church without relying on money (buffaloes) from America. They indeed built their own church with a sense of dignity.

God cured unhealthy dependency within one pastor's church through a dream about a buffalo on the side of a coin. We need to take seriously what God takes seriously. Through his e-mailed comments to Glenn Schwartz, a missionary in Zambia really made me think hard about this:

> I just met a young missionary from Zambia who returned prematurely and rather discouraged about the situation in which he found himself. He came to the conclusion that the mission has assumed the role of provider of the church. Not Jehovah Jireh, but Mission Jireh! He believes that the mission stepped in between the bride (church) and the groom (the Lord). It is as if the mission said, to the bride, this groom will not be able to meet your needs, we will do it for you.[32]

Mission Jireh! How often do I cause people to rely more on me than on God? How many opportunities have I stolen away from God to reveal his sovereignty? To be honest with you, when recipients receive financial gifts from those outside their respective countries, they often do not view the gift as a miracle from the hand of God. Rather, they merely see the money as someone else's surplus and duty. When God mobilizes local believers who share the streets with one another to provide for themselves and others, the hand of God is more easily recognized.

A TRIBUTE TO GLENN PENNER

Voice of the Martyrs is an organization that mobilizes efforts for the persecuted church. Glenn M. Penner was the CEO of The Voice of the Martyrs in Canada. For his last twelve years, Glenn traveled to thirty countries to offer practical help and encouragement to persecuted Christians. On January 7, 2010, Glenn went to be with his glorious Savior. I appreciate Glenn for all he has said and done to avoid unhealthy dependency. Here are a few of Glenn's motivational words:

> Merely stating that The Voice of the Martyrs in Canada believes in equipping without creating dependency and that we will maintain and promote the Persecuted Church's ability to be self-governing, self-supporting, and self-propagating and resist any programs or ministry that would detract from this does not guarantee that we will do it. The fact that such a statement exists in our Core Values is an admission that we have failed to do this in the past and that this remains a concern. Additionally, other missions with whom we partner in various ways have been and are engaged in dependency creating programs that we must step away from and refuse to support if we are to be true to our values. Often we inherit situations that we did not create. But this does not mean that we must settle for the status quo or excuse ourselves and continue engaging in activities that we know are detrimental. As servants of the Persecuted Church, we have no business adding to the suffering of our brothers and sisters by maintaining or creating dependency that will only hinder their witness and even threaten their very existence.[33]

Glenn has been known to state that unhealthy dependency on Western funds is a greater threat to the growth of the church of Jesus Christ than persecution. Glenn has left this earth, but he left us with a challenge: "We must not settle for the status quo or excuse ourselves and continue engaging in activities that we know are detrimental."

TWELVE SUITS AND THE FRIENDS MISSIONARY PRAYER BAND

Pastor J. Charagu of Kenya told me an inspiring story of how he has been trying to reverse idleness and apathy among the families that attend his church: Being able to own and wear a suit is a sign of dignity in Nairobi, Kenya. Within Pastor Charagu's church, the majority of the men did not own suits and never imagined that owning a suit was possible. Pastor Charagu told the men of his church that they were capable of owning and wearing a suit. He invited twelve men to give a certain amount of money to create a savings fund. When there was enough interest accumulated in the fund, one man per week bought a new suit. At the end of twelve weeks, each man owned his own suit.

On one particular Sunday, all twelve men wore their suits and were responsible for leading the Sunday gathering. These men led with a sense of confidence and purpose. Pastor Charagu said that the wives had the biggest smiles on their faces!

Pastor Charagu intentionally led the men through this exercise in giving, faith, and accountability to cultivate their desire and capability to serve as responsible heads of their households and the church. He did not stop there. Pastor Charagu has guided his church members through a series of faith-building opportunities. With each success, the members grow more confident and capable of sustaining their families and contributing to the stewardship of their church.

Pastor Charagu has refrained from allowing foreign money to accelerate the growth of his church. He realizes that such help would only compound a mentality of inferiority and helplessness among his people. From Pastor Charagu's perspective, he desires to heal his people so they are able to serve as givers rather than takers.

Pastor Charagu is a local champion who knows that all his people need are five smooth stones and a sling to take down the giant of unhealthy dependency. Part of my role as a missionary is to discern how I can come alongside people like him as an affirmer rather than undermining what he has set in action—to discern how can I cultivate local champions like Pastor Charagu who mobilize people around them rather than setting myself up as an external provider.

Beyond Pastor Charagu, there are many other local champions who have experienced the benefits of mobilizing their own resources through dependency on God. Ralph Winter, the founder of the U.S. Center for World Missions, gives an example of such a group:

> Furthermore, the largest mission agency in the India Mission Association (IMA) is the amazing Friends Missionary Prayer Band (FMPB) with close to a 1,000 missionaries being supported by some of the poorest populations in the world. Can you believe it? The FMPB will not accept a cent from abroad. Probably a single large U.S. church could provide their entire FMPB missionary budget. And why not do that? Because they value spiritual discipline more than money. They have prayerfully concluded that relying on foreign funds would spiritually damage their 30,000 prayer partners. These dear, poor people are members of the FMPB because they are willing to pray all night one night a week and give 20% of their meager incomes.[34]

The Friends Missionary Prayer Band denies donations from abroad because they value spiritual discipline more than money. Pastor Charagu steers away from dependency on outside funding because he wants to disciple men and women who have a godly work ethic and give their firstfruits to God. Where do missionaries fit into such a paradigm? We could join up in prayer with the Friends Missionary Band while leaving money out of the experience. We could serve as coaches to men and women like Pastor Charagu by facilitating them to discover creative ways to serve as local champions of sustainability in their realm of influence. We really, truly can be effective missionaries without presenting ourselves as Mission Jireh or external saviors.

MISSIONS AS PILGRIMAGE

If I were to invite you to go on a pilgrimage with me—a journey to some treasured destination—what would that mean to you? I remember the day I wanted so much to help the newly settled Cambodian refugees in St. Paul-Minneapolis with their problems. It dawned on me that the best way to help was to live with them in such a way that their problems became my problems. In this manner, I wasn't solving their problems; we were solving our problems together on equal footing. I entered their journey to the best of my ability, sojourning with the Cambodians instead of trying to fix them from within my own comfort zone.

Recently, Christian Vision Project (CVP) conducted an interview with Emmanuel Katongole, an African Catholic priest and a professor of theology at Duke Divinity School. The interview was targeted for American readers. CVP asked Katongole about how he viewed God's mission in the world. Katongole talked about two dominant models of missions and suggested an alternative. The first model he identified was "the model of mission as aid." According to Katongole, this model involves Americans who recognize their affluence, helping others in the world who face poverty, famine, AIDS, and other life-troubling issues. Katongole recognizes that this model helps to a degree, but he reveals its shortcomings:

> A lot of people are being helped by this kind of mission. But the problem is that from this mission, Christians return to a tower. Their world remains their world, and Africa's world remains Africa's world.[35]

The second model described by Katongole is "the model of mission as partnership." This model refers to American churches partnering with churches in Africa for the sake of world Christian unity and empowering one another. Again, Katongole acknowledges that this model does some good, but he enlightens us to this often overlooked reality:

This model also overlooks the difference in power between America and the rest of the world. One gets the impression because of the numerical strength of Africa's church, African Christians can be equal partners with their Western counterparts. But we cannot pretend that the power of America does not exist. There is a new desire to learn from one another, but how deep does learning go? I have a hard time getting a serious answer when I ask American churches what they have learned from their African "partnerships."[36]

Katongole's attempt is not to degrade these two models: "mission as aid" and "mission as partnership." Rather, he, as an African, wants to share with us what may be a better model for his people:

I'm not saying that either of these models is heretical—they have biblical foundations. Mission as aid often draws from the story of the Good Samaritan, and mission as partnership invokes Paul's image of the Body, which has many parts. It is only that these models do not go far enough in bridging the neat divisions or tribalism between "us" and "them." That is why we need to learn another model—mission as pilgrimage, which is based on a vision of the Christian life as a journey. This model grows out of a sense of being pilgrims together, pilgrims who feel the dust under their feet and come to know the places where they sojourn …this kind of journeying is slower than mission done as delivery of aid, slower than even partnership. But when we take time for that, it begins to transform the pilgrim. You have learned the names of people and places; you have inhaled the dust.[37]

Perhaps God needs to cultivate a new generation of dust inhalers. Our missions endeavors have been so much about what the missionaries and Western churches can do for others—what we can fix, what we can save, and what we can offer. By contrast, Emmanuel Katongole challenges you and me to be fellow pilgrims—sojourners who go on a journey with people instead of "doing to" or "doing for" people.

"One of the surest ways to cripple a Church Planting Movement is to link church production to foreign resources."

DAVID GARRISON

CHAPTER TEN

MAKE DISCIPLES OF ORAL LEARNERS:

USING ORAL STRATEGIES AMONG TWO-THIRDS OF
THE WORLD'S POPULATION

"Pastor Veasna, I learned how to preach at Bible school. Yet when I preach in the villages, people seem to be in a daze or prefer to talk to their neighbor."

"Pastor Sopheap, I notice at the temple that most of the people engage in chanting. So, I actually started having those in my church memorize the Bible by chanting Scripture. We do not promote the chanting as having any magical or merit-earning elements; rather, we use the repetition and a simple melody to assist in remembering God's Word. We use storytelling, drama, proverbs, poetry, response singing, and other modes of communication common to Cambodians. Maybe we could do an event for New Years together, combining some of the customary Cambodian forms of communication."

One day while I was still living in Cambodia, I returned to my home in Phnom Penh and immediately emptied my shelves of all the teaching resources I had either written or translated into the Cambodian language. I put these Western-style workbooks, Bible studies, and manuals in a cabinet and locked the door. What led to such an unusual action? That morning, I had gone to a Cambodian church in Phnom Penh. As the Cambodian pastor preached a sermon, I looked around at the faces of the listeners. The majority of the Cambodian listeners had that glassy look in their eyes. You know, the look that says, "I'm asleep, but I want you to think I'm listening."

The pastor preached quite well (at least by my standards, for he had learned how to preach such an articulate three-point sermon from me). Later in the day, I asked a Cambodian woman who attended the church the following question, "How was the sermon?" She answered without hesitation, "It was great!" I followed up with, "What was the sermon about?" She thought to herself for a few moments; then she began to speak and stopped midsentence. Eventually, she responded, "I don't know exactly what the sermon was about, but I do know it was good."

This experience caused me to ask a serious question: "How can the redemption message of God Almighty reach every city and village in Cambodia if life-changing, relevant, and reproducible communication is not happening?" I knew something was amiss in the cross-cultural communication style I was modeling to Cambodians. The Cambodian pastor was merely using a preaching mode that I had imposed on him—and it wasn't working.

Dr. Avery Willis, the former senior vice president of International Missions Board and developer of Master Life, once hosted a team of eight specialists. Each man who came to the table had abundant experience in the areas of oral learning, communications, and chronological Bible "storying" in cross-cultural settings. Dr. James Slack, J.O. Terry, Dr. Grant Lovejoy, and others dialogued about the topic of making disciples among oral cultures, thus creating an audio module to train others. Below is part of their verbal dialogue:

> The Western witnessing approaches all are geared to proceed according to a Western form of logic: a certain beginning point, followed by a next assertion, and a next and a next. Not everybody follows the Western logic. So that what may seem clearly logical to those of us who share that intellectual history, may not be clear at all to somebody who's from another philosophical background. In fact, it might be argued that the more effective a witnessing approach is in the West, the less likely it should be used in other places in the world. Because its effectiveness in the West probably shows it has been closely adapted to Western situations and patterns of thought. We tend to conclude just the opposite. The more effective it is in the West, the more confidence we have that we found the universal. But I would argue that the other is just as likely to be true. Having found the niche here almost guarantees it will not be widely adapted to lots of other places. If it turns out to be useful in other places, of course we celebrate that and are pleased. Yet we need to recognize that we have so often developed something with our set of

assumptions in our mind, and other people don't share those assumptions.[1]

I made the wrong assumptions, and I operated out of those wrong assumptions until an encounter with glassy-eyed people woke me up! I had to actually back up before I could go forward—I had to retrain myself to learn and communicate in culturally relevant ways among oral learners. I did this by intentionally observing how Cambodians communicated in the home and in community, religious, and entertainment settings. It did not take me long to realize I had overlooked the innate communication styles of the Cambodians. Cambodians mostly transmit their beliefs, heritage, and social values through rituals, chants, sayings, stories, drama, dance, music, symbols, and real-life experiences—a recognized and popular mode of communication and culture called "orality."

With my new zeal to learn, I paid attention to how they told stories. I learned their stories. Then I began to storytell the Bible.

What an amazing change! Glassy eyes were filled with enchantment, anticipation, and sometimes tears. People related to the characters in the biblical stories and strove to apply what they learned among their families, in their fields, and in the midst of their trials. For Cambodians, passing on these biblical stories became as natural as passing their babies into the arms of loved ones around them.

Beyond adapting to communication styles, experiencing orality changed my relationship with God. Like so many Westerners, I originally related to the Word of God with my left brain—dissecting and categorizing content. When I approached the Word of God with my right brain—imagining the story, feeling the emotions, and somehow participating in the story—my faith became less about information and more about transformation.

Mark Batterson, author of the book *Primal*, expresses the following:

> One of the great mistakes we've made in modern Christianity is approaching God deductively as an object of knowledge instead of approaching Him inductively as the cause of wonder...the mind is educated with facts, but the soul is educated with beauty and mystery.[2]

Through oral means of learning and communicating, I personally remembered, internalized, and applied God's Word more than ever before. My image of God became less abstract and aloof; rather, I viewed God as relatable and followable. And you can imagine how freeing it was for the Cambodians when they didn't have to drudge through someone else's learning style to experience God!

THE ORAL MAJORITY

Oral communication is not unique to Cambodia. The book Making Disciples of Oral Learners joins its voice to many other legitimate resources in conveying that 70 percent of the world's people are oral learners by necessity or by preference. If that is the case, how many Christian workers are using communication paradigms that are relevant to oral learners? The answer should shock you: 90 percent of existing Christian workers use strategies for evangelism, discipleship, church planting, and training that are based on print orientation, time orientation, individualism, and abstract reasoning among receptors who are oral, event-oriented, community-oriented, and concrete relational thinkers. These figures reveal that there is a massive imbalance in missions efforts. If we are to affirm and equip the approximately *four billion* oral learners throughout the world, we need a good dose of missionaries who intentionally understand and prepare their communication strategies for oral cultures. This is the only way we will truly fulfill the Great Commission of making disciples of all nations.

Even those people who consider themselves to be members of highly literate societies are experiencing the emergence of secondary orality, also referred to as post-literacy. In this case, people prefer non-book mediums of communication due to the influence of the electronic age.

Trent Batson, PhD, is the executive director of the Association for Authentic, Experiential, and Evidence-Based Learning (AAEEBL). Batson shares thoughts shaped by Walter Ong, an expert on orality and literacy:

> In the large picture of human history, the brief few centuries when print reigned unchallenged as the most revered form of knowledge will be seen as a mere parenthesis. Before Gutenberg, knowledge was formed orally and, now, in this post-Gutenberg era, knowledge is formed— increasingly—through "secondary orality" on the internet.[3]

Just as Johannes Gutenberg's modern printing press ushered in literacy for the masses, media-digital technology is generating a new era of "secondary orality" (media-digital culture). The fast growth of media-digital technology (Facebook, blogs, wikis, podcasts, YouTube, texting, and whatever else is coming next) is leaving the Gutenberg era behind.

Secondary orality is interesting in the fact that it is neither strictly oral nor strictly literate, but rather a hybrid of both. Secondary orality is inviting back components of orality, including some of the lost communal and storytelling aspects of culture, while still depending on the written word. In other words, orality in print-oriented societies is resurfacing from its Gutenberg burial. In fact, through my research, I have discovered that storytelling associations are becoming more popular and in demand for organizations and businesses in America.

The fact that a majority of the world's population are oral learners and that significant numbers of print-oriented people are converting to secondary orality means that cross-cultural communicators need to be abreast of primary orality and secondary orality and tailor their communication strategies accordingly.

EFFECTIVE COMMUNICATION ESSENTIAL FOR MULTIPLICATION

Effective communication that will impact lives requires all of the following: hearing, understanding, remembering, internalizing, applying, and reproducing. What I saw that glassy-eyed day in the Cambodian church was only a partial fulfillment of this effective communication cycle: the receptors were only semi-hearing and semi-understanding. Communication methods which are foreign and abstract to the culture stifle the multiplication process of making disciples who make disciples.

During my initial years in Cambodia, I worked diligently to train pastors to be preachers. Elaborate preaching outlines were not a part of their experience, so I taught them again and again until they could preach a topical or expository sermon similar to my Bible school experience. In this way, I made the spreading of the gospel message far too dependent on official clergy. The average Cambodian believer left church nodding his head in agreement but saying nothing. They were not able to tell others about the Word of God with any degree of persuasiveness.

Among oral cultures, it can take a long time to produce Western-literate leaders (leaders who process and communicate using Western patterns of thought). And once there finally are trained Western-literate leaders, those leaders are not effective among members of their oral society. Their communication forms are alien to the people. "A long time" and "alien" are not friends of multiplication and movements! It is not fair to expect rich oral societies to convert to literacy before they can experience a movement for Christ. If we use an oral-friendly approach to train others, we empower clergy and laymen to retain and reproduce the gospel message and all that it entails in a relevant and expedient manner.

In the recorded dialogue with those experienced in making disciples of oral learners, Dr. Lovejoy relayed a story that he heard from a man in South Asia:

I talked with a man who is working in South Asia who had said they had some people who had come for their agriculture training. They weren't coming to be trained as pastors. But as part of the agriculture training, they learned the Christian stories. Eventually, they went on and worked as agricultural consultants for a couple of years. And then a couple of the guys hired on with a government surveying crew that had been employed to go back into a region that was rather mountainous and do survey work. They came out about six months later and they looked to some Christian leaders and said, "We need your help." And they said, "What do you need help with?" They said, "Well, we need you to come and do baptism and help us with some things." They said, "Why?" "Well, while we were back in there, we started six congregations."

They took what they had known from their training. They weren't sent as church planters, they weren't sent as evangelists, they weren't pastors. They didn't think of themselves as official clergy at all. But because they had the Christian message in a form that they could keep with them and that was always present in their minds, then off hours, nights, weekends, and whatever in addition to their surveying work for the government and crew, they led people to faith in Christ and established churches. Christianity never spreads rapidly as long as it depends on the official clergy to do the work. It spreads most effectively when the average believer is able to share their faith in a winsome and compelling way. And we think oral means are the crucial component in any kind of oral environment.[4]

Since locking up my Western-style teaching methods, I have made it a personal goal to share the Word of God "in a form people can keep with them and have always present in their minds" so they can share the gospel with others in any place or any time. Keep in mind that people from oral cultures are already adept storytellers, poets, and musicians. Additionally, they can use existing local resources to enhance these roles. This combination of organic skills and local resources ensures reproducibility. Using communication strategies that are natural and relevant to the host culture will empower the indigenous people to reproduce disciples and movements for Christ.

NAKED TRUTH AND PARABLE

ASK (Academy Sharing Knowledge) *Magazine* uses the storytelling approach to share knowledge. Annette Simmons is the president of Group Process Consulting and has written a feature for *ASK* called "The Power of Story: Dressing up the Naked Truth." Annette claims that her former cognitive approach to presenting content to organizations in order to assist them in improving in group cooperation did not work. Cognitive presentations that ultimately came across like a list of dos and don'ts shut down her listeners. Instead, Annette discovered the power of storytelling and uses it in her role as a consultant. She says, "We need stories because cognitive learning doesn't always cut it."[5]

Annette's article title derives from a Jewish parable-poem told by a rabbi in Eastern Europe. I have read different versions of this parable. Below is "Naked Truth and Parable" as written in poetry form by Heather Forest:

Naked Truth walked down the street one day.
People turned their eyes away.

Parable arrived, draped in decoration.
People greeted Parable with celebration.

Naked Truth sat alone, sad and unattired,
"Why are you so miserable?" Parable inquired.

Naked Truth replied, "I'm not welcome anymore.
No one wants to see me. They chase me from the door."

"It is hard to look at Naked Truth," Parable explained.
"Let me dress you up a bit. Your welcome will be gained."

Parable dressed Naked Truth in story's fine attire,
with metaphor, poignant prose, and plots to inspire.
With laughter and tears and adventure to unveil,
Together they went forth to spin a tale.

People opened their doors and served them their best.

Naked Truth dressed in story was a welcome guest.[6]

"It is hard to look at Naked Truth; let me dress you up a bit." Orality is a method of communicating truth by dressing it up in parables, poetry, riddles, stories, drama, dance, and song. In many settings, delivering "naked truth" through explanations, teaching points, outlines, diagrams, and abstract concepts renders that truth unapproachable and unwelcome. Like Annette Simmons, my usage of cognitive presentations did not work in Cambodia. Once I learned to dress up "naked truth" in Cambodian-style clothes, truth reached hearts, and those hearts ministered to other hearts.

RECEPTOR-ORIENTED MESSAGES

As Western missionaries, we need to slay our monocultural biases and rather breathe life into other people's ways of relating and communicating. Elder Dr. Jeanne Choy Tate, with the Presbyterian Church, quotes Virgil Elizondo, who is a Notre Dame professor of Pastoral and Hispanic Theology:

> Only when we encounter an-other culture do we recognize the existence of our own culture as distinct; prior to that, we simply assume that our way of life and our interpretative horizon are universal. Not until I am exposed to another culture do I recognize myself as a cultural being, that is, as someone who has a particular way of life; prior to that, I simply assume that my way of life is also everyone else's.[7]

In the area of communication, those who minister in "an-other" culture often assume that everybody cognitively processes and learns just like them. This assumption that "everyone learns the same" is false. There is a significant contrast between the communication modes and worldview characteristics of oral-oriented communicators and print-oriented communicators. Both types of communication are equally viable and complex, and both have strengths and shortcomings. The bottom line is not to compare communication styles for the sake of competition, but rather to understand that there is a major difference. Lack of recognition of this reality will lead to misunderstanding and miscommunication, as well as disregard for another's sacred culture and communication experiences.

The cross-cultural communicator bears the responsibility to adapt to the receptor's cultural frame of reference. Alex Smith, in *Communicating Christ Through*

Story and Song, quotes Donald Larson, an author who addresses the topic of missionary roles:

> The storyteller role is perhaps the easiest one to develop, though one often finds missionaries to be sermonizers, theologizers or lecturers.[8]

Storytelling is only one of many communication styles of oral cultures, but I believe that if a missionary could train in only one skill, it should be storytelling. Jesus was the greatest storyteller who ever lived, and he mesmerized his audiences with the greatest stories ever told. Let's commit to being receptor-oriented in our communication styles, which makes us effective and affirms our hosts in their inherent communication styles.

Using proverbs is another popular oral communication style. The African soul is rich with quick wit and wisdom expressed through narratives and proverbs. I am convinced that Africans could speak into every vein of life through their existing proverbs and pithy sayings!

> However far the stream flows, it never forgets its source. (Nigeria – Yoruba)[9]
> A tree that does not know how to dance will be taught by the wind. (Africa)[10]
> If you support the wife, you also support the child. (Ghana)[11]
> When two elephants fight, it is the grass that suffers. (Uganda)[12]
> A lion's power lies in our fear of him. (Nigeria)[13]
> One hand cannot lift a thatched roof. (Hausa)[14]
> The day never turns back again.(West Africa)[15]
> God is a great eye. (Balanda)[16]

Ethiopians say, "A proverb is to speech what salt is to food."[17] So, what is our responsibility as cross-cultural communicators of the Bible among people who have such a wealth of oral culture? Justin Ukpong sheds some light on this question:

> The theologian's task consists of re-thinking and re-expressing the original Christian message in an African cultural milieu. It is the task of confronting the Christian faith and African culture. In this process there is interpenetration of both ...There is integration of faith and culture and from it is born a new theological expression that is African and Christian.[18]

Faith does not exist in a vacuum apart from culture. I know without a doubt that my theology is wrapped in my North American culture. And because of that reality, I should not simply think and express the Christian message from my instinctual culture. Rather, as Justin articulates, my task is to "rethink and re-express" the Christian message in the cultural milieu of my host culture. Rethinking and re-expressing the gospel message is challenging work, but it is the work of a cross-cultural communicator.

Renowned Capability

I have often seen people from oral societies downplay their orality in the presence of print-oriented communicators. In addition, I have heard people from print-oriented societies degrade people of oral cultures. Only arrogance leads print-oriented communicators to think that their learning experiences are somehow superior and that everyone should follow suit. On the other hand, those people from oral cultures should not minimize their rich oral culture but rather join their voices with Gideon Kiongo in celebrating their renowned capability:

> It is important that we employ the ever so powerful mode of communication in which Africans are renowned experts. I am referring to African "storytelling."[19]

I cannot even begin to explain the treasures that exist within oral cultures that have been lost to conceptual thinkers due to writing systems: treasures such as the ability to store and retrieve information instantaneously, highly personal relationships, value of community, relevance, unity between speaker and audience, participation, and so on. I believe that every one of these treasures would be a blessing to a movement for Christ.

One day, I was teaching at a university in North America. I explained how storytelling is a vital oral communication form and that it is universal. One of the students likened oral storytelling to telling stories to children in Sunday school. My first thought was, "There is a bit of ethnocentrism." Most stories have an entertainment component and play an integral role in relating to children. However, storytelling in oral-dominated cultures is not child's play, nor is it merely entertainment. Dr. Walter Ong, who is a key researcher of orality and literacy, sets the record straight, as described by Harry Box in his dissertation on oral, event-oriented communication:

Ong helps us understand a little more clearly why ancestors and past events are so important in these societies; why song, music and dance are such priorities; why meetings in the 'men's house' extend for such lengthy periods; and why people are so hesitant to step out and be different from the group. These are not just little 'hobbies' that they have, or means of entertainment, or particular quirks of their personality because they are still not 'educated'. No, rather, they are important features demonstrating that there are viable options to the 'western' cultural perception of reality.[20]

Stories and oral mediums preserve cultural heritage, involve a complex system of communication, exist at the core of the worldview, allow for storing and retrieving knowledge, and permeate every level of society. Those who conclude that differences in learning merely come down to the ability or lack of ability to read and write have greatly misunderstood the art of communication.

It has been a habit of literate cultures to view oral cultures simply in terms of their lack of the technologies of writing. This habit, argues Ong, is dangerously misled. Oral cultures are living cultures in their own right.[20]

Dr. Ong admonishes us not to put oral cultures in a box made up of our misunderstanding. Oral learners have the same intellectual capacity and learning ability as literacy oriented communicators.

PRIMARY AND RESIDUAL ORALITY

My biggest misconception was to assume that if a Cambodian could read the Bible, he or she would process and comprehend it through analysis, categorization, and clarification. This was not the case. Some Cambodians are strictly primary oral learners:

"Primary orality" refers to thought and its verbal expression within cultures "totally untouched by any knowledge of writing or print."[21]

Other Cambodians are residual oral learners:

"Residual Orality" refers to thought and its verbal expression in cultures that have been exposed to writing and print, but have not fully "interior-ized" (in McLuhan's term) the use of these technologies in their daily lives.[22]

Dr. Walter Ong describes primary oral cultures as "totally untouched by any knowledge or writing or print" in his prominent book *Orality and Literacy*.[23]

In his studies, Marshall McLuhan valued Dr. Ong's writings and added his own flavor of experience to the research process. He specifically expounded on technology's influence on the cognitive and social arenas. People within primary oral cultures learn through oral means by necessity. Residual oral cultures learn through oral means by preference. Some Cambodians, especially the younger generation, are bypassing literate-oriented methods straight to secondary orality. Secondary orality refers to thought and its verbal expression in cultures that have been exposed to modern communication technologies.

Ultimately, cross-cultural communicators cannot assume that the receptors of their communication process will take in and express information just like they do. We make assumptions based on our own experiences and allow those assumptions to become dark glasses hindering our ability to truly see the cultures around us. Let us affirm, celebrate, learn, and use oral forms of communication among the 70 percent who deserve the gospel within their own framework.

BIBLICAL COMPATIBILITY

Ezekiel, a prophet of God, stated the following: "The word of the Lord came to me: 'Son of man, set forth an allegory and tell the house of Israel a parable'" (Ezekiel 17:1–2). The parable in this case, revealed by God, was a message to Israel through an allegory of two magnificent eagles and a luscious vine. The Old Testament is loaded with genealogies, poetry, psalms set to music, prose, metaphors, proverbs, narratives, symbolic acts, and prophetic utterances—and all of them were originally delivered in the context of an oral community.

The Bible as a whole is 75 percent narrative and 15 percent poetry and proverbs. The remaining 10 percent is presented in a more propositional and apologetic manner. Yet, even the majority of that 10 percent—communicated in letter form—is a hybrid of propositional and oral styles. Paul did not sit down for a length of time to write a systematic theological document. He wrote letters that flowed from concrete experiences and relationships with others. He wrote letters rooted in his missionary journeys in order to tell his missionary story, to greet others, to set up appointments, to introduce people, to exhort, to encourage, and to address issues that arose within various communities of Christ.

Jesus never wrote a book. He trained his disciples, challenged the religious leaders, and delivered his kingdom message through oral communication forms. Tom Steffen, in his book *Reconnecting God's Story to Ministry*, reminds us that Jesus never wrote a book on systematic theology, yet he taught theology everywhere he went through parables, stories, life experiences, apprenticeship, demonstrations, conversations, prophecy, and symbols. Steffen emphasizes Jesus's mode of communication:

> As Jesus' listeners wrestled with new theology introduced innocently yet intentionally through parabolic stories, they were challenged to examine traditions, form new images of God, and transform behavior. To remain content with past realities became uncomfortable; yet to take up Jesus' challenges to step out of the boat, taste new wine, display golden lamp stands, turn from family members, extend mercy to others, search for hidden objects …Jesus' stories, packed with theology, caused reason, imagination, and emotions to collide, demanding change of allegiance. Jesus' example forcibly demonstrates that stories can effectively communicate theology.[23]

As cross-cultural communicators, our duty is to discern and investigate how certain people groups view and interpret life and how they process and relate their experiences. Subsequently, we present the Bible in an approach that will organically encourage a dynamic and relevant relationship with God in accordance with their worldview. If a specific people group is used to receiving and internalizing meaning through dramatic scenes, we do them an injustice to present life in a series of propositions.

Tom Steffen challenges missionaries to embrace and maximize the use of oral communication:

> The Bible begins with the story of creation and ends with a vision of God's recreation. Peppered generously between Alpha and Omega are a host of stories. While stories dominate the scriptural landscape, they rarely enter the Christian worker's evangelism-discipleship strategies intentionally.[24]

Steffen continues this line of thought by quoting Leland Ryken:

Why does the Bible contain so many stories? Is it possible that stories reveal some truths and experiences in a way that no other literary form does—and if so, what are they? What is the difference in our picture of God, when we read stories in which God acts, as compared with theological statements about the nature of God? What does the Bible communicate through our imagination that it does not communicate through our reason? If the Bible uses the imagination as one way of communicating truth, should we not show an identical confidence in the power of the imagination to convey religious truth? If so, would a good startpoint be to respect the story quality of the Bible in our exposition of it?.[25]

Jesus and the Bible are ripe and relevant to people of oral cultures, and yet sometimes Westerners make Jesus and the Bible into a blurry and abstract phenomenon that forever remains on the peripheral edges of life. People of oral cultures are able to quickly connect with Bible stories like connecting to a long-lost dance partner—as long as we do not stifle them by forcing the Bible into a tool of propositions, logic, and abstract concepts.

ORAL COMMUNICATION STYLES IN CHURCH PLANTING

The Togolese of Africa are an example of a people group who enthusiastically set aside their daily activities to hear about God through their oral forms of music and storytelling. As North Americans, we try all different kinds of programs to call people into our church buildings. In this case, the storyteller entered the world of the Togolese and connected the people to the reality of God among them. Carla Bowman—who is a founder, along with her husband, of Scripture in Use, a tool for Bible storytelling—sets the scene:

> Harmattan winds have hovered over desert Africa for weeks picking up the sands of the Sahara and filling the sky of sub-Saharan Kpele-Dafo with brown haze. In this sand-gray dusk, the hushed, unnatural silence of the windswept village is spellbinding and disconcerting …But the silence of this Togolese town is about to end. THE STORYTELLER IS COMING! And into the quiet hamlet the clear, resonant voice of his recitation will emerge, startling and powerful, heralded by the drums.
> The listeners are electrified as the biblical story of creation begins; "In the beginning God created the heavens and the earth" …the poetic,

melodious pattern of the story flows from Antoine's lips. When he reaches the repeating phrase, "And God saw that it was good," he sings a song composed by Timothee Ayivi in call and response style. The song is designed to reinforce the story; the words of the song are: "In the beginning God created heaven and earth. It was empty and darkness was over the surface of the deep." The call and response is choreographed by the composer in a traditional style that glorifies God the creator. As the villagers quickly memorize the song response and join Antoine, their voices become a chorus of blissful harmony. Then dancing intercepts the story. The headman dances as well, thus placing his approval upon the story and the event. The drum language continues. Amidst the steaming Equatorial heat sitting stiffly upon the air, the pulsating rhythm of the drum reaches to the stars and sounds deep into the tropical night. The storytelling and singing continue in this way. As the fire dims, the story ends. There is not one villager that wishes to leave that place. The story in this setting has connected them to the word and to their history. It has involved and inspired them as they interact with the story through song and dance.[26]

I don't think it can get much better than that! In Bowman's article "Story and Song in Kepele-Dafo: An Innovative Church Planting Model Among an Oral Culture of Togo," she shares the overall results of such a storytelling process. I have summarized these in list form below:

- The Word of God brought alive in the cultural context
- Felt needs addressed
- Worldview shaped
- Extended families converted by the Holy Spirit
- Obedience to Christ practiced
- People released from strongholds
- House churches established

Storying and singing among the Togolese was not an end in itself. Rather, these oral forms were used to plant churches in ways that were congruent to the culture. North Americans consider using storying and music as an innovative way to plant churches, but to the Togolese it is completely natural. Natural generates passion; unnatural produces passivity.

Keep in mind that 70 percent of the world's people are oral learners by necessity or by preference. Those of us who do not come from oral-oriented societies have a responsibility to learn and use methods to plant churches that are relevant to the context.

Let us feast on the richness of oral cultures rather than trying to overturn peoples to be someone else—to be like us. It's time we turn the mirror away from our own ethnocentric reflection and see the reflection that other cultures have to offer.

"For too long, Western Christianity has emphasized thoroughly rationalized doctrinal formulas over narrative and diminished the power of story to form Christian identity and create movement. An apostle is a theological storyteller, and apostolic movements understand and skillfully navigate the power of stories."

ALAN HIRSCH

INTERLUDE

At the end of this section, I rest my eyes and daydream. As I draw one or two deep breaths, I think of Paul, an apostle who premeditated multiplication, indigeneity, and sustainability.

As a missionary, how would you fill in the blank: "Our gospel came to you with__"? Paul gives his answer:

> For we know, brothers loved by God, that he has chosen you, because our gospel came to you not simply with *words*, but also with *power*, with the *Holy Spirit* and with *deep conviction*. You know how we lived among you for your sake. (1 Thessalonians 1:4–5, emphasis mine)

Is it possible that, at times and to some degree, we have replaced power, the Holy Spirit, and deep conviction with coaxing, donations, and superficiality?

Read Acts 28:1–10 when you have the opportunity. When Paul was shipwrecked on the island of Malta, he went from being a victim of a shipwreck and snakebite to being a so-called murderer, then a god, and then a man of God. Furthermore, Paul went from the shore, to the campfire, to the estate, and finally to the chief official of the island. Now that is missions—spreading the gospel through word, power, the Holy Spirit, and deep conviction.

As I think over the issues facing missions today, I think of the council at Jerusalem. Some men came down from Judea to Antioch in order to force the Gentile believers to become culturally Jewish. Paul, Barnabas, and Peter emphatically convinced the council members that God had thoroughly accepted the Gentile believers due to their faith. Paul did not point to cultural abandonment as proof of their sincere conversions; rather, he pointed out what God had done among them (miraculous signs and wonders and the giving of the Holy Spirit) and the Gentiles' faith. I remember Glenn Schwartz's sentiments from a previous chapter: indigenous churches should not stand out as something culturally alien, but rather should stand out because of their love and obedience to God. These thoughts bring me back to Paul's affirmation of the Thessalonians:

> We continually remember before our God and Father your work pro-
> duced by faith, your labor prompted by love, and your endurance
> inspired by hope in our Lord Jesus Christ. (1 Thessalonians 1:3)

Paul knew how to model to others for the sake of reproducibility and multiplication:

> You know how we lived among you for your sake. You became *imitators*
> of us and of the Lord; in spite of severe suffering, you welcomed the mes-
> sage with the joy given by the Holy Spirit. And so you became a *model
> to all the believers* in Macedonia and Achaia. The Lord's message rang
> out from you not only in Macedonia and Achaia—your faith in God *has
> become known everywhere* …They tell how you turned to God from idols
> to serve the living and true God. (1 Thessalonians 1:4–5, emphasis mine)

Is not that the dream of every missionary—that a people group would turn
to God from idols to serve the living and true God? To Paul, it was not enough
that the Thessalonians served God, the Most High. He expressed joy in the fact
that the Thessalonians became a model to other believers and that the message
spread from them to others. A people group that not only believes, but multiplies
the message in their context and beyond, is even a sweeter dream.

Paul understood how easily the prophetic voice of the apostle, disciple, and
church could be distorted. He did all in his power to protect the purity of the
message and the messenger. He shared the gospel and lived in such a way as to
protect the gospel and God's redemption work from suspicion, confusion, dis-
tortion, ulterior motives, and opposition:

> With the help of our God, we dared to tell you the gospel in spite of
> strong opposition. For the appeal we make does not spring from error
> or impure motives, nor are we trying to trick you. On the contrary, we
> speak as men approved by God to be entrusted with the gospel. We are
> not trying to please men but God, who tests our hearts. You know we
> never used flattery, nor did we put on a mask to cover up greed—God
> is our Witness. (1 Thessalonians 2:2–5)

We loved you so much that we delighted to share with you not only the gospel of God but our lives as well, because you had become so dear to us. Surely you remember, brothers, our toil and hardship; we worked night and day in order not to be a burden to anyone while we preached the gospel of God to you. (1 Thessalonians 2:8–9)

More than anything, I am concerned that unhealthy dependency and its multiple consequences will crush the prophetic voice of the church. If unbelievers see manipulation, jealousy, competition, secrecy, complacency, superficiality, idleness, and double-mindedness within the church, what will draw them to Christ, the head of the church? If unbelievers are convinced that believers within their society preach the gospel merely because they receive foreign benefits, how will they be attracted to God?

It is time we take account of how we "do missions." Are we, like Paul, doing all we can to live and share the gospel in a way that presents a pure gospel and allows for pure conversions to it? Or do we slip into a donor approach, in which subsidized nationals of various countries are viewed as Western Christian agents? Melvin Hodges shares the words of former Missionary J.J. Cooksey, who had missions experience in West Africa:

The employed national Christian agent makes the Moslem smile in the beard; the foreign missionary he indulgently tolerates. He will only furiously think …when Christ really and utterly captures some Moslem heart in sacrificial power, fills it with the Holy Spirit, and consecrates it for the task of building an indigenous North African Christianity.[1]

Perhaps we could put our heads together and find ways to capture the Muslim heart, the Buddhist heart, the Hindu heart, the Jewish heart, and the only-in-name Christian heart with Christ. Sacrificial power and the work of the Holy Spirit will change a man's heart more than any gospel seen as wrapped in mixed motives. Let us take inventory and ensure that we speak as men and women who are entrusted with the gospel.

"For the appeal we make does not spring from error or mixed motives, nor are we trying to trick you. On the contrary, we speak as men approved by God to be entrusted with the Gospel."

1 THESSALONIANS 2:3–4

PART III:

MULTIPLICATION, INDIGENEITY, AND SUSTAINABILITY IN ACTION

CHAPTER ELEVEN

MULTIPLICATION IN ACTION

"The key is to think 'movement'—and act 'multiplication.'"

BOB ROBERTS JR.

We need to plan for the multiplication of disciples. Perhaps ironically, as we plan for multiplication, we will find that we probably need to do less rather than more. Multiplication needs a spontaneous component, and humans tend to impose their own agendas. In this chapter, we will discover premeditated actions that open the way for multiplication.

AIM FOR PREMEDITATED MULTIPLICATION

Can you imagine trying to put together a puzzle from a mixture of pieces randomly taken from various puzzle boxes? Missions work often feels like everyone is trying to make one big puzzle with pieces from various puzzles. Instead of connecting pieces that fit tightly together, we join random pieces, leaving gaps and never completing a coherent picture. A mishmash approach to missions is like running on a treadmill—forever moving but never going anywhere. There are at least five instigators to this treadmill missions approach:

1. Institutionalization Maintenance

As missionaries, we tend to start complex projects and institutions that over the long run require high maintenance, consume our human resources, and do not have the multiplication of disciples at their core. The glue trap called maintenance prevents us from applying ourselves to the heart of movements for Christ. The sad reality is that many of our goals are swallowed up by the very institutions we established to meet those goals. Charles Kraft, in his article "Ethics of Change," expounds on the problem of institutionalization and asks several good questions:

Our western propensity for starting institutions has been mentioned.

Our intention is to go to the ends of the earth to demonstrate the love of God. To do this, we often set up an institution and then get captured by it to an extent that the real (as opposed to the stated) purpose of the institution changes imperceptibly from serving to demonstrate God's love to the need to perpetuate itself. Institutions are not intrinsically bad. The question however: Just what does the institution now stand for? What is it really communicating? And what now is its real purpose?

The history of institutionalization is that almost inevitably the institution becomes primarily a means for perpetuating itself, no matter how worthy the goals that brought it into being.[1]

I concur with Charles Kraft that institutions are not intrinsically bad. But the message of the love of God that we want to send is often not perceived by those who are served by the institution. Not only that, but the institution itself becomes like an elephant with a huge appetite: it needs to be fed big meals. Maintenance of the institution often becomes the driving factor behind decisions, and the original goals get shuffled aside.

Our Western partiality toward establishing institutions often becomes the ropes around our hands that prevent us from intentionally making disciple-makers, which is the key to movements for Christ. Jesus, the disciples, and Paul steered clear of creating institutions to fulfill the Great Commission. If we desire to follow in their footsteps, perhaps we need to be more cautious of implementing project-driven missions.

2.   Inherited Maintenance

When new missionaries arrive on the field, they are often appointed to fulfill roles in mission-established, non-sustainable ministries or projects which other missionaries have left behind in order to conduct their furloughs or return to living in their home countries. I call this phenomenon "the black hole." New missionaries are often prevented from intentionally applying themselves to the goal of multiplication because the black hole sucks them into maintaining the same old mission-established projects.

I have met and co-labored with many missionaries who have lost motivation under the burden of inherited projects and the unachieved goals of multiplying disciples. The demands of the projects and institutions position and direct missionaries rather than the same Holy Spirit who set apart Paul and Barnabas to minister to the unreached Gentiles.

3. Energy-Stealing and Time-Consuming Extras

Far too many times, I have seen local believers in various countries who have the mandate and capability to multiply organic disciples, leaders, and churches, but who are completely consumed with serving on committees, solving project-related problems, running errands to assist missionaries in their endeavors, and keeping mission-established institutions afloat. These energy-stealing and time-consuming extras prevent locals from getting around to an indigenous movement for Christ! As missionaries, we should do everything in our power to protect local believers from being distracted from the heart of the Great Commission: making disciples who obey all that Jesus commanded.

4. Hodgepodge

Naturally, missionaries often set up ministries based on what we see as the needs of the host country and/or our personal interests. But if these aspects drive how we conceptualize and conduct cross-cultural ministry, we will most likely conduct the missions task in a hit-or-miss fashion. Tom Steffen, a professor of Intercultural Studies and the director of the Doctor of Missiology program at Biola University, calls this phenomenon a "needs-based strategy" or a "piecemeal approach."

Steffen encourages people at the team level, field level, and agency level to adopt an intentional church planting strategy, rather than approaching missions in a piecemeal fashion:

> My analysis of the Philippine field situation revealed a number of factors that no doubt contributed to the lack of even one church being placed completely in the hands of nationals. (1) On the team level, members lacked a comprehensive church-planting strategy; one that incorporated role changes for withdrawal, dealt with key questions and faith objectives for each stage of the church plant, and provided a checklist to determine progress made toward the overall goal. (2) On the field level, a piecemeal strategy had developed over the years which meant that the strategy employed was determined by the changing needs of the various field members. (3) On the agency level, the candidate selection and training process tended to perpetuate and reinforce paternalistic church planting procedures.[2]

Weaknesses and gaps on one level affect other levels. It takes much fore-thought, planning, and commitment to synchronize the team level, field level, and agency level to work in a strategic manner. But the effort is well worth it. As Steffen reveals, piecemeal approaches can be responsible for the lack of even one active indigenous church.

5. Forced Competition

In reference to post-genocide Cambodia, the church was being reestablished while at the same time, numerous parachurch organizations were implementing their efforts. The parachurch organizations had come with their big budgets and demands to fulfill big agendas. The churches were growing slowly but surely at a more grassroots level. This is what I saw happen again and again: pastors worked hard to mentor volunteers and leaders in their churches. The parachurch organizations sought well-trained Christians to fill positions in their organizations, so they offered jobs and salaries to the very volunteers and leaders whom the pastors had intentionally trained. For the most part, the salaries offered by the parachurch organizations were more than the local churches could match. Consequently, the pastors struggled to build teams and sustain coworkers in their churches and ministries. The parachurch organizations operated as a big vacuum, sucking vital people out of the church and leaving a country with minimal laity volunteerism and few pastors paid by the local church.

In some cases, the hope is that both the local church and the parachurch organization will benefit: the parachurch organizations gain competent employees, and the employees give back to the local churches, both through advanced skills and increased offerings. However, more often than not, employees of parachurch organizations offer less and less to the local churches. This isn't necessarily intentional; often, the less is due to frequent travel and exhaustion from serving as "professional Christian workers."

It is true that the generous salaries given to locals by parachurch organizations often go back into the church through tithes and offerings. Unfortunately, this may serve as an artificial prop that gives the local church the illusion that it is sustaining itself. What will happen to local churches that expand their ministries through indirect dependence on parachurch employees when those parachurch organizations leave for one reason or another?

Artificial props and drawing workers out of the church are not merely problems related to parachurch organizations. Missions organizations create their own projects in which they need employees, and they often hire key people from local churches. Parachurch organizations and mission-established projects need to make sure they are empowering the church rather than unintentionally weakening their ability to carry out their core biblical functions.

This brings me back to premeditated multiplication. How much of what we do actually jams up multiplication? If we, as missionaries, are getting our puzzle pieces out of different boxes, we may never see the big picture. Like fishermen, we have a way of tangling our own lines. We create projects and ministries to facilitate the making of disciples, but often find those ministries serving as distractions. Haphazard quantity suffocates quality.

All people and entities who contribute to the missions task need to seriously evaluate their work and ensure that they are truly empowering the local church to be a multiplying force for the kingdom of God.

After a degree of stubbornness, I finally cleared away all the good things I was doing in my own missions work in order to apply myself to the best things of multiplication. I was doing numerous activities and fulfilling a variety of roles, sometimes all at once. One day, I stopped long enough to smell the orchids and realized I was involved in many activities, yet a significant extent of my work did not contribute to strategic multiplication. It was time for a serious change in course.

Making changes is not easy. In some ways, the need to change is a reflection of our own personal shortcomings. At the same time, we're usually set on not altering that which we deem sacred—that which is "how we have always done it." Erwin Raphael McManus words it this way:

> Bringing about change isn't simply programmatic—sometimes it is personal. When you alter the methods of the church, you are, in effect, trampling memories. Often, you only discover what is sacred once you have moved it.[3]

In my mind, I see a picture of a tightly fitted puzzle that reveals the best things of multiplication for Cambodia: 1) Cambodian communities of Christ that give birth to other communities of Christ that give birth to even more communities of Christ—in other words, multiplying churches; 2) churches that have an indigenous nature, which are viewed by members of society as a reflection of their culture instead of a foreign import; and 3) churches which believe the spread of the kingdom of God is dependent on their relationship with the Holy Spirit, their intercession, their sacrifice, their unity, their faith, their giving, their resources, their devotion, and their passion.

Albert Einstein astutely stated, "The definition of insanity is doing the same

Jim

thing over and over again and expecting different results." Think about that for a second and ask yourself, "Does this quote apply to the way I conduct my missions work?" Dissatisfaction with the status quo is a critical motivator for moving something that is stuck. Somewhere along the line, we may need to revamp what we are doing to achieve movements for Christ. May God cause a disquieting in our hearts until we notice where we are basking in complacency while something under our noses is in danger!

How will you conduct or adapt your work so you can be intentional about multiplication?

ASSUME NOTHING…PONDER EVERYTHING

I have frequently heard Glenn Schwartz, author of *Charity That Destroys Dignity*, say, "Beware of our assumptions. Our assumptions can become self-fulfilling prophecies." For example, if we assume a certain people group is too poor, then we will conduct ministry in accordance with that assumption. There is a very good chance that the specific people group in question never considered itself too poor until someone from the outside communicated that message.

Wikipedia defines an assumption as "a proposition that is taken for granted, as if it were true based upon presupposition without preponderance of the facts." As cross-cultural workers, I wonder how often we make assumptions without pre-pondering how something will work or not work in regard to multiplication among our host culture.

In my early stages of ministry, I assumed that Cambodians would take what I implemented and make the appropriate adjustments to their own cultural setting. However, those who learned under my tutelage made their own assumptions. They presumed that whatever I did was a mandate from the Bible. They were not able to decipher what was biblical and what was merely my own culture. Eventually, I ceased taking for granted that Cambodians should adjust what I modeled to them to fit their own culture; instead, I became the one to adjust.

Pondering everything involves discerning where *biblical* and *cultural* divide in our own experience. If my church experience has always entailed a church building in a specific location in which people meet on a specific day of the week, I may assume that a church is only legitimate when there is a dedicated building facility which holds Sunday services. This assumption could very well undermine the principles of multiplication, the existing worldview of my host culture, and the Bible itself. Time and time again, I have seen effective evangelism stop as soon as a building is erected. The building needs to be utilized: thus, program evangelism (you come to us in our building) replaces relational evangelism (we go to where you live and work). People become so busy with what happens in the building that they disconnect from unbelieving communities. On top of that, church buildings are an oddity to certain indigenous communities—the church buildings are not a central part of the society's value system, and thus, they may cause people to be standoffish or even hostile toward those who meet in them. Lastly, the Bible does not mandate or even model the construction of church buildings.

I am not trying to make a case for or against church buildings. Rather, I am suggesting that we be careful when operating out of own assumptions, which are rooted in our home-cultural experiences. If we give the impression that church buildings are necessary even when church buildings may actually be a hindrance, we have allowed our assumptions to mislead others and ourselves.

Before we open our mouths or activate our hands, we need to give ample preponderance to the elements of multiplication and the indigenous culture in which we work. Assume nothing, and ponder everything.

What assumptions do you need to dissolve to achieve multiplication?

CREATE SPIRITUAL DNA THAT ALLOWS THE HOLY SPIRIT TO WORK

The term "movements for Christ" is merely descriptive of what God is doing though the Holy Spirit—transforming people into lovers and followers of Jesus. Bob Roberts Jr., a pastor and church planting movement (CPM) practitioner, expresses his thoughts, along with referring to David Watson's input:

> Watson went on to say, "CPMs are our hope and prayer. Our part of that is making disciples, equipping leaders, and starting churches with the right DNA that is based on obedience. God's part is blessing our obedience in his time with the rapid and regular multiplication of disciples, leaders, and churches." Watson likes the term "gospel planting" because we plant the gospel and train obedience and the result is churches. The focus is not on the act of church planting itself.[4]

According to David Watson, we create spiritual DNA through obedience, but it is the Holy Spirit who blesses that obedience, which results in church planting movements. The transforming power of the Holy Spirit and transformed people are at the core of movements for Christ. What does this mean in a practical sense? It means we must be cautious so as not to make movements our idol or cause them to be dependent on us or our formulas, but rather lean on and promote God in every aspect relating to movements for Christ.

What will you do to create a spiritual DNA for the Holy Spirit to impart a movement for Christ?

Encourage Disciples to Retain Their Identity with the Community

Americans can adhere to any religion or faith and still be considered Americans. For the most part, religious affiliation and faith commitments do not sever Americans from their social identity or community. One can be Catholic and still be considered an American. One can be Mormon and still be counted as an American. One can be an evangelical Christian and still be considered to be red, white, and blue. Social identity and religious identity are not viewed as an integrated whole. This is not the case in many parts of the world. To be Thai is to be Buddhist, and to be Afghan is to be Muslim. In these nations, to become a Christian is to become non-Thai or non-Afghan. One of the biggest existing barriers to accepting Jesus as Lord among Buddhists and Muslims is not theological in nature; rather, it is the fear of losing one's social identity and community. For many, becoming a Christian is interpreted as forsaking one's nationality to become a different nationality while still living in one's homeland.

This barrier did not arise without reason. Missionaries who come from individual-oriented societies and Western church experiences often conceptualize and organize the church in other regions of the world in ways that create identity crises. You may recall the "one-by-one out of the social group" method described by Donald McGavran in an earlier chapter. McGavran's description can be expanded: "one-by-one out of the social group into the church." Missionaries who favor this method do not usually see a problem with forming Christian communities that are centered on a church building. Through the church's services and programs, the missionary leaders try to knit the people into a Christian community. Believers become a part of a new social group while they are more and more estranged from their own social community and identity.

I realize from my own experience that missionaries who use this church model urge believers to share the gospel with their friends and families, but their method actually hinders that process. The "one-by-one out of the social group into the church" model creates a competing community within a community. The church community becomes the believers' focus, and they become loosely connected to those in their everyday community. The believers feel estranged from their own community, and their community views them as "one of them."

The goal is to facilitate the natural growth of the gospel within the existing community, allowing the members of that community to express their faith within their context, not in a newly created and socially disconnected church context. Donald McGavran words it this way:

> The principle is to encourage converts to remain thoroughly one with their own people in most matters. They should continue to eat what their people eat. They should not say, "My people are vegetarians, but now I have become a Christian, I'm going to eat meat." After they become Christians they should be more rigidly vegetarian than they were before. In the matter of clothing, they should continue to look precisely like their kinsfolk.[5]

I recall the man who was healed from a legion of demons. He begged Jesus to allow him to go with him. Jesus told the man to go back home and tell those in his community about God (Luke 8:38–39). When new believers disconnect themselves from their kinsfolk, it causes confusion and disillusionment among those who did everyday life with them. Our churches will not multiply when people within the community say such words as:

> "They think they are superior now that they have aligned themselves with the foreigners."
> "They are traitors who joined a foreigner's religion."
> "They are no longer a part of us."

McGavran states that believers in Christ should say on all occasions:

> I am a better son than I was before; I am a better father than I was before; I am a better husband than I was before; and I love you more than I am used to do. You can hate me, but I will not hate you. You can exclude me, but I will include you. You can force me out of our ancestral house, but I will live on its veranda. Or I will get a house just across the street. I am still one of you; I am more one of you than ever before.[6]

What powerful words! If such words are actually backed up by action, imagine the impact of this type of commitment.

Gavriel Gefen, the founding director of Keren HaShlichut, an Israeli association of emissaries who serve around the world, gives us a tangible picture of what an intact community of Christ looks like:

> There is a growing phenomenon taking place concurrently within at least every sizeable region of the world today. People within numerous differ-ent tribal cultures and also people within the cultures of each of the major world religions are increasingly accepting Jesus without converting to Christianity and without joining churches. They are encountering Jesus in ways that change their lives forever, without them leaving one group for another. They are learning to discover for themselves what it means to be faithful to Jesus within their own cultures and within their own birth communities. Conversion for them is believed to be a matter of the heart and not one of joining a different, competing cultural community.
>
> It is usually the case that after a number of these individuals within the same community are following Jesus, they begin meeting regularly as a small group. Over time this expands into multiple small groups among the same people group or within the same country. Eventually, it becomes established as a full-fledged movement of believers in Jesus that is outside of Christendom. It becomes a Jesus movement within another tradition. Does this mean they are living their lives outside the boundaries of biblical faith? Or, are they merely living beyond the boundaries of Christendom as a competing community?[7]

I would like to answer Gefen's questions. First of all, the way North Americans do church—with a special building, a special day, a special leader or two, and a special service conducted for those who attend the church—does not have God's stamp of approval as the way to live out biblical faith in fellowship with others. In fact, there are plenty of North Americans who believe the come-to-church model is not working even in North America! "The quickest way to 'church the unchurched' may very well be to 'unchurch the church.'"[8] This comment is merely one in a million that expresses the concern that the common model of church in North America is failing to make disciples that make disciples.

Yet we take this pattern of worship and carbon copy it in places of the world that are communal in nature. Would it not be utterly more amazing if Buddhist, Muslim, Hindu, and Animist people lived out transformed lives in Christ in the midst of their birth communities, remaining intact in their social and cultural identities rather than becoming Western in their expression of faith? We work so hard as missionaries to acculturate ourselves to the cultural groups we live among, so why do we use church planting models that cause local believers in those groups to disengage from their culture and society? Rebecca Lewis, who spent fifteen years working among the Muslims, paints a picture of an intact identity-based church:

> Meanwhile, the New Testament also affirms an alternative church model, the oikos or household-based church, where families and their pre-existing relational networks become the church as the gospel spreads in their midst. The God-given family and clan structures are thereby supported and trans-formed from unbelieving communities into largely believing communities. Decisions to follow Christ are often more communal rather than individual (see NT examples in Acts: Cornelius, Lydia, Crispus, etc.) The destruction of the families and the creation of semi-functional, extracted, new com-munities of believers-only is thereby avoided, and the gospel continues to flow along preserved relational pathways. The movement to Christ has thus remained inside the fabric of the society and community.
>
> In "insider movements," therefore, there is no attempt to form neo-communities of "believers-only" that compete with the family network (no matter how contextualized); instead, "insider movements" consist of believers remaining in and transforming their own pre-existing family networks, minimally disrupting their families and communities. These believing families and their relational networks are valid local expressions of the Body of Christ, fulfilling all the "one another" care seen in the book of Acts, and so they do not need to adopt the meeting and program struc-tures common in Western aggregate churches.[9]

As missionaries, we are challenged with fulfilling the Great Commission, and an integral part of that Great Commission is for people around the world to live out their discipleship within existing communities rather than becoming elusive, disconnected disciples.

What can you do to ensure believers will remain well-connected to their preexisting identity and communities as much as possible?

MAKE DISCIPLE-MAKERS

Discipleship is something we live out, not merely someone we are. Jesus's Great Commission centered on active disciples making active disciples. An active disciple is one who obeys everything Jesus commanded and also teaches others to do the same (Matthew 28:20). Bob Roberts Jr. drives home the fact that disciples are a key to the multiplying church:

> The lowest common denominator is not a pastor, planter, or prophet—but the disciple.[10]

Disciples who make disciples under the authority of Jesus Christ are vital to any true movement for Christ. Pastors, church planters, and organizations have a role, but at the very core of multiplication are disciples making disciples that result in movements for Christ.

Gathering people for events and programs is easy. There is always a beginning and end in such a process—usually the start and closure of the event or program. Making disciples is hard work; it is a never-ending process. Bob Roberts Jr. expounds:

> Our time, effort, energy, and focus must be on how the gospel is spreading and how disciples are being made. If we do that, we will get to the church planting movement. It's a lot easier to build buildings, fill them up, and have special events than it is to pour into lives of people and make multiplying disciples. But it is the only thing that will really work.[11]

Allow this diagnostic question to regularly be a part of your evaluation: "How do I unfold ministry in such a way that I am making disciple-makers?" I have seen so many churches create "Sunday disciples" and use Sunday services as their discipleship means. The problem with that is that Sunday disciples live as followers of Christ within a predictable church setting, but do not know how to live as everyday followers of Christ within an unpredictable society. Discipleship confined to the Sunday church setting produces Sunday disciples.

If a church measures success by attendance, spacious facilities, high-financed programs, and fancy equipment, those desired results will drive the church's methodology. Not one of these standards is mentioned or modeled in the New Testament as a sign of success. In Cambodia, many people thought discipleship involved inviting someone to a polished church program, coaxing that person to go forward and repeat a "sinner's prayer" and then allowing the church to take over from there. (As an aside, I'm not sure where the whole concept of a sinner's prayer came from. I wonder if instant Christianity and passive involvement on

Sundays has led us to make mere superficial converts, rather than seeing people with radically transformed lives who love God with all their hearts, souls, minds and bodies.) We may need to redefine our paradigms of discipleship to ensure multiplication: disciples making disciples, the common denominator of a movement for Christ.

Over the years, I have tried to fine-tune discipleship that leads to multiplication. Below are a few principles that have become a part of my fine-tuning:

1.   Tony and Felicity Dale, authors of *The Rabbit and the Elephant: Why Small is the New Big for Today's Church*, challenge us with statistics revealed in "Active Study" by Dartmouth College: "Being a passive listener of a Sunday sermon produces spectators, not active and relevant participants of the gospel. I read somewhere once that people remember only about 20 percent of what they hear, 50 percent of what they see and hear, and 70 percent of what they say themselves."[12] Thus, I conduct participatory Bible study methods that involve hearing, seeing, saying, and application for all participants.

2.   A pastor who does not model discipleship to his congregation outside of what he considers a church setting has neglected Jesus's approach. Thus, I mentor pastors and disciple-makers to be with the members of their church in everyday life: in their homes, markets, noodle shops, fields, and social events.

3.   Just because we have trained church members as volunteers to make Sunday services and church programs happen does not mean we have made disciple-makers. Thus, I train disciples to share their faith and live out their relationship with Christ within their everyday network of relationships.

4.   Transferring information or doctrine does not lead to transformation. Thus, I implement ministry in such a way that participants can increasingly love God and others, as well as discover and apply Christ's commands in their communities.

5.   Those who see their vocation as merely a way to earn a living will miss an opportunity to love, serve, and lead people to Christ. Thus, I coach disciples of Christ to see their vocation as a ministry.

6.   Emphasizing a tithe of 10 percent may actually lock people's minds into only giving 10 percent. Rather, I challenge disciples to live a lifestyle of sharing and giving of resources, possessions, skills, time, experience, and knowledge.

The gospel flows through the establishing of significant relationships that are authentic and healthy, disciples making disciples. When we rely on professionally staffed churches, pastoral programming, and Sunday services, we end up with institutions. Erwin Raphael McManus expounds on this concept:

> The gospel flows best through the establishing of significant relationships that are authentic and healthy. When relationships become stagnant and the community of Christ closes itself to the outside world, the result is an institution rather than a movement.[13]

The book of Acts speaks of the unfolding of a movement—not an institution—and authentic relationships were a part of that movement. Peter was a disciple-maker of Cornelius; Paul and Silas were disciple-makers of the jailer and his family; Lydia was a disciple-maker of her family and friends; Aquila and Pricilla were disciple-makers of Apollos; and the list goes on (see Acts 10, 16, 18). Each relational opportunity for evangelism and disciple-making occurred in a natural setting and continued in the home, creating a movement for Christ—a fluid movement that could take shape in homes, in jails, and along riverbanks, not bound by the walls of institutions.

What can you do to make disciple-makers?

EXPERIENCE ACTS 2:42 IN A COMMUNAL SETTING

Acts 2:42 says, "They devoted themselves to the apostles' teaching and to the fellowship, to the breaking of bread and to prayer." Instead of relying totally on the method of one or two leaders conducting a church service, consider meeting together in an atmosphere in which everyone participates. According to the pattern of the disciples in Acts 2:42, seize the opportunity to do the following:

- Have a meal which everyone helps prepare. Before or while eating the meal, have communion/break bread together. You may be surprised at how rich the communion experience is when it is wrapped in true fellowship and an authentic meal versus instant communion tagged on to a Sunday service.
- Allow for a time of fellowship in which people share about their faith experiences and application of God's Word from the previous week.
- Teach one another God's Word. Use a method that allows for participation—seeing, hearing, and saying. Allow the participants to consider ways to apply what they have learned.
- Pray together and for one another.

Why do I suggest such practices for multiplication? Again, at the core of multiplication is disciples making disciples. A communal setting is conducive for making active disciples and is much more reproducible than Sunday church.

How can you encourage a group of believers to intentionally interact with one another to cause mutual growth under the lordship of Jesus Christ in a communal way?

EXPERIENCE INTERACTIVE BIBLE STUDIES

A Chinese proverb says, "Tell me and I'll forget; show me and I may remember; involve me and I'll understand." Sermons transfer information but do little to transform people into disciples and disciple-makers of Jesus Christ. Jesus taught his disciples through ongoing dialogue, integrated with showing and involving them in his work. Lectures that involved passivity of the people were few and far between in Jesus's ministry.

David Watson, who has been involved in CPMs and has taught globally on them over the last fifteen years, states that interactive Bible studies have been a key to generations of healthy churches. I love his simple but powerful account of a seventy-year-old man who practices an interactive Bible method to plant churches:

> "Brother, I need to learn from you. Teach me about church planting." He looked puzzled and replied, "It's not hard. Every morning my great niece reads from the Bible for one hour—I can't read so she reads to me. Then I think about what she read until lunch. I think about what it means and what God wants our family to do. When everyone comes for lunch, I tell them what God said through his Word to our family. Then I tell them to tell everyone they know what God said to our family that day. And they do. That's all."[14]

It seems so simple, but we have a propensity for complicating things. This seventy-year-old man has much to teach us. Did you notice that planned services and programs did not bind his method? Rather, his family's experience of the Word of God was wrapped in their natural setting and everyday lives.

Interactive Bible studies are a reproducible way to multiply obedient disciples. Below are a few samples for your consideration:

METHOD 1: David Watson's Obedience-Based Discipleship through a Discovery Bible Study[15]

Read, obey, and share are the core steps within the discovery process. To lead such a study, you unfold the process with four key phrases: Scripture, My Words, Discovery Study, and I Will.

1. SCRIPTURE:
Select a Scripture passage and then invite some of the participants to read it out loud.

2. MY WORDS:
Invite the participants to retell in their own words what they have read to reveal understanding and to practice sharing God's Word from their own mouths.

3. DISCOVERY STUDY:
After participants share the Scripture passage in their own words, study the passage through questions. David Watson and his team give some example questions:

- Did anything in this passage capture your attention?
- What did you like about this passage?
- Did anything bother you? Why?
- What does this passage tell us about God?
- What does this passage tell us about man?
- What does this passage tell us about living to please God?

4. I WILL:
The participants discover how to obey the Scripture passage and commit to share what they have learned with others. The participants create "I Will" statements. "In light of this Scripture passage, I will…"

METHOD 2: Dialogue
Many cultures are oral and community-event oriented. Among such groups, concrete questions that are relevant to everyday life are more effective than questions that are abstract and deductive in nature. I created a method of dialogue to accompany chronological Bible storying (CBS) for usage in Cambodia. You can find more details on this type of dialogue and CBS in a book that I wrote, *World Strategic Church Planting Among Oral Cultures*.[16] The method is based on four cues: characters, event, emotion, and application.

After a Bible story is told, the church planters/storytellers guide the dialogue in the following manner:

1) Invite the participants to identify the characters in the story. (Who are the characters in this story?)
2) Invite the participants to retell the events. (What happened in this story?)
3) Invite the participants to share their emotions as they relate to the story and/or characters. (How do you feel about the story or certain characters?)
4) Invite the participants to share how they want to act/behave based on the story. (How do you want to apply what you learned in this story to your everyday life?)

METHOD 3: Tony and Felicity Dale's Three-Symbol Pattern[17]

Church planters Tony and Felicity Dale advocate a pattern based on three symbols: a question mark, a lightbulb, and an arrow. In this pattern, the group reads out loud a portion of Scripture. After the reading, participants look for things that correspond to the following symbols:

The *question mark* represents anything that a person does not understand and wants clarification about. A person may say, "I have a question mark about these verses. What does it mean when...?"

The *lightbulb* signifies a portion of Scripture in which a person feels like a light has gone on. In other words, this symbol represents any portion of Scripture that illuminates understanding, inspires, or relates to one's own experiences. A participant may say, "I have a lightbulb on this Scripture. Yesterday, I experienced something similar with my son..."

The *arrow* represents God piercing one's heart to take action based on what the participants have read together. One might say, "Based on this Scripture, I plan to visit my father and ..."

Note: the Dales are church planters within North America. I suggest that if you use this pattern, you discover and use symbols relevant to the respective culture where you are working.

All of these interactive Bible studies follow a pattern. Some people may deduct that such patterns are redundant and static. But remember that we want people to repeat the process we teach in other settings for multiplication purposes. The simplicity and repetition of these patterns build others' capabilities to reproduce. The pattern may be static, but as long as there are people and the Holy Spirit, the process will always be dynamic and creative.

What can you do to encourage understanding and application through interactive Bible studies versus mere passive listening?

ENCOURAGE CONVERSATIONAL PRAYER OPPORTUNITIES

When we pray long and lofty prayers, we create a feeling among others that they will never be able to pray in such a manner. If we rely on strictly sermon-type prayers, others will withhold and simply wait for the same few people to pray.

In Cambodia, we practiced a conversation-type prayer. For example, if we had just finished a Bible story on creation, each person would pray one or two sentences thanking God for something they appreciated in his creation. This style of conversational prayer removes the intimidation of other prayer styles, which allows all participants to express themselves to God and multiplies disciples who pray.

What can you do to encourage every believer to have a prayer life?

PRACTICE "ONE ANOTHER" COMMANDS AND "EACH ONE" PARTICIPATION

The Bible is full of "one another" commands, and the practicing of them is a vital part of living out our faith as disciples—although they are often neglected in large church settings. To truly make disciples who practice these "one another" commands, we need to practice them in a group intimate enough to truly interact. If the lowest common denominator to multiplication is the disciple-maker, we need to do all in our power to create an atmosphere that empowers disciples to proactively live out their faith.

A variety of these "one another" commands can be found on various websites. Below I will share a particular list provided by mentorandmultiply.homestead.com:

Building loving fellowship one with another:

- Love: Love one another: John 13:34–35; 5:12, 17; Rom. 12: 10; 1 Thess. 4:9; 1 John 3:11, 14, 23; 4:7, 11, 12; 2 John 1:5; 1 Peter 1:22. Love one another to fulfill the law: Rom. 13:8. Increase our love one for another: 2 Thess. 1:3. Abound in love for another: 1 Thess. 3:12. Love each other deeply, to cover a multitude of sins: 1 Peter 4:8.
- Interact with care: Have fellowship one with another: 1 John 1:7. Forgive one another: Eph. 3:13; 4:32; Col. 3:13. Greet one another

with a holy kiss (an embrace in some cultures): Rom. 16:16; 1 Cor. 16:20; 2 Cor. 13:12; 1 Peter 5:14. Wait for one another to break bread: 1 Cor. 11:33. Bear one another's sufferings: 1 Cor. 12:26.

Serving one another:

- Serve: Serve one another with the gifts each person has received: 1 Peter 4:10. Serve one another in love: Gal. 5:13. Be kind to each other: 1 Thess. 5:15. Care for one another: 1 Cor. 12:25. Bear the burdens one for another: Gal. 6:2. Wash one another's feet as a sign of humbly serving: John 13:14. Work with one another: 1 Cor. 3:9; 2 Cor. 6:1.
- Teach: Teach one another: Col. 3:16. Instruct one another: Rom. 5:14.
- Encourage: Encourage one another: Col. 3:16; Heb. 10:25. Exhort one another: Heb. 3:13, Speak the truth to one another: Eph. 4:25. Lay down our lives one for another: 1 John 3:16. Spur one another to love and good deeds: Heb. 10:24.
- Edify: Edify (strengthen, build up) one another: 1 Thess. 4:18 & 5:1, 11. Edify one another gathering together each one with a hymn, a word of instruction, a revelation, a tongue or its interpretation: 1 Cor. 14:26.
- Give spiritual care: Confess our sins one to another: James 5:16. Pray for one another: James 5:16.

Cultivating unity one with another:

- Act with humility: Honor one another: Rom. 12:10. Be of one mind one with another: 2 Cor. 13:11; Rom. 12:16; 15:5. Do not criticize one another: Rom. 14:13. Do not speak bad one of another: James 4:11; 5:9. Submit to one another: Eph. 5:21. Be clothed with humility toward one another: 1 Peter 5:5.
- Live in harmony: Have patience one with another: Eph. 4:2. Live in peace one with another: Matt. 9:50. Receive one another with hospitality: Rom. 15:7; 1 Peter. 4:9. Glorify God together: Rom. 15:6.[18]

Another important component of discipleship is facilitating opportunities for each one to participate in strengthening the church. According to 1 Corinthians 14:26, Paul reveals that when coming together, "each one" contributes through a hymn, word of instruction, a revelation, a tongue, or an interpretation. In 1 Peter 4:10, Peter invites "each one" to use whatever gift he or she has received to serve others.

Again, to do this successfully means that the setting needs to be intimate and feasible enough for "each one" to contribute. The professionalism of institutional church, combined with a typical congregation size, often minimizes the practice of "one another" commands and "each one" participation. This negligence tends to produce acquaintanceship versus community and passive believers versus active disciples.

If disciples actually practiced the Bible's many "one another" commands, mutually building up others, people would ultimately become the church rather than merely going to church.

May God teach us how to multiply our communities by making disciples who live out the "one another" commands and give "each one" opportunity to participate with intentionality. A Chinese proverb says, "Make happy those who are near, and those who are far will come." A key to multiplication is a faith that works.

What can you do to encourage the "one another" commands and create the opportunity for "each one" participation?

ENCOURAGE VISIBLE TRANSFORMATION

Whenever we had an interactive Bible study in Cambodia, the lesson always ended with a mandate of action. In other words, we never ended with theory, but with a plan of action to obey Christ in society.

Pastor Mark Batterson shares how Christianity was never meant to be a noun:

When Christianity turns into a noun, it becomes a turnoff. Christianity was always intended to be a verb. And, more specifically, an action verb. The title of the book of Acts says it all, doesn't it? It's not the book of Ideas or Theories or Words. It's the book of Acts. If the twenty-first-century church said less and did more, maybe we would have the same kind of impact the first-century church did.[19]

If those from afar see us living out our faith—which equals visible transformation—they will join us. Church buildings and polished programs do not impress the onlooking world. They are looking for the active presence and transformational work of God.

Neil Cole, executive director of Church Multiplication Associates, shares the type of questions that "transformation seekers" ask:

> A better question is "Where is Jesus seen in our midst?" Where do we see lives changing, and communities transforming simply by the power of the gospel? Where do we see fathers restored to a life of holiness and responsibility? Where do we see daughters reconciling with fathers? Where do we see addicts who no longer live under bondage of chemical dependency? Where are wealthy businessmen making restitution for past crimes that went unnoticed? These are the questions that lead people to recognize the living presence of Jesus, loving and governing people's lives as King.[20]

Superficial conversions stimulated by hopes for betterment (services, jobs, and money) through connections with missionaries do not produce transformational lives. In such cases, the apparent believer aligns himself or herself to the Christian scene to better his or her physical and social life. He or she often speaks Christian lingo and participates in church, but does not "do life" with Christ on a day-to-day basis. The unbelieving community observes this dichotomy and develops distaste for both Christians and Christianity. In his book Church Planting Movements, David Garrison states that "unsavory salt" is one of the destructive elements hampering many church planting movements.[21]

I believe that superficial conversions have a lot to do with the fact that missionaries have removed the cost of following Christ and have made it about bettering one's temporary life. Garrison also discovered that a high cost for following Christ actually fueled church planting movements.[22] Disciples who live genuinely transformed lives in the community through thick and thin, among believers and nonbelievers, are vital to a movement for Christ.

What can you do to make sure transformation is a part of your multiplication?

IMPLEMENT THE TWENTY-ONE CRITICAL ELEMENTS OF CHURCH PLANTING MOVEMENTS (CPMs)

Church planting practitioner David Watson has created a list of twenty-one critical elements of CPMs. Watson learned these critical elements through many trials and tribulations. After eighteen months of hard work among the Bhojpuri in India, six people trained by Watson were martyred, and the government expelled Watson and his family from the country.

As you can guess, Watson pleaded with God to show him another way to plant churches. Through Scripture, Watson gained a new understanding about church planting. He started by training five men in the strategies that God had revealed to him. By the fifth year, these men saw one thousand legitimate churches planted within a year! In over fifteen years, over forty thousand churches were established. Some of these churches are tenth-generation church plants, and these churches are as mature as the first generation. His account can be found in "A Movement of God Among the Bhojpuri of North India" in the book Perspectives.

Since then, David Watson has made his experience available to others through training, equipping, and consulting. Below, I offer the "21 Critical Elements of CPMs" as presented by David Watson:

1   *Persistent Prayer:*

- Prayer is the starting point for all ministries.
- Know the mind of God and join Him in His work.

2   *Scripture:*

- Scripture is foundational and the source of all teaching.
- Scripture-Principle-Practice.

3   *Disciples:*

- Make Disciples, not converts.
- Converts focus on religion. Disciples focus on Jesus.

4   *Teach Obedience:*

- Teach Obedience to the Word, not doctrine.
- Doctrine is our church's teaching from the Bible. It may be highly interpretive, and may not consider the full counsel of the Bible.

5   *Communities of Believers (church):*

- Form new believers into minimum Biblical practice groups that will become Communities of Believers (churches) who transform families and communities.

6   *Authority & Holy Spirit*

- Authority of Scripture and the Holy Spirit are all that is needed to start. Church Planting is an act of God through His Spirit and His people who are obedient to the Word and the Spirit.

7 *Persecution:*

- Persecution is part of being a Christian. In pioneer work it is expected and response is trained.

8 *Spiritual Warfare:*

- In areas where the Gospel has never been preached, or in areas where traditional religions have reigned for a significant amount of time, it is not unusual to find those engaging in CPM activities confronted by Spiritual Conflicts that range from annoying to life-threatening.
- Living in obedience is the best preparation for spiritual warfare.
- One does not have to seek out spiritual warfare when planting churches. It will find the one doing the church planting.

9 *Groups:*

- Groups/communities learn more quickly, remember more things and better, replicate more quickly and often when correctly led, protect against heresy, and protect against bad leadership.

10 *Plan/Be Intentional:*

- Plan your work and work your plan.
- Be intentional in Access Ministry, Prayer, Scripture, Appropriate Evangelism and Church Planting.

11 *Access Ministries:*

- Access Ministries open the door for Church Planting and lead to community transformation.
- Ministry should precede evangelism and evangelism must always be the end result of ministry. Timing is important and necessary.

12 *Man of Peace:*

- Start with the Person of Peace or an existing relationship that will permit a Discovery Bible Study or Witness.

13 *Evangelize Households/families:*

- Focus on households/ families, not individuals.
- Households include non-related people living together as family.

14 Appropriate Evangelism:

- Evangelism is an intentional calling to a family to study the Word of God in order to move from not knowing God to falling in Love with Him through Jesus. The primary method used is the Discovery Bible Study in relationship with maturing believers. This makes disciples, not converts.

15 Reproducing:

- Reproducing disciples, leaders, groups and churches becomes a part of the group DNA.

16 Reaching Out (Missions):

- Reaching out to "ALL" segments of society becomes a part of the group DNA as a result of obedience to the Great Commission (missions).

17 Redeem Local Culture (Embrace the Local Culture):

- Do not import external culture, but redeem local culture by embracing all you Biblically can in a culture and transforming/redeeming the rest.

18 Inside Leaders:

- Keep all things reproducible by inside leaders and directed/led by inside leaders.

19 Outside Leaders:

- Model, equip, watch, and leave. Outside leaders introduce new concepts that are contextualized by inside leaders.
- Outside leaders deculturalize, inside leaders contextualize.

20 Self-supporting:

- Self-supporting, local leaders start and sustain all work — including groups, fellowships, and churches.
- Self-supporting may mean the worker has a job or business. This improves access and breaks down the barriers between clergy and laity.

21 *Education/Teaching—Training/Coaching—Equipping/Mentoring:*

- Discipleship and leadership education and training are "on the job," continuous and primarily through mentoring. This builds communities that hold each other accountable for obedience to the Word of God.
- Education increases knowledge through teaching. Training increases skill sets primarily through coaching. Equipping increases capacity through mentoring relationships.[23]

For further understanding of these twenty-one elements, you may want to participate in the seminars that David Watson offers. Learn more at www.cpmtr.org.

I have come to believe that the more we intentionally implement these critical elements of church planting movements, the greater the potential is for a genuine church planting movement to arise. The more we compromise, on the other hand, the greater the potential for elephant churches.

What can you do to implement these twenty-one critical elements for the sake of multiplication?

I hope that the suggested action steps for multiplication will give you some ideas and help to stimulate your own creative ideas. My prayer for those of us who "do missions" is this:

Dear God,

I recall when the man in his right mind—from whom you cast out a legion of demons—asked to join you and your disciples.

You gave a "multiplication" response: "No, return home and tell others about my mercy." Grant us the wisdom to know how to multiply your kingdom upon this earth.

May the story of your mercy transform people in every nook and cranny of this vast world.

CHAPTER TWELVE

STRATEGIC BEGINNINGS IN ACTION

"Day 1 affects Day 100."

JEAN JOHNSON

Beginnings can rarely be undone—or should I say, the effects of beginnings can rarely be undone. The beginning is when we lay the foundation, yet it's also where we're most tempted to act unwisely. How often are we tempted to take shortcuts to get to the good stuff? How often do we begin ministry in another country from our instincts and find ourselves in a tough spot halfway through because we didn't take time to get past instinct to intention? The purpose of this chapter is to provide some principles for implementing strategic beginnings for the sake of multiplying disciples in communities throughout the world.

RECOGNIZE WHERE THE BEGINNING BEGINS

Have you ever tried to untangle a rope? You were likely talking to yourself as you thought through the untangling process, saying, "Where does this thing begin?" Recognizing the beginning of a tangled rope is a key step in untangling it.

Recently, I read a Q&A about church planting. Within it, the following question was posed: "Is it possible for every new church to be self-supporting, self-governing, and self-propagating from the beginning?" The responder revealed that there is no example of a New Testament church that did not operate this way. No New Testament church was dependent on others for support, governance, or propagation.

Another question that became a part of the dialogue was "*When* is the beginning?"

"The beginning is at that point in which the group decides to become a church" was one of the responses—but from my perspective, that time frame is too late. Rather, I challenge us to consider that church planters need to be strategic from the very first intentional act toward planting the church and/or movement.

A church does not pick up the "selves" of the three-self principle on one special day or time; rather, a church grows into these practices from its conception. We would all agree that a great deal happens before a group declares itself a church. If we are not adamant about cultivating the three-self principles from our first action, "later" may be too late.

Some would even say that the beginning begins before missionaries even leave their own countries. I agree. Mentalities start at home; thus, home is a good place for missionaries to premeditate multiplication, indigeneity, and sustainability. In some ways, that is why I have written this book: to provide a tool to begin shaping our ability to cultivate indigenous movements for Christ before we begin life and ministry in someone else's country.

The minute we walk off the plane, our decisions and actions will contribute toward a movement for Christ or detract from it. The number of bags we carry, the size of our shipment, and our dealings with service people upon our arrival—all these things speak before we do.

Levy Moyo, who was born in Zimbabwe, wrote a book entitled *The Gloved Handshake*. In it, he shares about a missionary couple who estranged their Zimbabwean hosts through their very first actions—from Day 1. An entourage from the Zimbabwean church met the missionary couple at the airport with a mini-celebration. The host pastor proceeded to tell the missionary couple that they had arranged transportation for them and a temporary place to stay. The missionary couple declined the offer and informed the host pastor that their sending organization had already arranged for those details.

Turning down the host church's well-thought-out and sacrificial plan started the relationship off in the wrong direction. From the first few minutes of arrival, the missionary couple sent the message that they were somehow superior and didn't need to be dependent on the locals. This first paternalistic action began a long-term relationship of control and disappointment—control on the missionaries' part and disappointment on the locals' part.

Day 1 truly affects Day 100. The beginning starts the minute you take your first step and breathe your first breath in a host country, and every subsequent word and action becomes a powerful source for or against the spiritual DNA of movements for Christ.

What can you do to strategically cultivate an indigenous movement for Christ from the beginning?

START AND FINISH WITH AN INCARNATIONAL LIFESTYLE

Two major activities of missionaries who arrive fresh on a foreign field are to find housing and learn the language. Setting up living quarters and learning the language are Day 1 activities.

I wish I could tell you that the missionary couple to Zimbabwe realized their mistake and quickly made amends. It almost looked that way: just before departing from the airport to their mission-arranged accommodations, the missionary husband asked the host pastor to find them a house. He specifically asked for one that would be accessible to those with whom he and his wife would be interacting on a daily basis. The pastor and members of the church earnestly looked for a house in accordance with the missionary's request. Eventually, the host pastor called the missionary couple with the good news: "We found you a house!" The missionary replied, "Oh, I am sorry. We found a house already based on our missionary cohorts' advice." The missionary couple not only shunned the efforts of the host church, they broke their own criteria as well—they rented a house in a well-to-do neighborhood which was not easily accessible to the church members among whom they had come to serve. The gap between the missionaries and the locals grew wider and wider.

The Western missionary journey often goes like this: A new missionary family arrives on the mission field. They immediately visit and assess how and where the other missionaries live. Within weeks, they set up their household with some degree of resemblance to their lifestyle in their home country. In the beginning, they use the other missionaries as their point of reference instead of ascertaining what lifestyle or location would best contribute to the DNA of a church planting movement.

Compared to their Western lifestyle, these missionaries have made significant sacrifices, but compared to their host culture, they are still affluent. There is an immediate and obvious difference in status between the missionaries and the local people. This economic gap may seem like a blessing—our economic advantage will be an advantage to them, won't it?—but the disparity erodes cross-cultural interpersonal relationships in a big, big way.

In actuality, this is not solely a Western missionary's problem. Various countries and regions send out missionaries or church planters who are more affluent than the people among whom they live and minister. Merely sending someone from an urban area to a village area presents a potential lifestyle gap between the sent ones and the hosts. The bottom line is that missionaries and church planters need to seriously consider gaps of disparity as they formulate their strategies.

I am a North American missionary, and I have struggled with the tension of desiring to create a comfortable and efficient atmosphere for myself while also desiring to live a truly incarnational lifestyle. We all have our rationales for why we allow—to whatever degree—a lifestyle gap: for the sake of longevity, health, the well-being of the family, the social and educational development of our children, efficiency, influence, and capability to provide goods and services to others, among others. Yet I believe in my heart that the cost of economic inequity between Western missionaries and host cultures needs to be counted. Jonathan Bonk, in his book *Missions and Money*, reveals that Western missionary affluence and social advantages have relational, communicatory, and strategic consequences. Bonk makes two haunting statements:

> In exchange for the comforts and securities of personal affluence, missionaries sacrifice apostolic effectiveness and credibility . . .
>
> Since biblical faith is above all a relational faith, it is not only sad, but tragically wide of the mark (sinful), when personal possessions and privileges prevent, distort, or destroy missionary relationships with the poor. But this is an almost inevitable price of personal affluence.[1]

The messenger is equally as important as the message. Our presence among a people needs to be good news not because of a pocket full of money, but because we practice our faith in a realm that makes sense to the people we have come to serve.

For the majority of missionaries who come from the West, heat, noise, and lack of privacy become an instant personal battle. I remember, as a resident of cold, snowy Minnesota, when I walked off the plane my first time in Cambodia. I felt like the sun was at eye level with me, breathing right into my face. I found myself instantly surrounded by the inescapable noise of shouting and horns and haggling. The very word "inescapable" denotes the reality that a Minnesotan is accustomed to being able to escape heat and noise at will.

Ravi Zacharias, in his book *Walking From East to West*, talks about his boyhood in India. One of his boyhood memories was of the ceiling fans that swirled about in his home. The fans were no match for the aggressive heat. To assist the fans, his family would spray their thatched-straw drapes with water. No matter what clever tricks the family executed, it was sweltering hot. Ravi's family mostly learned to live with the hot weather conditions; it was a part of life in India. Furthermore, Ravi tells how his neighborhood was filled with unrelenting noise. In his own words, he says, "Silence was at a premium," and "There was no privacy to speak of."[2]

> Every morning at sunrise, any seeming quietness was broken by the shouts of the street vendors, hawking the items they were selling. "Onions! Milk! Vegetables! Knife sharpeners!" When these sellers came to our door, they would look through our open but barred windows ... We stepped outside on to the street, and the road itself was so narrow that a car couldn't pass through but only hand-pulled or cycle rickshaws. Outside were stray animals and people, each about some pursuit. Sometimes it was a beggar at the door, sometimes a leprous hand reaching for a handout with a plea of compassion. Life with all its hurts and pains squinted at you, squatted before you, and stared you down daily. This was the street where I grew up.[3]

Now, contrast Ravi's portrayal of his everyday life in India with Jonathan Bonk's description of the Western missionary's life in most cross-cultural settings:

> That insularity to which the privileged assume entitlement manifests itself in virtually every facet of a Western missionary's life. Comfortable, well-furnished residences; closets with several changes of clothing; cupboards stocked with a great variety of nutritious foods; medicine cabinets brimming with efficacious prophylactics and drugs; medical plans to deal with a child's crooked teeth or a parent's failing kidney; insurance policies providing for the well-being of loved ones in the event of an untimely emergency; retirement savings plans which, by taking careful thought of the morrow, are calculated to assist the aged missionary through the final transitions between this life and the next; the costly mobility—by means of personal motor vehicles—to which every Westerner feels entitled; resources sufficient for expensive local and international flights to whisk one's own away from danger or to take oneself on a much-needed furlough; for children, educational opportunities unmatched anywhere in the world; fun-filled, exotic vacations for the family; an abundance of ingenious technological aids, each promising and sometimes delivering efficiency in fulfilling personal and professional objectives; such derivatives of personal affluence constitute the "nonconducting material" of which missionary insulation from the "heat" and "sound" of poverty is fashioned.[4]

According to Bonk, Western missionaries tend to deal with extreme climate and noisy surroundings by resorting to insulation and isolation. Both of these actions create definite barriers between the missionaries and their hosts, no matter how much we want to believe they don't have any negative consequences.

Beyond shielding ourselves from the wear and tear of poverty, North Americans have a drive for privacy that is deeply rooted in our psyche. Jonathan Bonk quotes Philip Slatter on this issue:

> We seek a private house, a private means of transportation, a private garden, a private laundry, self-service stores, and do-it yourself skills of every kind. An enormous technology seems to have set itself the task of making it unnecessary for one human being ever to ask anything of another in the course of going about his daily business. Even within the family Americans are unique in their feeling that each one should have a separate room, and even a separate telephone, television, and car, when economically possible.[5]

It is really, really hard for those of us who grew up with this worldview of insulation and isolation to change. The more our privacy and comfort are compromised, the more we feel disconcerted. However, the more we try to maintain our privacy and comfort on the mission field, the more the local people in most places will feel disconcerted. John Walker, who wrote a contemporary view of Bonhoeffer's writings, *The Cost of Discipleship*, asks the following questions:

> Can you imagine the apostle Paul deciding where to go next based on the cost of living in a particular town? Why should we be any different? We serve the same Lord; we're infused with the same Holy Spirit? Are the standards of discipleship different now than they were in the first century A.D.? Are we called to a lesser (second-tiered) discipleship? Do we serve a lesser God?[6]

Jesus's lifestyle is worthy of emulation. Jesus was constantly moving into his receptor's frame of reference. Living on the move did not give Jesus opportunity to set up a stationery life that created an economic and social gap between him and his receptors. From the beginning, Jesus started his new life in a cross-cultural setting (heaven to earth) in a stable. He ensured there was no interpersonal communication gap based on status or affluence. The disciples and Paul clearly understood Jesus's statement: "Foxes have holes and birds of the air have nests, but the Son of Man has no place to lay his head" (Matthew 8:20).

How can you be intentional about an incarnational lifestyle?

PUT THE BRAKES ON A PERFORMANCE-DRIVEN MENTALITY

This book is a reflection of what I did differently after several years in Cambodia, what I do differently now, and what I strive to do differently with each new opportunity. What drove me to do missions in a way that I now deem counterproductive? For me, it was operating out of a performance-driven mentality that served as a deterrent to Day-1 planting of a truly indigenous church with evidence of self-image, self-functioning, self-determining, self-supporting, self-propagating, and self-giving. Within me, I had a sense that I had to produce results in an efficient manner. We tend to declare a ministry successful by that which we can see and count: immediate tangibles such as buildings, conversions, and members. My pressure for success was self-imposed, influenced by my North American culture and stressed by my church culture experience—and it led to several wrong approaches.

What happens when we function from a performance-driven mindset in a cross-cultural setting? We do things in the beginning to rush results; and when we rush results, it is almost certain that we will lay a foundation that undermines indigeneity, multiplication, and sustainability.

Shortcuts to the finish line mean negligence of the rules of the race: 1) be a learner of worldview, 2) contextualize, 3) maintain a low profile, 4) multiply, 5) be receptor-oriented, and 6) mobilize local resources. A missionary who spends his first term as a learner will ultimately produce more than the missionary who immediately throws himself into his work. The missionary who *learns* first will approach ministry as an insider. The missionary who *works* first will approach ministry as an outsider. A ministry that has an "insider feel"—that is indigenous—will multiply.

There is a saying that goes, "A wise old owl sat on an oak; the more he saw the less he spoke; the less he spoke the more he heard; why aren't we like that wise old bird?" Because I started my missions career unlike the wise old owl, I eventually had to backtrack in order to take the owl's advice: spend ample time seeing and hearing while speaking less.

My prayer for all of us who apply ourselves to the task of planting churches cross-culturally is that we will be expert builders. In the forefront of our minds, we always want to build the foundation on Jesus Christ (1 Corinthians 3:10–15).

206 · JEAN JOHNSON

I have to wonder how often we slip gold, silver, stones, wood, hay, and straw into the foundation. Paul was an expert builder by the grace God gave him; we need that same grace. I become quite sober when I think of "the Day" when God will test the quality of my work by fire. Sometimes the very thought makes me want to bury my talents and stay safe, but Jesus revealed to us that reserved thinking is not God-thinking according to the Parable of the Talents in Matthew 25:14–30.

How can you guard against the pitfalls of a performance-driven mentality?

I have in no way reached perfection in any of these practices! Like Paul, I press on to do better, striving to leave mediocrity behind. Together, we can make a supreme effort to strategize on Day 1 for the sake of multiplication on Day 100. My prayer for those of us who "do missions" is:

Dear God,
   Your beginning was humble and strategic.
   The Son of God became the Son of Man,
   A human being for the sake of human beings.
   You always had the future in mind as you lived in the present.
   Empower us to begin with wisdom and intent.

CHAPTER THIRTEEN

REPRODUCIBILITY IN ACTION

"Every Christian could sit in a church meeting thinking, 'I could do this.'"

TIM CHESTER

If every cross-cultural worker merely aimed for reproducibility, we would be well on our way to cultivating indigenous movements for Christ. Throughout this chapter, we will discover how to put reproducibility into practice.

MODEL THAT WHICH LOCAL PEOPLE CAN EASILY REPLICATE AND PASS ON

Picture this scenario: After six months of learning the language, Josiah, a missionary from North America, decides it is time to launch a church plant. Josiah takes a walk in the community to think through his strategy. He considers intently the question, "What do I have to offer these people so I can build relationships with them?" As Josiah looks up, he sees several colorful signs posted on a fence that read, "English classes." His heart beats faster, and he says under his breath, "This is it! I will start an English training center and include teaching the Bible in English."

Within hours, Josiah enthusiastically connects with his supporting churches in North America to request that they send as many English books as possible. Josiah and his wife, Theresa, find the perfect location to rent a building for the English training center—right next to a popular restaurant for expats. "Perhaps the students can practice their English with expats at the restaurant," says Theresa. Josiah's wife, who is quite artistic, paints the walls with English idioms to create a fun atmosphere for learning. Josiah busies himself with attaching whiteboards and preparing shelves for the books to add to the learning environment. With each improvement, Josiah and Theresa are filled with anticipation.

Upon the first day of English classes, twelve young people arrive, anxious to learn English from Americans free of charge. During the evening—as Josiah and Theresa unwind from a long day—Josiah says, "They even stayed to learn English from the Bible. I think our idea is working."

Picture another scenario: After twelve months of learning the language, Trevor, a missionary from North America, decides to launch a church plant. Trevor strolls through the community to consider his potential strategy. He smiles as he sees a noodle shop full of people chatting about their day. As he walks, Trevor kicks a small rock forward as if playing soccer. Trevor hears a commotion and quickly lifts his head to see what is happening. A group of people are standing in a semicircle around a man. The man has some props and seems to be telling a story. Trevor moves in closer to see the action. Sure enough, the man is story-telling, mingled with singing and dramatic gestures. Trevor's heart beats faster, and he says under his breath, "This is it! I will storytell the gospel."

Trevor immediately applies himself to learning as many local stories as possible. He keeps a journal of the styles, gestures, wording, and so forth utilized by the local storytellers. In addition to learning local storytelling techniques, Trevor practices telling Bible stories and implementing what he has learned from the local storytellers. He begins collecting props from everyday life to include in his storytelling. Although he cannot carry a tune, Trevor practices singing from his throat, unlike the way he was taught in his home country. Eventually, Trevor sets out with a bag full of props, storytelling enthusiasm, and a sore throat from overextending his voice. Young and old gather, listen, laugh, cry, and invite Trevor back.

Which scenario is easier for the locals to replicate? There are five elements within the first scenario that makes reproducibility impossible, which I call "the Five Es": Extraction, Expertise, Expensive, Extraneous (coming from outside the culture), and Exclusive (creating an "us and them" dichotomy). Josiah and Theresa created a ministry atmosphere that was comfortable for them and invited (extracted) people into their cultural frame of reference. This missionary couple relied on their expert skills in English to conduct their evangelism ministry. They spent a significant amount of money and solicited funds from abroad to implement their expensive practices. The setting and activities were centered on the English language and North American culture. (In fact, using English as a medium to introduce people to God may have compounded the local belief that Jesus is the god of the foreigners.) Lastly, their free English classes drew people from existing English classes through which locals were trying to earn a living, exacerbating the "us-and-them" dichotomy. (By the way, the Merriam-Webster's online dictionary defines the word "exclusive" as "snobbishly aloof.")

When the locals who have come to know Christ through the English training center are ready to launch a church plant, they will reflect on what was modeled to them. Questions will begin to bombard their minds: "How will we obtain funds to develop an English center? Who knows enough English to serve as teachers? Will people be drawn to us like they are to the missionaries?" After reflecting on such questions, the local church planters will most likely resolve, "We can't do this! We will have to ask Josiah and Theresa to assist us."

When we model ministries that are not easily replicated, we set up those who imitate us for failure and dependency. It is quite possible that Josiah and Theresa may be successful in planting a church while using this nonreproducible and culturally counterproductive strategy, but they will make it extremely difficult for that first church to plant another church.

Now let's consider Trevor's approach. As a storyteller, Trevor went to where the local people congregated. He utilized the common role of a storyteller, which did not require him to offer his expert services. Expenses were not an issue, because Trevor used local resources available to the everyday person. Storytelling was innate and feasible for those in his host culture. Since Trevor allowed for the typical audience response and created an atmosphere of inclusion for whole families, he worked within the social values of the community. The community was seeking God together in their natural circles, rather than creating something artificial and intrusive from the outside. Trevor had the great beginnings of a movement for Christ.

I would hope that Trevor saw it that way. But there is a good chance that he would default to his own worldview: his experience of church in North America. In other words, he might feel a driving sense to gather the various storytelling groups into one group, acquire funds from North America, and build a stationary church. In this case, Trevor's storytelling method, which worked within the framework of the existing community, will morph into reliance on a stationary building that creates an us-and-them scenario. Ultimately, Trevor's provision of a church building will create another scenario that local people cannot replicate with their own local resources.

As missionaries, sometimes we feverishly implement the guidelines of reproducibility in the evangelism stage, only to abandon such principles in other stages. Our tendency is to minister from our instincts, and that includes a sense of expediency and a desire for accomplishment. If we indeed operate with this mindset, we will ignore reproducibility, which is necessary for multiplication. Our challenge, then, is to weigh everything we do in the light of reproducibility for the sake of spontaneous multiplication.

How can you ensure reproducibility as a component to your modeling?

CONSIDER REPRODUCIBILITY AS IT RELATES TO MATERIAL THINGS, STRATEGIES, AND STYLES OF LEADERSHIP

(My thanks to Charles Brock for this threefold challenge, as laid out in *Indigenous Church Planting.*)[1]

When considering reproducibility as it relates to material things, avoid using anything that the people cannot or will not provide for themselves. For example, as believers show interest in worship through song and music, missionaries may be tempted to use or provide instruments and equipment. Be patient. There are musicians in every community, and music is a part of every person. In due time, someone will join in who plays a local instrument. If we rush the process by prematurely providing imported or expensive instruments, we will create an nonreproducible worship ministry. *Consider reproducibility as it relates to material things.*

When I was in Cambodia, "preaching points" were popular. This meant that a trained minister gathered people and preached a polished homiletic speech, using many biblical references and apologetics. Missionaries introduced the term "preaching points" and made it a strategy of church planting. But we need to face the obvious: a preaching-point approach is Western, abstract, and complicated to reproduce. To ensure relevance and reproducibility within a Cambodian context, we conducted "storytelling points" instead. This meant that Christian storytellers—using a skill innate to the culture—gathered people and told or dramatized Bible stories. *Consider reproducibility as it relates to strategies.*

No matter how much missionaries are passionate about Bible schools, Bible schools modeled after Western systems are not readily reproducible in most cultures. Merely create a list of everything and everyone that it takes to operate an institutional Bible school, and you will see the complexity and limitations of this Western-style training strategy! Bible schools will produce ordained leaders, but if we also want to produce organic leaders at an exponential rate, we need to model and legitimize training methods that are reproducible within the cultural context. I personally used a Paul-Timothy style of training which is mobile, on-the-job, uncomplicated, and inexpensive—all characteristics of reproducibility. With this style of leadership training, the leader-in-training actually developed a community of believers as he practiced everything he learned in theory. The leader was a leader because he had followers. *Consider reproducibility as it relates to styles of leadership.*

How can you practice reproducibility as it relates to material things, strategies, and styles of leadership?

REALIZE THAT SIMPLE DOES NOT NEGATE DEPTH OR SIGNIFICANCE

Some people lament that reproducible characteristics such as simplistic, inexpensive, common, and organic promote shallowness and a lack of biblical soundness. From observation, I believe the absolute opposite is true. Relevant, practical, participatory, inclusive, and applicable methods produce passionate and capable disciples, leaders, and churches. Nothing is watered down; Rather, the meaning and content is presented in such a way that others can hear, understand, internalize, apply, and reproduce.

Tony and Felicity Dale wrote a book together with George Barna about multiplying small groups known as "house churches" or "simple churches." In their book they invite us to pay attention to reproducibility.:

> If we hope to see simple churches multiply, then we need to pay attention to what we model. All of the key elements of simple church are as basic as possible. It is not that the content is simplistic or shallow—it is often very profound—but the pattern for doing it is simple and therefore easily replicated.[2]

The pattern is simple for reproducibility's sake, but the content and outcome are valuable, far-reaching, and powerful.

Jesus trained his disciples through repetitive patterns of storytelling, parables, sayings, demonstrations, and participation. He did not produce shallow or wimpy disciples! His disciples had depth, and they impacted the world deeply and widely. Reproducibility serves the purpose of empowering locals to envision and conduct ministry with their God-given resources, local initiative, and natural abilities, without having to constantly extend a begging hand to missionaries.

How will you allow for patterns that are simple to replicate but encourage depth and impact?

USE DIAGNOSTIC QUESTIONS TO ASCERTAIN REPRODUCIBILITY

I have created two questions to assist myself in assessing whether something I am about to do is reproducible. These diagnostic questions help me to exercise self-control and think long term.

1) Will those we train be able to successfully implement the methods in their ministry context with their own resources and capabilities? (Or will they need to constantly come back to us as their source?)

2) How will our method impede reproducibility (too expensive, not relevant, too complicated, etc.) or how will our method enable reproducibly?

Perhaps you too will find these strategic questions useful in keeping you on the railroad track that leads to reproducibility.

How can you evaluate reproducibility?

I am convinced that if we deliberately practice reproducibility principles, we will avoid psychological and financial dependency in local churches, which is a guaranteed hazard to multiplication and indigenous movements for Christ. My prayer for those of us who "do missions" is this:

Dear God,
After your death and resurrection, your disciples made more disciples.
That cycle has not been broken to this very day.
Let us put away our man-made ways, ways that serve as distractions and delays.

CHAPTER FOURTEEN

INDIGENOUS CHURCH GROWTH IN ACTION

"An indigenous church, young or old, in the East or in the West, is a church which, rooted in obedience to Christ, spontaneously uses forms of thought and modes of action natural and familiar in its own environment."

DR. ED STETZER

Indigenous has much to do with organic growth. When growing food, organic farmers deliberately avoid introducing external substances, such as pesticides, synthetic fertilizers, hormones, and additives. The goal is to allow plants to grow within their intended environments, using only natural techniques to sustain health and production. Likewise, an organic church planter purposely avoids imposing external resources. Indigenous church sustainability and growth is much more about not doing than it is about doing. In this chapter, we will focus on how to contribute to the growth of organic indigenous movements for Christ.

ALLOW WORLDVIEW BARRIERS TO GUIDE YOUR INTENTIONALITY TOWARD INDIGENOUS GROWTH

As Christians, we all agree that the Bible and its theological content must serve as the foundation of what we do. But if we ignore the worldview of our host culture, we are essentially pushing a cart with one broken wheel—we will be arbitrarily all over the place and will not effectively reach our destination of planting indigenous churches.

The worldview of host peoples must have a role in guiding our approach if we desire to see a movement for Christ among them. The apostle Paul modeled this approach when he used the worldview of the Athenians to shape his strategy. Paul debated among the best of the philosophers in the Areopagus. He referred to one of the altars among the Athenians' objects of worship to launch his gospel message. Paul flavored his presentation with poetry well-known to the Athenians.

He intentionally spoke to the worldview barrier of the Athenians' religious and philosophical assumption that any god would do (Acts 17:16–34).

There are many definitions to the word *worldview*. Worldview is multilayered and affects everything. Worldview is not simple, but my simplest definition is to merely invert the word to *view world*. Worldview is how a people view the world around them.

J.O. Terry, who has international experience working among oral cultures, shared the following during a recorded dialogue: "If we don't consciously identify and speak to their worldview, by default you will speak to your own."[1]

Identifying and acting upon worldview barriers is one way to guide our content and methods along an indigenous path. A *worldview barrier* is everything and anything within a people group that prevents them from hearing, understanding, and responding to the gospel.

While in Cambodia, I helped facilitate a Cambodian church planting team to identify worldview barriers among the Cambodians of their area. The team recorded the worldview barriers through a picture of a road and boulders along the way—each boulder represented a particular barrier. Whenever the team planned a ministry activity, they would evaluate the activity based on those worldview barriers.

For example, one day the church planting team decided to perform a play for the community. The team members came up with a number of ideas for how to conduct that event. Then they evaluated those ideas according to the worldview barriers. One prominent worldview barrier was: "Jesus is the foreigners' God and religion." Based on that worldview barrier, the church planting team decided to exclude foreigners from high-profile roles, use indigenous music, wear traditional costumes, and create a communal atmosphere common to Cambodians.

Worldview barriers come in all shapes and forms. Ravi Zacharias reminisces about his childhood in India and shares about some of the worldview barriers he encountered:

> That's the way I remember first experiencing religion—as something involving fear: A man rolling down the street, chanting the name of his god. Men and women with deep gashes in their faces. Tales of goats being sacrificed in temples to procure answers to prayers. Each time I asked my mother about these things, she explained, "They do it to worship their god."
>
> Worship? It was an empty word to me, steeped in some mysterious

expression that didn't make ordinary sense. It was a magic wand to ward off tragedy. The one thing I learned from observing such rituals was a palpable sense of fear. Everything has to follow a certain sequence. If you didn't do it right, something bad was going to happen to you. If I didn't make my offering, what would befall me? If I didn't do this one thing correctly, what price would I have to pay to some sharp, implacable divine being? Was all that just superstition born out of fear, dressed up into a system, and embedded into a culture?[2]

Indeed, I saw the same forceful fear "dressed up in a religious system and embedded into a culture" in Cambodia. This should not be underestimated. A "palpable sense of fear" is definitely a worldview barrier. Awareness of the spirit world and behavior that accompanies that awareness makes up the daily experience of most Cambodians. Almost everything a Cambodian does involves an element of pacifying the spirit world: births, weddings, funerals, changing of seasons, travel, field work, commerce, a temple stroll, an unusual feeling, a spat with a neighbor, passing under a tree, and so forth. Who would dare deviate from generations of rituals that are meant to keep them safe and sound? Thus, an obvious worldview barrier is the fear that following Christ means to risk the wrath of spirits and divine beings.

From a Western worldview, we are quick to address and intervene on issues of political repression, human rights violations, human suffering, and poverty. But many people around the world are more concerned about spiritual, physical, and emotional oppression due to spiritual beings. We need to scratch where it itches. With this in mind, those who share the message of faith through Jesus Christ ought to habitually and consciously model how to do life victoriously, conquering fear that is "dressed up into a system." We cannot operate out of what our worldview informs us, but rather out of what our host culture's worldview informs us.

If we ignore or treat the worldview of our host culture lightly, people who have supposedly become followers of Christ will default to beliefs and practices that derive from their worldview, especially in a crisis. A crisis situation reveals what people believe to be real deep down inside of their being. For example: A father of four children regularly attended the Christian church close to the center of the village. When he conversed with other members of the church, he weaved Christian lingo into his conversations, causing his listeners to be in awe of his faith in Jesus. From their perspective, his commitment was confirmed by the fact that he worked for a Christian organization that assisted the poor.

One day, this gentleman's child became very ill. A missionary who had a role in this particular church received news that this man had taken his child to a traditional sorcerer who used incantations and offerings to appease the spirits responsible for making the child sick. The missionary was completely baffled and disappointed. "I don't understand! Why would a Christian take his sick child to the witch doctor?" Yet the North American missionary, who was deeply influenced by a scientific worldview, had rarely addressed the probing questions that derived from the local man's worldview.

Worldview is intricately linked to the questions that people internally ask themselves. How do I avoid sickness and misfortune? Who will faithfully help with my destiny after I die by making adequate offerings? How should I accumulate merit? How do I keep the territorial spirits happy? If our presentation of the gospel and subsequent discipleship process ignores questions driven by the worldview, we will grieve over people who are quick to abandon their faith in Jesus when life counts—daily life lived outside a religious building.

In chapter 17 of this book, I give examples of how Cambodians selected Bible stories and crafted the stories so as to address the worldview of their people. I encourage you to make a list of worldview barriers as you experience life among a particular people. As you make action plans, allow the list of worldview barriers to inform you of dos and don'ts.

Worldview barriers serve like a railroad track, keeping the indigenous train on target. The decisions do not comprise of "he said, she said," but are shaped by the worldview of the respective people. Methods that strategically consider the worldview empower missionaries to keep from defaulting to their own worldview and direct local leaders to keep from being sidetracked by the missionaries' worldview.

How can you use worldview barriers to guide you in cultivating indigenous growth?

VIEW CROSS-CULTURAL MINISTRY WITH "PHASE-OUT EYES"

As I write these words, emergency teams are headed to Haiti to offer relief to earthquake victims. There is no water or food available in Haiti; thus, anyone entering the country has to be able to supply his or her own necessities, and this includes fuel. Do you know what that means for planes entering Haiti? Pilots need to ensure they have enough fuel to return home, or their planes will be stuck at the airport. And this cannot be allowed because other planes, loaded with supplies, are waiting to land and contribute to the relief effort. Any pilot that looks at his entrance to Haiti with only "phase-in eyes" (not "phase-out eyes") is in trouble and will cause trouble.

Like the pilots of emergency flights to Haiti, we need to consider our arrival to a country with phase-out eyes, not merely phase-in eyes. We tend to be in such a hurry to establish our presence and ministry that we give little thought to how our approach will affect our phase-out plan. Phase-out eyes are absolutely necessary if we truly want to ensure an indigenous movement for Christ.

Tom Steffen coined the terms "phase-in eyes" and "phase-out eyes." During Steffen's first term of missionary work in the Philippines, he became alarmed as he identified a gap between verbal goals in pursuit of the indigenous church and that which actually happened on the field. Steffen makes this comment:

> Reluctantly, I had to admit that my mission agency lacked a successful "three-self model" in the Philippines. No church-planting team has successfully phased out of their ministries so that nationals could control their own churches—and this after almost a quarter of a century of sacrificial missionary effort.
>
> Individual team members, possibly because of an overall field strategy, tended to focus more on "phase-in" activities (e.g. evangelism and discipleship) than "phase-out" activities (e.g., activities that would empower nationals to develop leadership among themselves with an eye toward ministry that reproduces) ... Team members tended to view ministry with "phase-in eyes" rather than "phase-out eyes."[3]

Steffen points out that viewing ministry with "phase-in eyes" only, is a main reason why missions organizations fail to plant true indigenous churches. The mere fact that some missionaries in the Philippines were still in control of local churches after almost a quarter of a century reveals that there was something severely amiss. Steffen mentions the lack of leadership development—that aims for reproducibility—as one neglected component due to dull phase-out eyes. And there are many more obstructions to the growth of the indigenous church created by those who view ministry with only phase-in eyes while forgetting phase-out eyes.

A missions term used frequently these days is "creative access". This term is usually used in reference to countries which missionaries cannot easily enter; thus, missions personnel use as much creativity as possible to get in. Some of the ways missionaries creatively access countries are through humanitarian projects, orphanage work, and ESL projects. Although creative access is a worthy strategy in itself, I fear that in many cases, we cause an imbalance by working so hard to create a method of access (phase-in) that we neglect to examine how our means of entrance will affect our intentional phase-out. Lack of a phase-out strategy will negatively affect the development of the indigenous church. Ultimately, creative access has put the emphasis on phase-in eyes while neglecting phase-out eyes (creative exit).

What do many of the creative access projects look like? The missionaries are the dreamers, the founders, and the caretakers of the project, which usually has some degree of imposed foreign structure and mode of operation. The project is started and overseen by missionaries and funded by donations from abroad. Even if the missionaries fill positions with local employees, the missionaries spend ample time raising and disbursing funds, as well as giving some degree of oversight. Ultimately, creative access projects are heavily marked with foreign fingerprints.

Due to the foreign structure, expertise, and outside funding necessary for such projects, local people cannot sustain them. What is most troublesome about a creative-access, mission-established, non-sustainable project? Three issues come to mind: non-transferability, role confusion, and foreign dominance, which are all elements of dependency.

This generic (but typical) example will help us see these three issues play out: A particular missions agency makes a deal with the government to start and oversee an orphanage. A missionary couple with aspirations to plant local churches is assigned to run the orphanage. Providing oversight of an orphanage involves raising funds, building a facility, managing affairs, providing employment, disbursing salaries, keeping financial records, and the list goes on.

The missionary couple dutifully apply themselves to developing a state-of-the-art orphanage. They want the orphans to have the best care possible. The missionaries find local people to employ as cooks, caretakers, and dorm parents. The orphanage adventure is underway, and within a year, seventy beautiful children grace the orphanage.

Because most of the missionary couple's daily relationships are with the orphans and the hired staff of the orphanage, they decide to plant a church starting with these specific people. For the sake of ease, they use the mission-established orphanage facility as a meeting place. The staff at the orphanage, little by little, invite their contacts to the church. A key employee of the orphanage serves as an interpreter and eventually a key leader in the church. The church does not have any pressing financial needs, as the leaders of the church receive adequate salaries from the mission-established project and the orphanage provides the church's ministry resources.

Eventually, the missionaries sense a need for a church building located outside the orphanage grounds. They raise funds from their home country to build a church facility. The members of the church do collect special offerings to apply to the building expenses; nonetheless, the missionaries cover the majority of the cost. The church is now official and ready for advancement.

Although the church is not on the orphanage property, the church and the mission-established project are intimately intertwined. This interconnection creates confusion and dysfunction within the church. When someone is fired from the orphanage, the relatives of that employee cease coming to church. Others come to the church hoping that the church members will help them find employment at the orphanage. If the orphanage has problems, the church has problems; if the church has problems, the orphanage has problems. Many of the members of the church lack respect for the local church leaders because they view them as hirelings of the missionaries. The pastor of the church, who is also an employee of the orphanage, doubts his calling as a pastor but doesn't dare say anything for fear his role in the orphanage could be compromised. The members of the church give obligatory and small offerings because they feel that the missionaries and the orphanage should fund the church's expenses and salaries.

After many years of hard work, the missionaries want to transfer the orphanage to the locals. After trying out different ways, they discover it is impossible for missionaries to totally disengage from the project—at the very least, they have to fund the orphanage ministry. However, the orphanage staff are trained enough that the missionaries can take planned absences. In regard to the church, the missionaries decide to maintain a low profile. They work hard at this goal because the church members are so accustomed to their presence. They are diligent about keeping their boundaries so that the church members will develop healthy relationships with their local leaders and each other.

Now it is time for the missionaries to go on furlough. Another missionary couple replaces them at the orphanage. They love church work and immediately apply themselves to high-profile roles in the church. The wife notices that the local members struggle to play the electric keyboard. She offers to teach them, and she plays on Sundays. The local pastor invites the missionary to train his elders instead of doing it himself. This pattern of confusion and unhealthy dependency becomes a trademark of this creative access ministry.

If we really want to see how a missions project established through phase-in eyes can detract from the authentic growth of the indigenous church, try completely closing such an orphanage for six months. Members of the church feel less obligated to attend a church that is not connected to their employment. Tithes go down. The pastor's support decreases. The church flounders and struggles to have a true impact on making disciples within its community. From this example, we can see that while the orphanage (the phase-in project) helped some children with very real needs, it trapped the local church into a paternalistic and non-indigenous condition for the long term.

Upon entering Cambodia, if I had been assigned to develop and oversee an orphanage, I would have implemented the undertaking exactly as described above. Missionaries don't go into cross-cultural ministry with intentions to stifle the local church. The missions task is not a color-by-number endeavor. The work is dynamic and involves discovery, adaptation, more discoveries, and more adaptation. I am thankful for people like Tom Steffen, who has dedicated his time to share with us about phase-out eyes. His principle gave me a microscope to see that which I would normally not see.

Ministries conceptualized and organized without phase-out eyes, dependent on the expertise and funding from the missionaries' home country, create a myriad of trouble spots. Such a ministry:

- Blurs the delineation between salaried project roles and church roles.
- Creates immediate and ongoing dependency on foreign funds and supplies.
- Generates mixed motives (job security versus authentic commitment).
- Influences the community to see other believers as people who have forsaken their culture to align themselves with foreigners and foreign benefits.
- Makes phase-out nearly impossible for the missionaries.
- Demands missionary presence in one form or another, which perpetuates paternalism in local churches.
- Produces a sense of obligation to give local roles to missionaries.
- Results in a non-sustainable project that is nontransferable (locals do not want to take indigenous responsibility for such a complex and expensive ministry).

The fallout from ignoring phase-out eyes for the sake of overemphasizing the phase-in eyes of missions work is significant. If we want to truly promote and contribute to an indigenous church movement, we need to view our cross-cultural ministry with phase-out eyes. This frame of mind includes applying ourselves in such a way that we empower the local entities to fulfill Dr. George Patterson's words:

> To start a movement for Christ among unreached people groups, which includes the planting of churches and the training of leaders that from the beginning have the spiritual authority, vision, and capability to multiply themselves without any necessary reference to the missionaries.[4]

The apostle Paul was an expert in entering a city or province with phase-out eyes. He intentionally planted churches in such a way that the recipients were not dependent on him. The longest time Paul stayed anywhere was in Ephesus, and he stayed there no more than three years. Paul was a tentmaker and deliberately left doses of money and mission-funded projects out of his plan. As much as it was up to him, Paul planted culturally relevant churches instead of imposing the sending church's culture. Paul trained capable leaders on the job for both expediency and quality. All of these actions were part of his phase-in strategy so that he could easily phase-out, leaving an indigenous church behind.

Some missionaries have discovered the troublesome consequences of creative access projects and have decided to keep mission-established institutions and projects separate from local church planting. This does decrease some of the icky stuff, but it does not necessarily encourage indigenous churches. As I mentioned a few paragraphs back, the presence of a mission-established and foreign-funded project requires the presence of missionaries, some who will stay away from local churches and others who can't help but be involved. Furthermore, the local churches will see how much foreign money goes into the projects, which causes them to claim, "The missions organization spends thousands of dollars on projects but ignores us as the church."

As missionaries, when we enter a field of service we are challenged with the task of considering all phase-in plans with the equally important partner of phase-out plans in mind. How many times did I conduct phase-in ministry because of some pressing need, only to find out later that I had made phasing out difficult and sometimes impossible? In this new day, we need healthier phase-in paradigms. When I came to understand the hindrances of operating without phase-out strategies, I implemented practices such as microenterprise, tentmaking, low-profile coaching (being versus doing), on-the-job training, and chronological Bible storying. These practices made it much easier for me to phase out without negative consequences to indigenous growth. We will explore these methods more thoroughly throughout this book.

How can you plan with phase-out eyes?

BUILD IN RESPONSIBILITY RATHER THAN TRANSFERRING RESPONSIBILITY (NATIONALIZING)

When I was serving in Cambodia, the missionaries (including myself) planted the first few churches. Eventually, we decided that there were enough churches to form a national executive committee according to our practice in North America. As missionaries, we initiated the committee, served in key roles, and invited one or two Cambodian leaders to serve along with us. In all honesty, we created the policies, procedures, and constitution while receiving minimal input from the local leaders.

Over time, we decided to transfer leadership responsibility of the national church to the Cambodian pastors. Over the years, I watched how the Cambodian leaders struggled with procedures, policies, and structures that had been passed on to them from our own church culture in North America. The Cambodians did not have psychological ownership of the ways to function imposed upon them. They felt obligated to continue with polices and structures even when these were unproductive. William Smallman defines this transferring of ministry as *nationalization*, the "transfer of administrative authority from the foreign founders of a mission church or institution to capable national leaders."[5]

Of course, if the administrative authority of a church or institution is under the control of foreign founders, it is a worthy cause to transfer that administrative authority to capable national leaders. But what I am suggesting is that we facilitate ownership and responsibility from the foundation up, rather than nationalizing ministries down the road.

If we do this, I envision the following scenario unfolding: A local Cambodian pastor says to a national colleague, "Makara, we have several churches now. Perhaps we need to find a way to network our churches. Let's ask a missionary for his help!" After seeking out the missionary's advice, the missionary responds, "Why don't you gather the leaders of these churches—with Bibles in hand—to begin discussing how you can relate to one another?"

The hope is that if they are able to take responsibility and ownership from the start, local believers and leaders will recognize their own growth needs, search out biblical guidance, and address those needs through their own indigenous strategies and God-given human and financial resources—rather than continually relying on foreigners and outside help.

I recently read a missions article in which the author was encouraging reluctant missionaries to realize that their fears of entrusting governance to the locals were unwarranted. The author explained that the locals would succeed beyond and above their imagination. I appreciate the fact that this author was encouraging missionaries to let go of the reins and entrust local leaders with full responsibility—better late than never—but his word choice disturbed me somewhat: "When responsibility is put on the nationals, they will rise to the challenge." I would like to believe that we can avoid "putting responsibility" on locals. Rather, I am convinced that we can and should encourage local churches to grow at the pace of their own willingness and ability to take responsibility for each phase and role of ministry. In such a case, the ministry would grow up and around the local leaders, with no missionary needing to "put responsibility" on those in their host culture.

We often imagine that we will transfer leadership when a group of believers is "mature." But maturity is way too late to transfer psychological ownership, responsibility, and authority. A national church that has looked to missionaries for leadership and support for a significant amount of time will find the transfer of ownership a shock to its system. Moreover, the formal transfer of ownership and authority doesn't guarantee automatic psychological ownership and follow-through. How many of us have merely treaded water in ministries we inherited?

Ultimately, we are challenged with the goal of building responsibility into the roots of the church rather than transferring it at some later stage of growth. Missionaries who desire to generate an indigenous ethos will refrain from creating and filling positions for the local national church. Rather, they will allow the local believers to identify needs and roles and fill those roles from the beginning.

How will you build in responsibility from the beginning onward rather than trying to transfer it later?

STIMULATE A HEALTHY SELF-IMAGE AND A HEALTHY COMMUNITY IMAGE

Missionaries Tim and Rebecca Lewis had been settled into their new life in a North African city for just a few months. Yet within that short amount of time, they had managed to gather a group of women and men at their home for church. Eventually, some Muslim-background believers joined their meeting. This gathering surely looked like the beginnings of a church plant, an opportunity to form a community of believers.

Tim and Rebecca worked hard to create a local-style atmosphere within their home. The scent of mint tea filled the house, and couches provided seating. A variety of people with different backgrounds attended the church: Berber, Arab, French, Spanish, Scottish, and American. The worship and Bible studies were conducted in Arabic, French, and English. Tim served as the pastor of this multicultural church. All seemed well—for a while. Then the church started to struggle. The participants interacted on a superficial level because they had little in common. When Tim traveled, the church members did not take the initiative to meet.

Eventually, the church plant failed, but Tim and Rebecca treated failure as a stepping-stone to success. They allowed this church planting experience to guide them in transforming their church planting paradigm. They are candid about their discoveries through various articles and help us to keep self-image and community image in the forefront of our minds as we plant churches.

Even though Tim and Rebecca diligently invited people and created an atmosphere with local flavor, they planted a church with no self-image or community image. These elements are necessary to any movement for Christ. A church with a self-image says, "We are committed to one another's growth and responsible to connect, love, and disciple our neighbors." A church with a community image is surrounded by a community that has a positive attitude toward the church, rather than seeing it as a foreign import.

Many of the lessons of the Lewises' story should sound familiar by now. Tim and Rebecca, North American Christians, gathered random people they knew around them. Meeting in their missionary home with Tim functioning as the pastor sent the message to the surrounding community that foreigners drove the church. The actual members of the church had no authentic bond and no influence in the surrounding community. The church members viewed the church as the missionaries' responsibility; thus they lacked self-motivation for the life and function of the church.

Through their struggle, Tim and Rebecca learned a key revelation about church planting:

> God overhauled our concept of church by planting a church Himself within our people group. To be accurate, He didn't really plant a church; He planted the Gospel into a community that already existed.[6]

Adapting to this new mindset, Tim and Rebecca facilitated an Arabic-speaking believer to visit a community in which two brothers had finished a Bible correspondence course. The brothers had requested that someone come to them and share more about God. When the Arabic evangelist arrived at their house, the house was full of family and friends. The Arabic evangelist thought he had interrupted a wedding. In actuality, people from the community were waiting for him! Those who were gathered at the brothers' house put their faith in Christ and committed to follow Jesus as a group.

Do you see the beauty of this development? No one had to contextualize or form a church here. The gospel life began and grew out of an organic setting and among an indigenous people. The believers' natural network of relationships provided instant community, and they continued multiplying among other communities through their extended relationships. They naturally conducted biblical ministry in a way that was relevant to their culture. This church never sought leaders or resources from outside their community; thus, dependency did not enter the picture. Yes! Tim and Rebecca's struggle brought about a healthy, thriving, and multiplying church (perhaps even a movement), and through their vulnerability, they have taught other cross-cultural church planters key gospel-planting principles.

> We can begin by telling our Muslim friends that worshiping God in spirit and truth does not require them to change religious systems. If some receive this news with joy and invite us back to tell their whole family, we can go into their community. As happened in Hassan's family, those who decide to follow Jesus can grow in faith together. Instead of trying to get believers from different communities to form a lasting new group, we could, like Jesus, establish a church inside their natural community...
>
> We needed to find a person of peace who would invite us into their own community to share the Gospel. Jesus was welcomed into the Samaritan village. The 70 disciples were welcomed into a home. In the same way, Peter was welcomed into Cornelius' household, and Paul was welcomed by Lydia into her household.
>
> In each case, they were welcomed into a cohesive community, so the Gospel was shared with the whole group. As a result, people already committed to each other came to faith together. A church was born within a natural community, without creating a new group just for fellowship. It reminded us of something Ralph Winter had said, "The

'church' (i.e. committed community) is already there, they just don't know Jesus yet!"[7]

I want to join with Tim and Rebecca and learn to cultivate from within instead of imposing from the outside or forcing into existence through extraction. Creating artificial communities, giving the impression that the church is foreign-driven, and practicing superficial contextualization rob the church of a healthy self-image and community image. On the other hand, facilitating a natural, organic group of people to reorient themselves to the lordship of Christ will promote a healthy self-image and community image.

How can you cultivate a self-image and a community image?

AVOID LOANING YOUR THEOLOGY

William Shakespeare avowed, "Neither a borrower, nor a lender be; for loan oft loses both itself and friend, and borrowing dulls the edge of husbandry." Shakespeare's expression reveals to us that a borrowing-lending relationship can hamper both the relationship and the ability of the borrower to manage his or her resources in a healthy way. I find this to be true when missionaries loan their theology, culture, and structures. For example, Cambodians who have borrowed North America's theology, worship, and structures have dulled the edge of their own spiritual husbandry—that is, their ability to steward their realm of ministry.

Glenn Schwartz describes how local churches often borrow theology, worship, and structure from the missionaries' distant cultures. The trouble? All of these things have to do with the fundamental nature of a church:

- An indigenous theology has to do with how a church thinks.
- An indigenous form of worship has to do with how a church feels.
- An indigenous form of structure has to do with how a church works.[8]

I use these three statements to guide my cross-cultural work. For example, if I am in Mongolia, I desire the Mongolian church to think, feel, and work like a Mongolian church, while allowing the Word of God to ultimately direct them. Dr. Alan Tippett links this to "missionary identity," which he defines as learning to leave the West behind when in a foreign land. Gailyn Van Rheenen, with the help of Dr. Alan Tippett, states that too many missionaries never achieve their missionary identity:

Too many missionaries never learn to differentiate Western domains of culture from the domains of the host culture in which they minister. Tippett rightly says, "Far too many missionaries never achieve their missionary identity because, though sent to a foreign land, they never learned to leave the West behind them."[9]

To reach our missionary identity—leaving the West behind—is no easy task, but it is a necessary task nonetheless.

An indigenous theology has to do with how a church thinks. The theology of persecution is a good example of this. North Americans often view persecution as an interruption and surprise that should be tamed, avoided, and solved. Our passion for equality, personal rights, liberties, and freedom drives us to "solve" persecution and rescue the persecuted. Power is important to us, and it needs to be exercised to keep away that which makes us vulnerable. In accordance with this mindset, I have seen missions organizations and leaders make it their agenda to convince governments to legalize the church within particular countries.

While I understand their deep concern for the persecuted, I wonder if we should allow God to work this out from within. Working from our worldview of persecution, we may undermine what God is doing. What do I mean by that? Well, Bible writers, disciples of Christ, and Jesus tell believers to expect persecution as the norm. The apostle Peter exhorted believers not to view persecution as some strange happening, but consider it of value (1 Peter 1:6–9). Jesus said that the persecuted are blessed and should rejoice for the honor (Matthew 5:11–12). The early church spread beyond Jerusalem to Judea and Samaria because of persecution (Acts 8:1–3).

Eric Bridges, with International Mission Board, reveals in his article "Worldview" that the caliber of persecuted believers is instrumental to the fruitfulness of church planting movements:

> Some Chinese house-church leaders actually dread the day persecution ceases. They fear their strong, faithful congregations will become flabby and complacent—like so many in the West …If we truly want to serve our suffering brothers and sisters, it's time to embrace a biblical—and not necessarily American—view of persecution.[10]

We may want to think twice before aiding our host culture to borrow our North American theology of persecution. If North American missionaries live and minister among a persecuted people, we will definitely need to shed our world-view and think like the persecuted, promote a biblical worldview of persecution, and include perseverance as a key theological and discipleship component.

Another worldview mindset that Westerners often unconsciously loan to other cultures is our way of viewing and interpreting life through secular eyes. Imagine the following scenario:

"My husband is very sick," says Chantha. "What are his symptoms?" inquires George. Chantha replies, "He is hot and then cold!" George promptly assesses the situation by checking vital signs. Neighbors look on, saying, "Her husband has a bad spirit." George goes to the pharmacy to find medicine for malaria. He returns and promptly gives Chantha's husband Doxycycline to treat his malaria. Then George says, "Let us pray."

Chantha feels a disconnection but is not sure why. What is the disconnection? The disconnection is caused by a conflict of two worldviews. George, who is from North America, compartmentalizes the secular (man, the church, science, the world) and the spiritual (angels, demons, and God). When George is in a church setting, he addresses life through theological sermons and spiritual activity, but when he faces a demanding situation in everyday life, he deals with what he would call the "empirical" world—in this case, his worldview is characterized by a pragmatic response to an illness.

Chantha, on the other hand, felt odd throughout the experience. Something was amiss. Chantha does not view the world in two nonrelated categories. Rather, Chantha and the Cambodians see nature, man, and the spiritual world as intimately interconnected. The average Cambodian is consumed with interacting and keeping harmony with the spirits. For this reason, Chantha has a very intentional relationship with the Holy Spirit. Chantha immediately understands when Paul says, "For our struggles are not against flesh and blood, but against the rulers, against the authorities, against the powers of this dark world and against the spiritual forces of the heavenly realms" (Ephesians 6:12). Chantha cannot help but pray for her husband as if the powers of the dark world are against them. Praying without ceasing is an important part of her everyday life with God.

In our example, George totally ignored a vital component of Chantha's worldview by compartmentalizing the secular and the spiritual. How does Western culture affect the theology of prayer for those who need supernatural intervention from God? Keep in mind that theology is an intertwining of what we believe and what we actually practice. For example, I have noticed how lightly Westerners (including myself) treat the presence and active work of the Holy Spirit. The scientific nature of our worldview is a main cause of this casual treatment of the Holy Spirit and faith for God's supernatural signs and wonders. When encountering a problem such as illness, we naturally look to natural causes and find tangible ways to solve the problem within our own power. We do eventually pray, but often prayer is a tag onto what we do. Westerners are definitely unaccustomed to the spirit world and often view it as little more than entertainment in movies.

Western Christians will most likely have a very watered-down theology about the Holy Spirit, prayer for God's supernatural intervention, and the demonic world. Our scientific approach to the world affects our theology, whether we admit it or not. I wonder how many times we unknowingly stifle Christians from other parts of the world in their intimate and active relationship with the Holy Spirit, their sensitivity to the spirit world, and their desire to rely on the power of God?

Dr. David Hesselgrave, the director of the School of World Mission and Evangelism at Trinity Evangelical Divinity School, reminds us to be adamant about not giving the Christian message wrapped in our own culture:

> The Christian message is, indeed, abiding and universal. It is for all people of every time in history and of every culture on earth. But the cultural contexts in which God revealed it and to which the missionary delivers it are all distinct and different. They cannot be superimposed upon one another. If Christian meaning is not to be lost in the communication process, contextualization is required.[11]

Ultimately, the goal as missionaries is to encourage the indigenous church to think within their own context along with God's Word, rather than borrowing theology that has been shaped by our culture. Those people groups who borrow Western theology will find themselves irrelevant among their own culture, which is detrimental to a movement for Christ.

AVOID LOANING YOUR FORM OF WORSHIP

An indigenous form of worship has to do with how a church feels. The operative principle here is this: avoid loaning your worship. Whenever I attend a Cambodian church which uses both Western-imported songs and Cambodian-style songs, I notice a distinctive difference in the worship expression of the participants. As the musicians pluck out notes of a familiar Cambodian tune, I see faces of satisfaction and feel the energy increase in the room. The Cambodians sing with an emotional connection and intensity that is unlike the style of many foreign-imported songs and music. When I walk the streets and pathways of Cambodia, I can hear the distinct music of weddings, funerals, ceremonies, mothers singing lullabies, and casual karaoke that tells me, "You are on Cambodian soil, and this music is an expression of the Cambodian heartfelt culture." Should not people who walk the streets and pathways hear the same sounds and expressions coming from churches and communities of believers? Should not they be able to declare, "This moves my heart and makes me feel at home?"

Chris Hale, a musician with experience in India, shares similar thoughts about the Hindu man:

> The average religious Hindu man—hungry for an encounter with the Ultimate Reality—responds to song perhaps more than any other form of communication. He wants to experience the Truth, to feel it. He is not content with mere intellectual understanding. Music is one of the best bridges from me, as a follower of Christ, to this Hindu man.[12]

Hale states that all kinds of music are played in India. An average man hums to a tune from a favorite Indian movie, a villager smiles as he watches a live performance using folk-style music, and a young man dances the night away to Hindi pop music.

Although Hindu youth and urbanites enjoy Western music and participate in contemporary Western worship styles, Hale also reveals the following:

> When it comes to his devotional life, however, the Hindu religious seeker wants bhajans, repetitious songs with a simple melodic line which the leader sings and devotees repeat ...The average urban Indian is attracted to Western modern music and Hindi pop (which is influenced greatly by the West). It makes him loosen up and enjoy himself. But if you introduce this kind of music in a religious context he would likely find the experience confusing. He may leave saying, "Tan halata hain lekin man ko kuch nahin karta" (or, "This music moves the body, but it does nothing for the soul").[13]

Remember, an indigenous form of worship has to do with how a church feels. Borrowed worship may move the body and the intellect, but indigenous worship moves the heart.

The Vaglas of Ghana, West Africa, borrowed their worship styles, melodies, and music from other cultures. With that fact in mind, Sue Hall and Paul Neeley served as coaches to facilitate the development of indigenous hymnody among the Vaglas. They refer to themselves as "midwives" because they help bring about the birth of heartfelt music that is culturally relevant to a specific people. Sue and Paul share about their experience:

> Now, the Vagla musical types of Maara, Zungo, Dugu and others are being used to communicate the content of the Gospel in a form that all Vagla people instinctively recognize as their own …John 3:16 was accompanied by a horn ensemble of seven antelope horns played in intricate interlocking patterns. To the uninitiated, it sounds remarkably like a traffic jam; but to the Vagla people, it's one of the sweetest sounds on earth—especially when coupled with those life-changing words.[14]

Sue and Paul spell out the aim clearly: we are to communicate the content of the gospel in a form that the people of a cultural group instinctively recognize as their own. An instinctive connection to the communication form leads to an instinctive connection to God.

In many cases, the people of Thailand reject Jesus because they view him as the Westerner's god. Churches, such as the Thai Isaan church in Northeast Thailand, compounded this misconception by using foreign forms, songs, and melodies when they worshiped. However, one day, the Thai Isaan church ceased borrowing worship from the West and worshiped in a manner culturally appropriate to them—all because a grandma among them danced.

Paul DeNeui shares about a life-changing event that involved an elderly Isaan woman:

> It was during one of these local-language Bible discussions, as people sat on straw mats in the home of a believer, that one elderly woman stood up from her squatting position, stepped into the middle of the circle and suddenly began to dance the traditional Isaan steps. Her thin arms and fingers waved gracefully back and forth in rhythm to her small, delicate steps. It was a familiar sight at drunken parties—but this was Christian worship! There was no music, only a stunned silence. Finally one voiced called out, "Grandma, sit down! What do you think you're doing?" Without a break in her motions she simply stated, "You don't tell your old grandma to sit down. I'm 90 years old, and I'm just thanking the Lord that you're here."[15]

From that day forth, the Isaan church incorporated indigenous Isaan dance, music, and worship into their gatherings. This Isaan grandma's impromptu and innate worship expression served like a prophetic voice, saying: "God is the God of the Isaan people. We have a responsibility to present him to the Isaan people as our God. God created us, and we have melodies and music in our Isaan hearts. Why should we become somebody we are not in order to worship our God? Our expression of faith and adoration needs to come from our indigenous soul, rather than borrowing superficial worship that is forced and awkward to our God-given ears, voices, and musical talents."

As a result of that grandma praising God from her heart, this Isaan worship song was eventually created:

From the Heavenly City the Word came down.
He was born right here where we live.
We Isaan people have new happiness now.
He loves us and that will not change!

From the City Above, he came down for us.
Full of love from the Almighty.
Now listen! The sound of the ching and the Kaen,
And who is that playing the pin?
Hear the clear tones of the ponglong as they join.
The sounds of the saw, "Eeee oon aaaw."
The melody of the saw is coupled with the sound of voices of praise.

The Lord Jesus Christ, the Victor over death,
Is born in our cultural forms.
Listen to the sounds of the flute and the drum
All Isaan rejoices in Him![16]

As I typed this Isaan-flavored song, a few tears trickled down my face. There is such a beauty when people groups express their faith to God in their heart music! The Vaglas of Ghana and the Isaan of Thailand deserve to relate to God in ways that move their hearts, not merely their intellects.

I believe there are at least two reasons why—in my early years—I imported my own worship expressions to Cambodia. First, I had personally worked hard to learn the heart language of a people, but I struggled to learn the heart music.

Learning both the language and the music of a people group is a daunting task! Language is of more obvious importance; thus, learning the heart music of a people group is usually neglected.

Second, I perceived church through my Western mindset. Thus, I surmised that for a church to be called an official church, it must have a formal worship service. As I planted the first church, I felt a need to have a worship component as soon as possible. With this mindset, I did not have time to learn indigenous music or serve as a midwife in the birthing process of indigenous worship. So I introduced translated songs and imported melodies and instruments, hoping to convert the worship to an indigenous style later. However, the church became accustomed to foreign worship, and they did not have a dancing grandma to redirect them.

I recently read in a blog hosted by Lausanne Global Conversation about a scenario in which indigenous worship was stifled due to imposed Western structures.[17] A specific people in New Guinea had produced Scripture-based songs in an indigenous style. The New Guineans were not able to maintain written versions of these songs because of the harsh conditions of jungle life. These conditions demanded that they commit their songs to memory. Unfortunately, Western missionaries had convinced them to learn and sing Western songs in the place of their indigenous songs so that they could easily participate in regional meetings. The missionaries' Western propensity to over-organize and form people into conventions, denominations, and structures swallowed up the New Guineans' opportunity to worship in their heartfelt style.

To turn this discussion around, what if the New Guineans were to plant a church in North America using New Guinean songs, melodies, and instruments? I imagine we would cringe and say, "It will never work." Why is it that we can see the downside of this method if it happens to us, but we'll go all around the world imposing our worship forms without a second thought?

Recently, I was leading a discussion in a class within the Intercultural Ministries and Language Department at a Christian university. The discussion was centered on the article "What Happened When Grandma Danced," and I had posed this question: "Why do some American missionaries tend to import their own cultural worship?" One student responded, "Because Americans often think they own Christianity, even though the gospel of Christ originated in Asia."

For those who do missions, we have the grand opportunity to serve as midwives, birthing indigenous expressions of worship instead of reinforcing a "foreign god" stereotype. I remember when I first went to another country, the country of

Belize: I did not understand the words people were singing in church, but I felt goosebumps when I heard familiar Christian tunes from my homeland. Now, I get goosebumps when I hear indigenous people worshiping God with their unique flavor of music and song.

The contributing authors of the manual *All the World Will Worship* equip people to serve as facilitators of indigenous worship and hymnody in cross-cultural settings. Within the introduction, Brian Schrag defines both catalyst and indigenous hymnology:

Indigenous hymnody is:

A body of hymns and spiritual songs which are composed by the members of an ethnic group and thought of as being their own.

A catalyst is:
The activity of a facilitator that causes another event, namely, the expanding and deepening use of indigenous hymnody within a specific culture.[18]

All the World Will Worship shares catalyst activities, background research techniques, tools, and applications for facilitating indigenous hymnody. I especially appreciate the "Worship Research Questionnaire," which trains facilitators to use questions to explore and facilitate indigenous worship. Tools like these prevent people like me from making excuses based on lack of understanding and ability in the arena of ethnomusicology. No particular ethnic group should have to go through the unnecessary process of adjusting and adapting to the missionaries' music and worship styles. Rather, missionaries can offer catalyst opportunities for specific groups to feel their worship and feel their God, like the average Hindu man "hungry for an encounter with Ultimate Reality," as stated by Chris Hale.

AVOID LOANING YOUR FORM OF STRUCTURE

An indigenous form of structure has to do with how a church works. Avoid loaning your structure. One of the most profound statements I've read was made by a camel herder in northern Kenya and shared by Malcolm Hunter, who is a specialist in ministry to nomadic pastoralists:

When you can put your church on the back of my camel then I will think that Christianity is meant for us Somalis.[19]

This herder's proclamation refers to how a church works. I have had the rare opportunity to teach pastors and apprentices in Mongolia, a nation known for its Gobi Desert—an ideal place to recline on your back and watch the stars perform.

Where there is immense space, there you will find nomads who know how to live with the land. The pastoral nomads of Mongolia move between pastures and consider being stationary to be like chains around their feet. The seasons mandate their schedules, and they live by and for their livestock. Children are practically born riding horses, which gives them freedom to navigate the steppes. Accumulating, storing, and decorating for permanency is frivolous to the nomads of Mongolia. Gers—transportable dwellings that are never fixed to the ground—assemble and dismantle within hours.

Now, imagine the typical church structure with walls and a ceiling, stationary benches, an altar that never moves, a place that dictates and demands that the participants be sedentary, an atmosphere of predictability, and architecture that cuts you off from the grand sanctuary of nature. It seems obvious that the typical Western church structure has no place among the nomads. In this sense, Western Christians are one-dimensional: theology locked up in a church building. As creatures of habit, we struggle to dream outside of the box and the structure of our own experiences.

David Phillips, who has thought inside and out about how to make disciples among the nomadic peoples of the world, emphasizes how the typical church structure serves as a faith-killer for nomads:

> The Western-style church is time-and property-orientated. Christian activity centered around a building with a weekly timetable is alien to people who live according to where the grass is growing. This structure therefore reinforces the nomads' misconceptions of Christianity. The relationship of the members and leaders can be conveyed, rightly or wrongly, by the seating arrangement—even in an informal camp meeting. Many times the building of a special meeting place or mission "station" (meaning something stationary) can be the death knell to work among nomads; it could either be ignored or distort or destroy the nomadic cycle, and demonstrates the workers' ignorance of the value of nomadism to the people. Christianity could easily become synonymous with disrupting their way of life...[20]

The Somali herder understood what church structure would empower his people to view God as their God: "When you can put your church on the back of my camel, then I will think that Christianity is meant for us Somalis." There are several possibilities for contextualizing a church structure among nomads: allowing the scenery and environment of the steppes to serve as a worship stimulant unto the Creator, enabling "church" to be viewed as "people on the move," emphasizing discipleship within the context of everyday relationships, oral Bible storying, apostolic visits, and apprenticeship training—to name a few.

Loaning our church structures in inappropriate cultural contexts is like putting snowmobile outfits on those who live in the tropics. Those with imposed snowmobile outfits will need to shed them quickly because wearing them just does not work. Let's plant indigenous churches that work within people's God-given context.

How can you avoid loaning your theology, worship, and structure?

DISCERN FUNCTION VERSUS FORM

Missionaries desiring to operate within the framework of their host cultures will pass along biblical principles instead of the practices and patterns of their own church culture. Once the host culture is exposed to and rooted in the missionaries' patterns and forms, it is nearly impossible for them to eventually develop their own indigenous theology, worship, and expressions of faith. Dr. George Patterson, who has thirty-five years of missions experience and has written books on church multiplication, encourages missionaries to teach Christ's commands and obedience to those commands as the foundation of discipleship rather than founding churches on the theology and church patterns dictated by the missionaries' cultures.

Aubrey Malphurs, a professor of pastoral ministries at Dallas Theological Seminary, advises Christians working in an "atmosphere of change" to have a "theology of change" which relates to function, form, and freedom. Malphurs writes:

I define the functions of the church as the timeless, unchanging, and nonnegotiable precepts that are based on Scripture and are mandates for all churches to pursue to accomplish their purpose.[21]

Professor Malphurs gives examples of five of the church's general functions found in Acts 2:42–47 and prescribed in other parts of the New Testament: teaching, fellowship, worship, evangelism, and service. (I differ slightly with him here; I prefer to consider evangelism as a component of discipleship.)

Malphurs points out that functions are ends, not means to ends, and that they explain why the church does what it does. Forms, on the other hand, are the means to functions. Ultimately, the functions of the church do not change with culture or time frames or circumstances. While the cross-cultural communicator should adamantly apply himself to passing on the *functions* of the church, he or she avoids passing on and imposing *forms*. Malphurs says:

> I define forms as the temporal, changing, negotiable practices that are based on culture and are methods that all churches are free to choose to accomplish their functions.[22]

For example, if evangelism is a function of the church, the form will relate to how the church implements evangelism. A cross-cultural communicator may teach a seekers Bible study among students at a university, whereas another may tell chronological Bible stories among people of a rural village. Both are valid ways of implementing function because they are appropriate for their respective context. Form is the means to fulfill the church's functions.

Missionaries have the important role of promoting the functions of the church without introducing and modeling their own cultural forms. Why do so many churches around the world think like, feel like, and work like Western churches? Why do so many people from various cultural groups declare Jesus to be the foreigner's god? Why do places like Thailand not move beyond 2 percent of adherents to Christianity after one-hundred-and-eighty years of missions work? Part of the reason is that missionaries have passed on their own cultural forms wrapped around the functions of Christ's church. This process creates a visibly Western-oriented ministry that is offensive to most people around the world.

We need the wisdom, patience, and self-control to encourage our host cultures to implement their own culturally relevant forms to fulfill the functions of the church of Jesus Christ. I believe that if missionaries understand and practice the "theology of change," as worded by Malphurs, we will intentionally plant indigenous churches instead of spiritual carbon copies of the Western church.

Another way missionaries impose their own cultural forms is through promoting and imposing extrabiblical requirements, which burdens the church unnecessarily. David Garrison notes that extrabiblical requirements are one of the main stumbling blocks to church planting movements. Mandating that an indigenous

238 · JEAN JOHNSON

church have a church constitution, a particular leadership structure, or a decision-making pattern based on one's own cultural version of the church are examples of introducing and imposing extrabiblical requirements and design.

> In many older mission fields, church planters labor under the weight of years of tradition-built definitions of church and church leadership. This happens when well meaning Christians come to believe that they are not a church until they have been constituted by the national denomination, or have reached a certain congregational size, employed a seminary-trained pastor, secured church property, or constructed a building. All of these requirements exceed and encumber the biblical ideal.[23]

The more extrabiblical requirements are modeled and imposed by the missionaries, the more the local churches of a nation are weighed down by man-made versions of the church and church structure. For example, requiring that acceptable pastors must be seminary trained or ordained is adding extrabiblical requirements that go far beyond 1 Timothy 3:1–7. And narrowing the pool of potential leaders due to extrabiblical requirements slows down a church planting movement. Some might argue that such requirements ensure quality control and minimize false doctrine. Yet, none of the leaders in the New Testament were seminary trained, and they impacted the world.

When missions organizations pass on extrabiblical requirements, those extras are most likely to come out of their own culture. Our traditions become so much a part of us that we sometimes cannot differentiate between biblically driven or culturally driven activities. We model what comes naturally to us, and those around us are unable to decipher what is biblical versus what is the culture of the missionary. Josh Hunt, who wrote the book *Make Your Group Grow*, explains what he experienced:

> The way they do missions today is totally different from the way it was done when I grew up in the Philippines.
>
> Forty years ago, it worked like this. An evangelist would go out and share the faith. Some would respond. After they responded, the evangelist would gather these new Christians into churches. (This order is important as we will see in a moment.) The churches would take on an approximate form to a church in America. They would have a choir and a Sunday School and a constitution. (How can you run a church without

a constitution?) They would have committees and Wednesday night supper, church counsel, & visitation. In the early days we even built buildings with red bricks, a tall steeple and white columns out front.

Then, we grouped churches together in Associations, State Conventions and National Conventions. We created institutions, seminaries, agencies and so forth. We sent our young ministers to our seminaries and they received degrees that duplicated the kind of degrees they can get here. In short, we not only exported the gospel, we also exported the whole form of the way we do church in America. We exported not only the wine, but the wineskins as well.[24]

Hunt's words support the idea that missionaries should present the biblical mandates and functions of the church while encouraging indigenous churches to have the freedom to form themselves in accordance with the Bible and their culture.

How can you decipher function versus form and apply what you discover?

CONSIDER PLANTING THE GOSPEL—NOT THE CHURCH

While I have addressed church planting in a traditional and nontraditional sense all throughout this book and used the term generously, I have to admit I am leery of the expressions *church planting* and *planting churches*. The term *church planting* carries within it preconceived ideas and experiences of what we call church in the West. In North America, church planters often start the process with a building or lead several people to Christ and then move into or buy a facility. They mobilize the church as the method to bring people into relationship with Christ. Neil Cole, founder and director of Church Multiplication Associates, reveals to us a typical (yet backward) mindset:

Mike Frost and Alan Hirsh have challenged the way we order our thinking about Jesus and the church. Typically, we think of church as something to mobilize so that people will come to Jesus. Instead, Jesus leads people in mission, who in turn bring forth fruitful churches.[25]

North American church planting has much to do with gathering people into a building on a fixed day and at a fixed time for a fixed program. The expression "I am going to church" is a revelation of the fact that in North America, church is viewed as a place to which we go at a designated time and with designated people—similar to membership in a club or organization. If you recall, David Phillips, who is the founder of the Nomadic Peoples Network, describes the Western-style church as time-and-property oriented. In other words, church planting in the West has involved securing property and conducting time-oriented programs that invite people into a church building to experience Jesus. Favoring a time-and-property-oriented church model has limited us in making disciples in many places around the world. Phillips, who longs for effective discipleship among nomadic people, reminds us that in many cases, buildings and planting churches have overshadowed making disciples:

> It is extraordinary that the first evidence of Christianity that people have today is an institution called a church. Unfortunately, the word "church" carries connotations of elaborate buildings, well-established timetables and rituals, hallowed traditions and unfamiliar structures of leadership— as if they are to last as part of this world forever. Most mission agencies are committed to reproduce the accumulated wisdom in the church structures of their home countries as the ultimate desirable result. This idea is congenial to the workers and entails a ready-made package to overcome the inconvenience of the converts' slow learning.
>
> How much does our own spiritual experience depend on the thrill of large congregations, professional music in comfortable buildings, surrounded by friends who do not disturb our convictions?
>
> Christ's Great Commission does not mention building or "planting" churches, but emphasizes the importance of being witnesses and making disciples. Discipleship means developing a close relationship with Christ, with a growing understanding of salvation and the progressive assimilation and practice of his teaching. The call of the itinerant Jesus was away from institutions and towards dynamic relationships in small groups.[26]

We need to be cautious with the concept of "church planting." No matter what we think, the term includes an unspoken push to plant the church for the outcome of a church, rather than for the outcome of followers of Christ who are part of their communities and transforming their communities.

While it might be beneficial for North Americans to rethink our own paradigms of church, I am not as concerned about the North American church as I am about those who think this form of church is for everyone, everywhere. Missionaries from the West, as well as from other places in the world that have experienced time-and-property-oriented church models, have reproduced such churches in their places of cross-cultural ministry. This style of church is ineffective in multiplying disciples in most communal societies, which includes much of the world. David Phillips shares that nomadic people have come to believe that God is only the God of sedentary people and has no interest in those whose lifestyles are centered on migratory cycles and movement. This is a sad conclusion, especially since Jesus and the disciples were "people on the move"!

Neil Cole urges us to differentiate between planting organizational churches and planting the presence of Jesus within communities:

> Our mission is to find and develop Christ followers rather than church members. There is a big difference in the two outcomes. The difference is seen in transformed lives that bring change to neighborhoods and nations. Simply gathering a group of people who subscribe to a common set of beliefs is not worthy of Jesus and the sacrifice He made for us.
>
> We have planted religious organizations rather than planting the powerful presence of Christ. Often, that organization has a very Western structure, with values not found in the indigenous soil. If we simply plant Jesus in these cultures and help His church emerge indigenously from the soil, then a self-sustaining and reproducing church movement would emerge, not dependent upon the West and not removed from the culture in which it grows.[27]

How does planting the gospel differ from planting the church? *Planting the gospel* means allowing the gospel (God's presence and transformational work) to take root within a community in such a way that the community expresses and spreads its faith in an organic manner, natural to the surrounding culture and context, under the lordship of Jesus and his Word. This organic expression may look very different from the cross-cultural communicator's church experience. Revisiting the nomadic people, we can see that their forms of living out their faith would be in complete contrast to Western forms of church. David Phillips states:

> We have to recognize that Christ himself is more at home in a nomad camp, with its humble hospitality, its small group fellowship and its storytelling way of exchanging news, than a Western church.[28]

Neil Cole wrote a book called *Organic Church: Growing Faith Where Life Happens*. The phrase "growing faith where life happens" spells out the goal of planting the gospel in preexisting communities. Finding God's fingerprints (discovering what he is already doing) among a preexisting community, stimulating what you discover, and allowing the faith experience of Christ and its expression to rise up among the community are all part of planting the gospel in an organic manner. Planting the gospel will naturally allow an indigenous nature to flourish, in sharp contrast to trying to create a cultural church experience and somehow convert it into an indigenous experience—a process which is really indigenization in disguise.

What can you do to plant the gospel organically?

CONSIDER MISSIONAL HOUSE CHURCH MOVEMENTS

Patrick Lai, the author of *Tentmaking*, tells us that house churches or small groups are a necessity in many places. He tells a story about some Muslim-background believers (MBBs) who planned to build a church in their rural community. A man in the community donated land, and everyone saved money for close to two years. The day came in which this group of believers could actually build their church. While they were building their church, two Muslim men walked by, and this is what happened:

> These men were known for their radical faith and hatred of us. They innocently inquired what we were doing. The leaders responded, "We are building the first church in this country!" To which the men answered, "That's good; work hard." The church members were surprised at their answer and discussed among themselves why would they be so encouraging. Finally, one of the leaders ran after the men and asked them, "Why were you so encouraging towards our building a church?" The men replied, "Because when you are done, it will make a good bonfire."[29]

When they realized that a high-profile church building was going to be counterproductive, the group of believers decided to meet in houses instead. More and more around the world, high-profile churches are neither feasible nor acceptable. North American missionaries who are used to church buildings may need to realign their thinking.

Josh Hunt expounds on what he did to avoid merely importing the way he did church in a cross-cultural context:

Around 20 years ago, we started experimenting with a different model, one that is now known as Church Planting Movements. It is the dominant model of missions around the world these days. I found this statement on the International Mission Board's web page: International Mission Board's Overseas Leadership Team adopted a vision statement: We will facilitate the lost coming to saving faith in Jesus Christ by beginning and nurturing Church Planting Movements among all peoples.

Now, the phrase "Church Planting Movements" is probably not all that clear to you, as it was not to me. I think of "Church" as "Church as I know it." These are more like house churches, as was made clear to me on a recent trip to Richmond and a conversation I had with an IMB executive there. These are not churches as we think of churches. The executive clarified this to me adding, "In fact, we try to keep them small and continually reproducing..."

...I am curious what comes to your mind when you think of the phrase "House Church." It has always had a bit of a negative connotation to me. It has always spoken to me of people who could not get along with the people in traditional churches and decided to just do church at home. But, these are not rebels. This is an intentional strategy. Those who follow this strategy are following the top leadership of the IMB.[30]

House churches are not merely a default to deal with persecution or accommodate remnant members of disgruntled churches, as Josh Hunt originally thought. House churches have proven to be a powerful key to indigenous church planting movements. House churches are designed to reproduce, are closer to the grassroots of the culture, and are able to work within the natural flow of relationships. The reason I put "missional" with the phrase "house church movements" in this section's opening suggestion is to emphasize the missional mandate of house churches. Some people meet as house churches simply because they favor the format and all that it provides. But *missional* house churches have it in their DNA to multiply and make disciples.

There are several reasons for this. House churches do not create the huge, cumbersome structure of most mission-established churches and ministries, a structure which needs to be transferred to local leaders. House churches are meant to be a light baton, easily passed from one to the other. There are several characteristics of house-church movements that empower indigenous leaders to plant, grow, and multiply. We do well to pay attention both to these characteristics and to the biblical basis for planting house churches:

1) House churches were prevalent in the New Testament, and a significant extent of the gospel narrative occurs in homes (Luke 10:5, 7; Acts 2:2; Acts 2:46; Acts 5:42; Acts 8:3; Acts 10:22; Acts 12:12; Acts 16:14; Acts 18:7; Acts 20:20; Acts 21:8; Romans 16:5; 1 Corinthians 16:19; Colossians 4:15; Philemon 2; 2 John 10).

2) House churches offer an ecclesiology which is compatible with New Testament practice, rather than imitating foreign church structures and extrabiblical practices. (There are no testaments to church buildings, constitutions, committees, etc.)

3) Believers gather in homes that are organic to the community, rather than extracting people to meet in an imposed building that creates division.

4) House churches offer groups that are small and intimate enough to sincerely practice "one another" commands.

5) House churches focus on personal discipleship and modest worship; thus, expensive and professional worship services are not necessary.

6) Building-centered, structural, or programmatic approaches, which demand energy, time, and money, are avoided.

7) Organic leaders come from within the house churches, are often bivocational, and learn mostly through on-the-job training instead of relying heavily on highly trained and staff-driven ministers who expect significant salaries.

8) Evangelism is relational and happens within networks of relationships; thus, glamorous and costly evangelism programs are not necessary.

9) House churches are relatively self-sufficient and are not dependent on complicated ties to a central leadership (accountability comes through networks, eldership, and apostolic visits, similar to Paul's methods).

10) Multiplication is the DNA of each house church.

11) House churches are able to focus on enabling "each one" ministry instead of professionalism and programs.

12) There is no need for resources to maintain buildings and staff.

Allow me to summarize the above characteristics with Stephen Atkerson's formula:

Simple – Meet in a home, share a meal, fellowship with others who love Jesus and who are like family.

Strategic – Grows naturally, replicates easily, fosters spiritual maturity, builds relationships, promotes unity, uses resources efficiently.

Scriptural – Established by the Lord through the Apostles, practiced by the early church and prescribed by the New Testament for today.[31]

In the New Testament accounts, the house was the center of a good deal of apostolic ministry. The disciples received the promise of the Holy Spirit in a house. The first believers broke bread and shared meals in their houses. Peter's mother-in-law was healed in a house. People were martyred in their houses during Saul's persecution. Day after day, disciples of Jesus went from house to house sharing about Jesus Christ. A house church fervently prayed for Peter's release from prison. Cornelius, head of the first non-Jewish Christian family, experienced salvation in a house. Paul often greeted house churches in his letters. Lydia opened her house to serve as a church. The house represents families, and families make up communities.

It is not my goal to explain in detail how to launch and oversee a missional house church movement. Rather, I invite you to consider the benefits of such a strategy in encouraging indigenous multiplying movements for Christ. There is so much more to learn about missional house church movements, and there are ample books to guide you. I suggest starting with books by Rad Zdero, Robert Fitts, Wolfgang Simson, David Garrison, Larry Kreider, and Steve Atkerson.

If you decide to plant multiplying house churches, how can you do it?

USE SIX QUESTIONS TO GUIDE YOUR INTENTIONALITY FOR THE INDIGENOUS CHURCH

I believe it is worthwhile to consistently use Dr. Alan Tippet's six marks of the indigenous church and the accompanying questions to keep us on track with facilitating the indigenous church:

1) Does the church have a healthy self-image?
   Does it view itself as the Body of Christ in its own community?
2) Is the church self-functioning?

Does it contain all the parts necessary for caring for itself and its own outreaches?

3) Is it self-determining?

Is the church autonomous—capable of making its own decisions?

4) Is it self-supporting?

Does it carry its own financial responsibility? Does it finance its own service project?

5) Is it self-propagating?

Does the church have its own missionary outreach?

6) Is it self-giving?

Does it manage its own service programs such as hospitals, seminaries, relief projects and so on?[32]

In missions circles today, the word *indigenous* seems overused, and perhaps its commonality has caused it to lose some of its appeal and influence. However, I am convinced that we should not relax the meaning, influence, or practice of aiming for indigenous movements for Christ. My prayer for those of us who "do missions" is this:

Dear God,
The floating water hyacinth is a rich ornamental plant,
But introduced into Uganda's waters has become a plant of torment.
Grant us the insight to not interfere and impose
But rather cultivate the indigenous expression of your kingdom.

CHAPTER FIFTEEN

LOW-PROFILE COACHING IN ACTION

"Keep your face towards the sunshine—shadows will fall behind you."

WALT WHITMAN

I have often heard or perhaps even used the idiom, "I don't want to be in his shadow for the rest of my life." We say this in a negative sense. It means that we don't want to be lost or forgotten because someone else is excelling above us and receiving more attention. We would never hear someone say, "I long to be in your shadow." Yet that is exactly what Jesus's life of submission and humility points to. John the Baptist certainly understood the process of being in the shadow of someone else. I suggest that commitment to living or serving "in someone else's shadow" serves an essential purpose when planting indigenous movements for Christ. Throughout this chapter, we will discover ways in which cross-cultural workers can serve in low-profile roles with high-impact results.

IMPLEMENT THE "SHADOW PASTOR" METHOD

The typical tendency of a missionary is to birth a ministry or church, assume leadership, and eventually transfer leadership to the locals. In earlier chapters, we looked at the huge disadvantage to transferring ministries and roles. This process has been referred to as nationalizing: to take an existing mission-established ministry and give it over to the locals associated with the ministry in that context. As you can imagine, the nationalizing process rarely passes on psychological ownership, nor does it develop an indigenous nature within these inherited ministries.

Although I cannot recall the resource, I remember Curtis Sergeant, an insightful writer on the subject of church planting movements, suggested that missionaries should serve as "shadow pastors." Shadow pastors intentionally keep the focus off themselves and allow local leaders to grow into leadership from the beginning. The shadow pastor coaches the new leaders to pray, prepare, and practice from behind the scenes. The shadow pastor does not regularly attend ministry activities, giving the local leader opportunity to build trust and community with those he shepherds. If the shadow pastor does join in at times, he or she keeps a low profile. Shadow pastoring avoids the delicate and often detrimental transfer of leadership from missionaries to locals.

There was a season within my missions work when serving as a shadow pastor would never have crossed my mind. Honestly, many missionaries struggle with serving in a low-profile role. It is not the nature of the beast to be in the shadows! We have this drive to be seen, to have control, to be tangibly active. It takes a highly dedicated and disciplined foreign man or woman to work in the shadows of the indigenous man or woman so as to promote the other's psychological ownership, dignity, and effectiveness. I appreciate the words of the poet Walt Whitman, "Keep your face towards the sunshine—shadows will fall behind you." In a poetic way, effective church planting happens when missionaries coach local leaders to keep their faces toward God and then serve in the shadows that fall behind the local leaders.

How can you serve as a shadow pastor?

ADOPT A LEARNER-SERVANT-STORYTELLER POSTURE

A number of years ago, Donald Larson wrote an article entitled "The Viable Missionary: Learner, Trader, Storyteller." Thomas and Elizabeth Brewster, well-known for their informal language learning techniques, have adapted Larson's three roles to learner, servant, and storyteller. I believe wholeheartedly that if we adopt a learner-servant-storyteller posture, we will avoid the many issues of paternalism and dependency. The very attitude and strategy surrounding this posture serves as a protective cocoon around the local people so that we will not bombard them with our leanings toward ethnocentrism.

The Brewsters' article, "The Learner-Servant-Storyteller Posture," encourages us that a learner-servant-storyteller refrains from ministering from a status of privilege or expertise. Rather, we lift the local people's self-esteem and emulate a ministry lifestyle which they can imitate. Beyond the good news of the gospel, the presence of missionaries on foreign soil needs to be perceived as good news as well. Do we come to intimidate and compete, or do we come to promote the message, "You can do all things through Christ who strengthens you"? Our very status, posture, and attitude speak volumes, perhaps even more so than any ministry project or message we may bring. Thomas and Elizabeth Brewster explain this concept well:

To have a discipleship ministry in postures other than Learner, Servant and Storyteller is to minister from the platform of a privileged, ascribed status. The model of ministry that is then provided may be perceived as out of reach of those who are ministered to. They may not view themselves as having the necessary credentials or resources to carry on the ministry, and may, therefore, feel that the responsibility of making disciples or leading ministry is something that only the expatriate missionary can do.

The high profile, high status administrative, educational, technological, or theological positions that many missionaries assume for themselves may seldom be perceived as Good News when viewed through the eyes of the local population. Often the missionary may be introducing a competitive health system or agricultural system or educational system or religious system …A better posture could be based on Philippians 2:3 "Let each esteem others as better than himself." The people themselves should have their self-esteem raised as they are affirmed through their relationship with the missionary.[1]

I cannot even begin to describe the riches of being an intentional and eternal learner in a culture not your own. There is a wise Cambodian saying: "Enter a river where it bends, enter a land by its customs." An Indian proverb says, "He who questions will not lose the path." East Africans say, "Learning is like sailing the ocean: no one has ever seen it all." The Chinese verbalize, "Learning is like rowing upstream: not to advance is to drop back."

As missionaries, we often learn the objective culture—that is, the noticeable culture, such as food, eating habits, dress, expressions, gestures, likes and dislikes—and then start ministering from the self-appointed position of teacher. Instead, we need to enter and live in a culture with "eyes in the back of our heads," observing and internalizing the subjective culture—the core of the worldview. The subjective culture includes the indigenous view of reality, values, driving forces, allegiances, and interpretations. I would have no problem with a missionary who completely dedicated the first four years to learning the culture and language while building relationships. Combining African and Chinese wisdom, the best posture from which to minister is a posture that views learning as rowing upstream and sailing an ocean all at the same time.

In chapters 10 and 17 of this book, I write much about the storyteller. During my initial years in Cambodia, I did not grasp the role of a storyteller. Now, however, I am converted. I believe wholeheartedly in the role of the storyteller and the role of stories in making disciples. You may have noticed that the storyteller is third in the Brewers' list. We do not start as storytellers in another man's land. Donald Larson makes this clear, as explained by Tom Steffen:

> Larson (1978) objects to those storytellers who enter a mariner's storyland and immediately begin to tell Bible stories or their own faith stories without scanning the mariner's storyland. He argues that mariners view such encounters as one of three entities: a schoolhouse, a marketplace, or a courtroom. When in school, the messenger becomes the teacher while the mariners become the students. When at the market place, the messenger becomes the buyers. When in the courtroom, the messenger becomes the accuser while the mariners become the accused. None of these are effective methods of communicating the gospel. Larson realizes this and asks, "Can an outsider teach or sell or accuse an insider?"[2]

If we present ourselves as teachers, traders, and accusers, will the people of our host countries feel drawn to our posture? More likely, if we go to foreign fields as learners, servants, and storytellers instead of leaders, principals, directors, and administrators, we will be perceived as "good news" and true messengers of the good news.

What are some practical ways you can be a learner-servant-storyteller?

GRACIOUSLY REDIRECT OFFERS TO FILL POSITIONS

A pastor of a local church in Cambodia constantly sought out missionaries to teach the children. When one missionary moved on, he sought another to serve in the same role. Within his fifty-member church, a Cambodian husband and wife had a burden to teach the children. But every time they had a thought toward this goal, they dismissed it by saying, "We can't teach like the missionary, and we don't have the resources she brings to the class." (By the way, the felt pieces of the flannel board that the missionary donated to the church were covered in mold within three months.)

Every time a missionary fills a position, he or she does a disservice to the development of an indigenous church in the area of self-functioning. Let's say that the missionary in this case graciously turned down the offer to teach the children. What would most likely happen? The pastor would be more motivated to seek out and train someone in his church. Furthermore, the ministry to the children would be more reflective of Cambodian culture if conducted by Cambodians.

Local leaders will be quick to ask you as a missionary to serve in certain roles. When you accept, you are stepping away from the goal of indigenous multiplication. Your filling a position prevents the pastor or elder from seeking out and training people from his or her own flock. It is awkward to decline a sincere invitation, but it is necessary for the greater goal.

How can you avoid filling positions for locals?

ALLOW THE CHURCH-IN-PROCESS TO STRATEGIZE ITS OWN DEVELOPMENT

Not growing a ministry beyond its people's vision and capacity is an important discipline in serving as a low-profile missionary-coach. The tendency is to develop a ministry based on the missionary's vision and resources. The more effective alternative is to facilitate a core group of families and guide them to incrementally add only those functions and activities which they have determined are necessary and which they can lead.

In other words, the missionary guides the development of the ministry based on what the local people can do, not on what he or she can do. The church grows at the pace of the local people in relationship to their own resources and capabilities. I remember when I added worship to a church-in-process because I deemed it important. I also had my own cultural standard of what worship should include. I had to impose my own forms and resources to meet that standard. Remember this quote from Patrick Lai:

> Cultural expectations concerning "what is a church" should be tried, not formed. Believers need to be discipled in the principles but not the forms of "church." Believers need to discover in the Holy Spirit and within their own culture, ways they feel comfortable practicing their faith and ecclesiology. There is a danger of new believers uncritically embracing western thinking and models. We should go to great lengths to ensure that the emerging church meetings can be readily reproduced by those who attend. This means even with the first gatherings of believers, the potential national leaders should be involved in leading. Time and effort is to be taken to teach leadership principles and allow believers to work out these principles within the parameters of their own culture.[3]

"Cultural expectations concerning 'what is a church' should be tried, not formed." Lai's insightful words give us a way to impress on our hearts an important goal: we should encourage the local believers to "try" their church within their own culture and under the guidance of the Holy Spirit, rather than "forming" church for them at our pace and expectations. Allowing the churches-in-process to strategize their own development in accordance with God's Word produces healthy members and healthy leaders within the churches.

What can you do to encourage the church to strategize its own development?

PLANT THROUGH QUESTIONS, NOT ANSWERS

Instead of implementing and modeling forms of church, the missionary may want to facilitate growth by combining Bible accounts with practical questions. This process allows the local believers to shape their church experience in accordance with the Bible and their own local culture. In my prior book, Worldview Strategic Church Planting Among Oral Cultures, I share a method of using Acts 1–11 and accompanying questions to implement this process:

	FUNCTION	BIBLE STORY	BIBLE VERSES	MAIN QUESTIONS
1)	Pray for the power of the Holy Spirit.	Believers receive the Holy Spirit (Acts 1:4–5, 8; 2:1–17)	Luke 3:15–16	What? Who? How? When? Where?
2)	Baptize new believers.	3,000 people believe and are baptized (Acts 2:14–15, 22–24, 29–41)	Matthew 28:19	What? Who? How? When? Where?
3)	Meet together to: - love one another - worship together - teach one another - pray for one another - share with one another - share meals with communion	The believers meet together often (Acts 2:42–47; 12:12; 16:40; 18:7; Romans 16:5; 1 Corinthians 16:19; Colossians 4:15; Philemon 1:2)	Ephesians 5:19–20 Colossians 3:16 Ephesians 6:18 1 Corinthians 12:7–10, 28–30 1 Corinthians 11:23–26	What? Who? How? When? Where?
4)	Pray for the sick and demon possessed.	Peter & John pray for the sick and tell the Good News (Acts 3:1–19)	Acts 5:12–16	What? Who? How? When? Where?
5)	Tell the Good News and make disciples.	Peter & John tell the Sanhedrin about Jesus (Acts 4:1–22)	Romans 1:16	What? Who? How? When? Where?
6)	Continue to pray for the power of the Holy Spirit.	The Holy Spirit enables the believers to share the Good News boldly (Acts 4:23–31)	1 Corinthians 2:4–5	What? Who? How? When? Where?
7)	Give and be good stewards of God's resources.	The believers give and share (Acts 4:32–35)	Proverbs 3:9–10 1 Timothy 5:3, 9, 16, 4, 8 Philippians 4:15–19 1 Timothy 5:17–18	Why? Who? How? When? Where?

	FUNCTION	BIBLE STORY	BIBLE VERSES	MAIN QUESTIONS
8)	Give and be good stewards of God's resources.	Ananias and Sapphira lie to God about their offering (Acts 5:1–11)	2 Corinthians 8:7; 9:6–7; 8:13–15	Why? Who? How? When? Where?
9)	Prepare to face persecution.	The disciples are put in jail (Acts 5:12, 17–41)	Matthew 10:24–31	Why? Who? How? When? Where?
10)	Prepare leaders and helpers to fulfill God's work.	The disciples choose seven men to help in the ministry (Acts 6:1–7)	2 Timothy 2:2 Ephesians 4:11–13	Why? Who? How? When? Where?
11)	Continue to prepare to face persecution.	The stoning of Stephen (Acts 6:8–15; 7:54–60; 8:1–4)	1 Peter 4:12–16	Why? Who? How? When? Where?
12)	Continue to baptize new believers.	Philip baptizes an official from Africa (Acts 8:26–39)	Romans 6:3–6	Why? Who? How? When? Where?
13)	Continue to tell the Good News and make disciples.	God prepares Saul to tell the Good News to others (Acts 9:1–22)	2 Corinthians 5:18–20	Why? Who? How? When? Where?
14)	Pray for the sick and demon possessed.	Peter prays for the sick (Acts 9:32–42)	1 Thessalonians 1:5	Why? Who? How? When? Where?
15)	Continue to tell the Good News and make disciples.	God gives Peter a vision to tell other nations about Jesus (Acts 10:1–48)	Romans 10:13–15, 17	Why? Who? How? When? Where?
16)	Continue to tell the Good News and make disciples.	Barnabas and Paul make disciples in Antioch (Acts 11:19–26)	Matthew 28:19–20	Why? Who? How? When? Where?
17)	Continue to give and be good stewards of God's resources.	The disciples give to help those experiencing famine (Acts 11:25–30)	Romans 15:25–28 1 Corinthians 16:1–4 2 Corinthians 8:1–7; 9:10–13	Why? Who? How? When? Where?

Using this method, I invite the church-in-process or key leaders to read (or tell) the Bible stories and the accompanying Scriptures. Then I facilitate them to pray and develop ways to implement the function revealed in the Bible story and Scriptures, with their culture and the Scriptures in mind. With this style of planting through questions, missionaries are able to impart the church's biblical functions while allowing the local believers to design indigenous forms to carry them out. Basically, missionaries avoid imposing their cultural forms on an indigenous group of people with this style of communication.

How could you use asking questions as a part of your planting strategy?

TRAIN AND MULTIPLY

How can we train with multiplication at the core? Jesus called twelve men to himself, and they became a mobile classroom with twenty-six legs. The disciples learned by observing, doing, and debriefing as they traveled from place to place with Jesus. Often, Jesus invited the disciples to participate in ministry with him, and at times he sent them out. Jesus spent time with the disciples, facilitating them to evaluate and discuss what they were experiencing. Jesus's method of training is not some ancient form that should be relegated to the archives of Christendom. I have to believe that Jesus knew what he was doing when he trained his apprentices. Nor was he the only one. Paul rarely traveled alone; he trained others, such as Timothy, on the job. Jesus's training methods are worthy of a second and third glance.

For the sake of movements for Christ, I am convinced that we need approaches that generate the maximum number of capable leaders within a reasonable amount of time. The reproducibility of a training method leads to multiple generations of capable leaders, and capability comes from systematic experience and practice. The more real an experience is, the more real the capability; the more artificial the experience is, the more artificial the capability.

Dr. George Patterson has created a system called "Train & Multiply" to meet the need for multiplying churches and leaders in Honduras.[4] Train & Multiply is not a program; rather, it is an interdenominational tool to empower the multiplication of leaders through Paul-and-Timothy-style reproductive chains of mentoring. This excellent training resource strategically guides a trainer to implement shadow pastoring.

Here, I introduce the six key transferable components of Train & Multiply. You may want to explore this system for your setting or implement the principles to your own training paradigm. Learn more at https://trainandmultiply.com.

1.   On-the-Job

On-the-job training includes opportunity to learn theory and practice simultaneously. The pastoral student is active, not passive. Instead of preparing for some future role, the pastoral student actually implements what he or she is learning within a community on a day-to-day basis. At the end of the training, the pastoral student will have a viable ministry, as opposed to a certificate and the need for a job! Fruit, not exams on paper, will provide evidence of progress.

2.   On-site

The training is conducted where the pastoral students live and minister. In other words, the community and real life serve as the classroom. This method of training allows those who have families, existing ministry responsibilities, and a livelihood to train for the ministry without severing foundational ties that are actually an asset to their stability, maturity, and ministry.

3. Menu Approach (Student-Centered)

Typically, a teacher prepares a systematic set of lessons and unwinds those lessons one by one as he or she determines is best. In the case of Train & Multiply, the pastoral students choose the topic of study in accordance with their current ministry needs and then apply what they learn immediately. This method is similar to that of a menu in a restaurant. In fact, the Train & Multiply system actually has a menu, listing and providing action-oriented guidelines for studying and practicing seventy-five pastoral activities.

To use this method, the trainer facilitates the pastoral students to evaluate their present ministries. As the pastoral students identify what they need to do to grow their ministries, they choose pastoral activities from the menu that address those areas of ministry. The pastoral students study the pastoral activity (such as discipleship) under the tutelage of their trainer while simultaneously practicing what they learn.

At the point when the pastoral students are capable of implementing the pastoral activity and there is obvious fruit, the trainers and pastoral students proceed to a new pastoral activity. The trainers and the trainees continue this process, adding pastoral activities one by one as the trainees learn, practice, and develop specific areas of ministry.

4. Paul-and-Timothy-Style Mentorship

In Train & Multiply, the trainer serves as a Paul mentoring a Timothy. The trainer and trainee meet on a regular basis to evaluate completed studies and pastoral work as well as plan for subsequent studies and pastoral work. These highly relational mentoring sessions are key to cultivating momentum, accountability, and progress.

5. Multiplication

The methods of Train & Multiply hinge on the 2 Timothy 2:2 principle of reproduction. Pastoral students who reveal dedication and capacity eventually become pastoral trainers, thus creating an ongoing network of new pastoral trainers and pastoral students. In addition, Train & Multiply imparts to newly planted churches the vision and the capacity to plant new churches, thus creating an ongoing network of new churches.

6. Reproducibility

The methods of training and resources within Train & Multiply are tailored to be manageable and economical for any group of people. The main resources are the Bible, "Paul," "Timothy," a pastoral training menu, and a real-life context. This grassroots training method enables a larger pool of people to reproduce training in various contexts with multiplication at the core.

Personally, I have used Train & Multiply in Cambodia, and the principles are forever a part of my coaching style. More than anything, Train & Multiply has given me a framework to train in a low-profile manner, encouraging the development of indigenous leaders and churches.

How can you effectively train and multiply?

CONDUCT LOW-PROFILE MINISTRY IN SHORT-TERM MISSIONS

Those who do missions on a short-term basis may ask, "How do I build the capacity of local leaders and ministries in a short amount of time in a low-profile role?" It is my belief that the most powerful thing a short-term visitor can do is to boost the self-esteem of the local believers. If we go and do big things with our resources and expertise, we often cause the local believers to feel inadequate.

Allow me to share a generic example of building dignity and affirming the local culture: A short-term visitor might say, "We diligently practiced three contemporary songs to sing to the churches in Mongolia. We really wanted to perform well, and we decided we would bring some of our own instruments. At the end of the trip, we would leave our instruments with the local churches. But upon being present in a Mongolian church, the Holy Spirit revealed to me: 'Don't perform your songs. Praise the Mongolians for their music and worshipful attitudes. Invite them to teach you a Mongolian song, no matter how long it takes you. Then, at the end of your trip, perform the song with them.'"

How can you remain low-profile in short-term missions scenarios?

I believe with my whole heart that appreciating our hosts and showing a willingness to learn from them will do more than all our polished and well-intended high-profile ministries. Sometimes I have it so backwards! I need the Holy Spirit to give me an acute sense of the context around me, how to encourage "local champions" and set aside my need to be an "external savior".[5] My prayer for those of us who "do missions" is this:

Dear God,

You were a God who became a servant.

You taught more through serving than lording over others.

Enable us to walk in the shadows of international leaders who face the Son.

CHAPTER SIXTEEN

SUSTAINABILITY IN ACTION

"We have reached the point at which almost every facet of
the American missionary enterprise is significantly impacted by
money, money, money."

DAVID HESSELGRAVE

During my college years, missions students were challenged to conceptualize and organize a potential ministry in a country they had never visited. I understand the educational logic behind this method of teaching, but it also preconditioned me to think that I could actually sit back in North America and plan *my* ministry in someone else's country. Inevitably, the conceptualized plan included the resources that I would obtain and invest in my plan.

This line of thinking carried itself into reality as I entered Cambodia. I conceptualized and organized ministry by drawing from the resources that I could access and provide, while trusting that those who benefited from the ministry would eventually take full responsibility. I am learning more and more that I need to take the word "eventually" out of my vocabulary! According to Merriam-Webster, "eventually" means "at an unspecified later time: in the end." Sustainability is not something a group can "at an unspecified later time" or "in the end" take responsibility for. Rather, sustainability needs to be inborn and part of the overall DNA of one's missionary work from the beginning onward.

AVOID CONCEPTUALIZING AND ORGANIZING THE MISSIONARY TASK IN A WAY THAT IS NOT SUSTAINABLE AND REPRODUCIBLE

Gailyn Van Rheenen shares his straightforward thought on the subject: "The Western temptation is to conceptualize and organize the missionary task on an economic level that can only be sustained by Western support and oversight."[1] To conceptualize and organize in this manner is a temptation to missionaries and a snare to those who are on the receiving end of the missionaries' plans, as stated by a Latin American theological educator:

Non-contextualized churches carry out a ministry not suited to their reality while seminaries perpetuate theologies, methods, and strategies best suited to churches in an opulent and wealthy society.[2]

As North American missionaries, we have a propensity to impose our visions and drive those visions with our own resources and capabilities. Ken Stout, whose thesis is entitled *Fostering Sustainability & Minimizing Dependency in Mission Finances*, redirects us to work in such a manner that the local people are the ones who conceptualize and organize ministry suited for their context and contribution:

> If they operate out of a paradigm that believes that God has given them in their own community or region the resources they need to advance the kingdom, then they are released to use the full scope of their creativity, ingenuity, and resourcefulness to bring together the various elements to fulfill the visions and plans God has given them.[3]

Our role is to lead people of other nations to believe that God has visions to give them and that he will provide all they need from within themselves and among their own people. Our goal should be to facilitate the dreams of others, rather than to unfold our own dreams in someone else's backyard.

Timothy Mitchell is a missionary who implements training and mobilization among the Xhosa in Transkei, South Africa. Timothy and his wife share about their temporary relapse into organizing the missionary task in accordance with their foreign funds and oversight:

> Fundamental changes took place in our life and ministry. We now found ourselves working hand-in-hand with a Xhosa pastor. However, in our enthusiasm, we slipped into the age-old mistakes Western missionaries have so often made in Africa. As a result, we began reaping the enormous frustrations and disappointments that this approach can bring.
>
> Much as we longed for the local African leadership to take full responsibility and ownership for the operation, it just never happened. We found ourselves increasingly responsible for all the financing of the program and all the headaches of managing and motivating the whole concern. Although we aimed at sending out missionaries, very little fruit resulted. And although we planned to hand over leadership of the train-

ing centre into local hands, it never happened. Our students graduated, but invariably went back into secular work. Eventually the school closed down and joined the long list of Western models in Africa that never worked—models which were never indigenized and often stood out as an embarrassment to the people.

We came to see that local initiative can come only from local vision and ownership. This can ONLY happen with local funding. Westerners struggle with this process, because it is initially much slower. There are any number of Western Christians in the world only too eager to sponsor projects in Africa, thus hastening a parasite mentality ...We determined not to look outside the local community for any ministry funding. This is now working with exciting results! We teamed up with a man with the same thinking as ourselves and have seen in the last three years a highly missions-minded local church being established which is fully self-funded with full support for the pastor and his family and an appreciable monthly allowance to me, the "missionary", although most of our family salary continues to come from our own people.[4]

In Timothy's case, he had to fail before he could succeed. Originally, the motivation, drive, oversight, and provision were all in the hands of the missionary. When Timothy eventually conceptualized and organized his missions task in order to promote self-reliance in the local church, he saw the African leaders excel. The local church did not only achieve sustainability, but they sent their own missionaries to Mozambique. I have done my share of slipping into "age-old mistakes." Along with Timothy, I want to learn from my failures and strive to be one who contributes to sustainability versus unhealthy dependency.

When we conceptualize and organize ministry in other people's countries, we inevitably pass on our cultural trappings. These cultural trappings put an unnecessary yoke upon those we are supposed to empower. In their article "Dependency," Ronnie Hahné and Wouter Rijneveld quote missionary Charles Cook:

In fact, in our modern missionary endeavors we have been doing for our converts what they well may never be able to do for themselves (...) pay big salaries and build big buildings. A church does not have to have a building, it does not have to have a paid preacher. Who taught them otherwise? These are western concepts which are not necessarily biblical. Ideally, those of us who do missionary work in foreign places should be giving our new converts a model they can imitate, not one they may never be able to match (...). If an ax must fall upon the root of this problem it must be placed at the feet of American missionaries.[5]

Before we go any farther, I want to talk briefly about artificial sustainability. Allow me to share a generic example: The local church looked reasonably healthy. The members of the church tithed and supported their own pastor. The church had resources to grow and expand. Unfortunately, one day it all stopped. The members dwindled, and the flow of giving decreased. The church could not carry out its typical functions or pay its bills. What happened? How did this seemingly sustainable church go backwards?

Well, a majority of the members of the church benefited from a nearby missions-established school, which functioned due to foreign funding. The members of the church were either teachers, who drew their income from the school, or their children, who went to the school. When the school lost its overseas funding, it had an immediate effect on the members of the local church.

This is artificial sustainability. Although the church appeared to be locally supported, its source of ample resources could still be traced back to foreign-injected funds. When those funds stop, the church also stops (at least in the sense of how they are used to doing church). A seemingly sustainable church was propped up by a behind-the-scenes source of foreign funding.

I think we need to be more conscious of the vulnerability of churches that are propped up by foreign-funded projects. We have the mandate to mobilize people, not immobilize them by conceptualizing and organizing ministries that are not sustainable or reproducible in their local contexts.

How can you conceptualize and organize the missions task with sustainability and reproducibility in mind?

PLANT AT A SUSTAINABLE PACE

To plant at a sustainable pace means to allow local churches to discover and grow ministries at their own pace with their own local resources. For example, let's say members of a church plant express compassion for those with AIDS. The North American missionary mind immediately thinks, "A benevolence ministry." He or she follows that thought up with, "We will need this and that."

At this point, the missionary is well on his or her way to envisioning and funding a full-blown ministry. I suggest that this is the time for premeditated sustainability and the opportunity for the missionary to become a shadow pastor—

to stay in the background to pray and cheer the locals on as they grow their church.

If the local church implements a self-sustaining benevolence ministry, the process may look something like the following: They choose one family who has a member with HIV. They offer companionship, assistance in the garden, simple medical tasks, and prayer. As they gain experience and credibility, they multiply their efforts by inviting others from the church to be a part of this compassion experience with a new family. The church members start small and allow the compassion ministry to grow naturally around their own experience and local resources. No, this isn't a high-profile project with beds and full-time caretakers. Yet it is their ministry, and it is reproducible!

This principle of sustainable pacing should be implemented in regard to all functions of the church. In other words, allow the church to add functions and organize those functions at a pace that is doable for the locals in accordance with local resources mobilized by the indigenous people.

How can you plant at a pace that is sustainable for the local people?

MODEL COMPASSION IN REPRODUCIBLE WAYS

Since compassion is so close to our hearts, we tend to act upon it without thinking about how our response will affect other important components of life and ministry. In several cases in my own ministry, I responded to needs by locking my thought processes into the issues at hand.

I well remember one example. As a missionary and church planting coach, I was walking along a road with a group of four Cambodian church planters. We met a young man who was ill.

Before I continue, keep in mind that I was standing among church planters who would plant other churches in the near future and among potential new believers from the church plant that would eventually plant other churches. In addition, I was an outsider who would return to my home in the capital city when all was said and done.

Together, we prayed fervently for the man. Upon not seeing any improvement, I so wanted to drive the ailing man to the hospital in the capital city and pay his medical bills! I wanted him to receive competent medical help. But I was learning to ask questions instead of merely acting on instinct. Would these church planters have the ability to express compassion in the same way? What would happen the next time, when I was not there and the local church planters could not provide in the same manner for others? What would the community think of them? Would the community bypass their genuine yet meager help to ask for me? And if the answer is yes, do I just move on and inhale my innate compassion?

Instead of doing either—jumping in to help with my resources or swallowing my compassion—what if I model compassion by first allowing the church planters to think of ways to minister and by implementing methods that they can emulate in the future? Could the church planters do chores in the man's garden while he is ill? Perhaps they could pray with the man through the night, or they could keep the man hydrated, show moral support, and allow the family to make the major decisions for his care. Maybe they could facilitate the community to collect a compassion offering. Such contributions of compassion may seem small in comparison to a missionary intervening with resources only he or she can obtain, but they are heartfelt, and they can be done by the local believers within the realm of their capability.

Glenn Penner, who was the communications director for The Voice of the Martyrs, Canada, said it well:

> Our role needs to change from being perceived as the white knight riding in to rescue to that of being a player-coach seeking to mobilize local resources to meet local needs.[6]

It feels great to be a white knight riding in on an impressive horse—until you see your actions robbing those you are training of credibility and respect among their own people because they are unable to secure a horse.

Every missionary will face the dilemma of what to do when it seems like a need is calling your name. When I am safely sitting behind a computer writing a book, it seems easy to delay helping others through immediate reaction in order to think through all the ramifications. The reality is not so easy to deal with. However, in most circumstances, the need is not an emergency—a life-and-death situation in need of immediate reaction. Additionally, God is present. He is sovereign over life and death. In most circumstances, missionaries have time to think purposefully before enacting a plan.

I recall reading an article by Phil Parshall called "Missions and Money."[7] Phil tells the story of a missionary named Gary who worked among Muslims in a South Asian country. Gary had led three men who were farmers to Christ. These men and Gary met together on a weekly basis to sip tea and discuss their faith in Christ. One day, the three men presented Gary with a request for blankets and warm garments. Their thatched huts were no competition for the cold winds. As a missionary, Gary did his best to live meagerly so as to not outdo his neighbors; nonetheless, these three men could see that Gary had ways of keeping his family warm.

Phil Parshall presents his readers with two questions. The first question is: "How would you respond to these seemingly legitimate requests?" There was a time in my life when I would have fulfilled the men's request without a second thought. But Phil then presents us with the second question: "What are the issues that complicate a response?" This question is loaded with insight—the question itself informs us that the response to legitimate requests is not always straightforward.

You may be surprised that Gary decided not to meet the three men's material needs. Rather, his response was based on a more holistic picture of how his help might meet one need but actually create another and more severe problem. Gary had the insight to realize that if those Muslim-background believers walked away with goods from a foreigner, their community would deem them as traitors to their own identity for the sake of material benefits. In communal societies, isolation from community members has all sorts of economical and social fallout.

We may ask, "But isn't that fallout part of being persecuted for Christ's sake?" Real discernment is needed here. In this case, the men would not have been persecuted for their faith, but for their alliance with a foreign religion for the sake of material benefit. If people perceive others in their community as aligning themselves with a foreign religion for the sake of material betterment (which is sometimes the reality), there is no credible testimony.

Gary did not simply deny the three farmers help. He directed them to seek God as their provider. Gary himself prayed fervently for these men. When the three men came back to sip tea and learn about Christ together, the men informed Gary that the Lord had indeed met their needs. Eventually, five hundred Muslim-background believers became the fruit of these three faithful men who knew that God was sovereign. Gary did not deny his heart the opportunity to show compassion; rather, his compassion challenged the men to give God full opportunity to meet their needs in light of broader community concerns.

Think out of the box when it comes to compassion. Meeting a material need with the missionary's means is not the only way to show compassion! Sometimes, our passing out of our surplus can be interpreted merely as our duty and not as an act of love driven by a God of love. Tears, sincere visits in cold huts, praying with someone through the night, working alongside, listening for hours, laughing for hours, and being a friend through thick and thin all reveal compassion in reproducible ways.

How can you model compassion in reproducible ways?

BE CAUTIOUS OF INVITING RESPONSIBLE ADULTS INTO A PATERNALISTIC RELATIONSHIP

I have read missions books that refer to one stage of cross-cultural church planting as "parenting." The writers liken the missionary's role to that of a parent and the church's to that of a child during the infant stages of planting. It is believed that because the church is only beginning, the participants do not have the resources or capability to be financial givers and stewards of their ministry; thus, the missionary has a legitimate reason to temporarily supply the funds for growth, as you would do with a child.

Although new church plants certainly do go through an infant stage, there is a danger in this analogy. New believers within a particular culture are adults who managed their homes, finances, and businesses before the missionaries came along. Moreover, they have a traditional system of sharing and giving ingrained within their society and religion. In Cambodia, members of society habitually give to the monks and temples as part of their religious practice. Monks' meals come from food donated by everyday people, and temples are built with the donations of Cambodian citizens. Why would missionaries want to invite new believers in Christ to regress in giving and stewardship practices?

I suggest we view such people not as children, but as already capable stewards, redirecting them to share and give under the lordship of Jesus Christ. And if circumstances are such that people lack a proven stewardship of their families and livelihood, we certainly do not want to compound that by developing a paternalistic relationship that drives them even deeper into apathy.

How can you avoid paternalism in regard to the giving and stewardship of the local believers?

TEACH BIBLICAL STEWARDSHIP

There is no doubt that good, old-fashioned teaching about biblical stewardship is vital. But merely teaching about biblical stewardship will not necessarily produce healthy, self-sustaining churches, especially if churches are growing up in models that breed unhealthy dependency. On the other hand, we can promote methods that promote sustainability, but self-sustainability without the equally important emphasis of biblical stewardship is unattainable.

Malachi 3:7–12 reveals to us that a lifestyle which involves keeping our resources to ourselves and not giving back to God brings about poverty in our lives. A missionary concerned about self-sufficiency in Mali writes the following:

> Poverty as such is not the primary problem behind our churches' inability to achieve self-sufficiency. Disobedience to biblical principles of Christian stewardship is a key factor behind the problem of personal poverty, both spiritual and material (cf. Malachi 3:7–12). Furthermore, there is no stipulation in the entire Bible that would exonerate even a materially poor believer from honoring the Lord with his/her tithe. For this very reason I have often encouraged the poor to tithe even their very poverty to the Lord, explaining that ten percent of a poor man's loaf of plain bread is equal, if not superior, to the ten percent of a rich man's truckload of fine pastries and cakes!
>
> I also believe that obedience in this area is an important step in achieving material emancipation. The Lord does clearly promise to open the windows of heaven and pour out his blessing upon the tither (Malachi 3:10). However, it should be noted that this blessing does not come ex nihilo from heaven, but is a blessing given within the context of work that generates material sustenance, for it says, " ...I will prevent pests from devouring your crops, and the vines in your fields will not cast their fruit,' says the Lord Almighty" (Malachi 3:11).[8]

One of the major consequences of unhealthy dependency is a lack of motivation and discipline to give back to God and his kingdom work. If obedience in giving firstfruits to God is a step in achieving material emancipation, North Americans need to be alarmed at how our pipeline of money to churches around the world is shutting down their obedience in giving and earning a livelihood with their own hands.

The church principle of self-reliance is revealed in three vital ways in the Bible. First, we have the church described in the book of Acts. This community of believers shared everything in order to achieve self-sufficiency as a community (Acts 2:42–47). Second, Paul deliberately provided his own income—through tentmaking—as part of his apostolic strategy (Acts 18:2–3). Third, the principle of reaping from your own harvest—"those who preach the gospel should live from the gospel"—is another means to self-supporting (1 Corinthians 9:7–11).

Two of the most vivid examples of giving in the New Testament relate to those sharing out of poverty. The Macedonian church gave out of extreme poverty to the mother church in Jerusalem, and a poor widow gave all she had (1 Corinthians 8:1–13; Luke 21:1–40).

Paul encourages a life of generosity that does not flow one direction. He states in 2 Corinthians 8:14: "At the present time your plenty will supply what they need, so that in turn their plenty will supply what you need."

I can hear the objections in my head now. "See, at this time the North American church has plenty, so we should give our plenty to those in need around the world." However, when will that "present time" pass? How long will we treat the rest of the world as recipients? We cannot forget about an equally important Bible verse: "As it is written: He who gathered much did not have too much and he who gathered little did not have too little" (2 Corinthians 8:15). And we need to remember that Paul's statement in 2 Corinthians 8:14 is wrapped around a poor church giving to a mother church that was facing famine—a relief situation. There is no example in the Bible of one church assisting with or covering the operational expenses of another church. These are part of the core biblical responsibilities of the local church.

As missionaries, we cannot preach stewardship to a people while at the same time crushing that very people's potential for stewardship. Believers who view themselves as stewards and God as the owner and provider will richly generate indigenous churches that are Christ-reliant.

How can you teach biblical stewardship?

AFFIRM THE APOSTLE PAUL'S MODUS OPERANDI

Why is it that we so rarely talk about what Paul did not do? He did not build church buildings. He did not give out money. He did not start humanitarian projects. Paul did not create institutions and fund ministries to widows, but instructed Christian families and churches to take care of their own widows.

Christopher Little, who has vast missionary experience, brings to our attention that we have "concentrated on 'orthodoxy,' right or correct doctrine and thinking, to the exclusion of 'orthopraxy,' right or correct practice and action."[9] For example, many North American Christians believe that affluent churches in North America should provide subsidies to pastors and evangelists in other countries where they are fulfilling the Great Commission. This thinking is based on the numerous Scriptures that speak of being compassionate and generous to those who are less fortunate. Yet there is not one practical example of the apostle Paul—the guru of church planting—paying the leaders or providing operational costs of the churches (communities of believers) he planted.

Paul did give something, though; he gave himself. Reading Paul's orthodoxy (his epistles), we can see his orthopraxy:

> We loved you so much that we were delighted to share with you not only the gospel of God but our lives as well, because you have become so dear to us. Surely, you remember, brothers, our toil and hardship; we worked night and day in order not to be a burden to anyone while we preached the gospel of God to you. (1 Thessalonians 2:8–9)

Reflecting on Paul's orthopraxy, I believe missionaries and those who do missions in any form or fashion need to affirm Paul's modus operandi. Paul did very little nonchalantly. He was an intentional apostle who considered how each and every one of his actions would affect the pure spread of the gospel and the building of God's kingdom on earth. Paul, who integrated missions with the trade of tentmaking, fulfilled his calling throughout the whole Greco-Roman world:

> I have declared to both Jews and Greeks that they must turn to God in repentance and have faith in our Lord Jesus …Therefore, I declare to you today that I am innocent of the blood of all men. (Acts 20:21, 26)

Paul's bi-vocational method does not seem to have impeded or slowed him down. On the contrary, his method of sustaining himself was a strategic means to share the gospel and make disciples. Paul told the Corinthians that one who plants a vineyard does deserve grapes from that vineyard—technically, the churches Paul served had a duty to support the planter-apostle among them. However, Paul revealed that he deliberately denied himself this right so as not to hinder the gospel. He went so far as to say that he would rather die than compromise this value (1 Corinthians 9).

Why did Paul view his livelihood as a means to sharing the gospel and making obedient disciples?

In Cambodia, because so many missions organizations and teams pay subsidies to Christian workers (pastors, Bible school students, church planters, translators, service workers, etc.), opportunists often become involved in church, Christian fellowships, and ministry for betterment purposes. Sometimes their motives are mixed—interest in the gospel mingles with a desire to improve their economic opportunities. In many cases, the drive for personal benefits overshadows the drive to love and walk in obedience with God or to fulfill a true calling.

Astute onlookers see through this masquerade, and they become antagonistic toward what they consider hypocrisy and manipulation. This progression veils the purity and the grace of the gospel. Paul did not want money to rob the gospel of its effectiveness. As you read Paul's words to the Corinthians, keep in mind that Paul purposely denied his right to collect support:

> But I have not used any of these rights. And I am not writing this in the hope that you will do such things for me. I would rather die than have anyone deprive me of this boast. Yet when I preach the gospel, I cannot boast, for I am compelled to preach. Woe to me if I do not preach the gospel! If I preach voluntarily, I have a reward; if not voluntarily, I am simply discharging the trust committed to me. What then is my reward? Just this: that in preaching the gospel I may offer it free of charge, and so not make use of my rights in preaching it. (1 Corinthians 9:15–18)

A story I told earlier bears repeating here: A Kenyan pastor told me that when a man has no job, he sometimes will obtain a Bible and go from house to house until he meets a white man to fund his "ministry." Paul labored determinedly to avoid such a disgrace to God's kingdom work:

> You know, brothers, that our visit to you was not a failure. We had previously suffered and been insulted in Philippi, as you know, but with the help of our God we dared to tell you his gospel in spite of strong opposition. For the appeal we make does not spring from error or impure motives, nor are we trying to trick you. On the contrary, we speak as men approved by God to be entrusted with the gospel. We are not trying to please men but God, who tests our hearts. You know we never used flattery, nor did we put on a mask to cover up greed—God is our witness. (I Thessalonians 2:1–5)

Paul said that it is more blessed to give than to receive. Pastors, evangelists, and church planters who receive funds from overseas are viewed as chasers of a foreign religion and of the foreigner's pocketbook—in other words, as covetous. Will we lock believers around the world into the position of receivers and thus rob them of God's blessing? How will they model to those they disciple that it is more blessed to give than to receive if they are perceived as leeches?

I have not coveted anyone's silver or gold or clothing. You yourselves know that these hands of mine have supplied my own needs and the needs of my companions. In everything I did, I showed you that by this kind of hard work we must help the weak, remembering the words the Lord Jesus himself said: "It is more blessed to give than to receive." (Acts 20:32–35)

Missionaries frequently invite potential leaders or lay leaders out of their livelihoods so they can train or serve God in full-time ministry. In many of these cases, the missionaries then provide subsidies for those who no longer have a self-generated income. In contrast, Paul used his role as a tentmaker to become an accepted member in a network of relationships within the community and to model a work ethic, which is a key value to a life of sustainability.

After this, Paul left Athens and went to Corinth. There he met a Jew named Aquila, a native of Pontus, who had recently come from Italy with his wife Priscilla, because Claudius had ordered all the Jews to leave Rome. Paul went to see them, and because he was a tentmaker as they were, he stayed and worked with them. (Acts 18:3–4)

Make it your ambition to lead a quiet life, to mind your own business and to work with your hands, just as we told you, so that your daily life may win the respect of outsiders and so that you will not be dependent on anybody. (1 Thessalonians 4:11–12)

In the name of the Lord Jesus Christ, we command you, brothers, to keep away from every brother who is idle and does not live according to the teaching you received from us. For you yourselves know how you ought to follow our example. We were not idle when we were with you, nor did we eat anyone's food without paying for it. On the contrary, we worked night and day, laboring and toiling so that we would not be a burden to any of you. We did this, not because we do not have the right to such help, but in order to make ourselves a model for you to follow. For even when we were with you, we gave you this rule: "If a man will not work, he shall not eat." We hear that some among you are idle. They are not busy; they are busybodies. Such people we command and urge in the Lord Jesus Christ to settle down and earn the bread they eat. (2 Thessalonians 3:7–10)

Did Paul know something we do not? Is it worth taking a serious look at Paul's orthopraxy and his orthodoxy? If we had an opportunity to sit with Paul over a cup of tea and ask him about the International Partnership Movement, which centers on the West providing salaries for Christian workers in other nations, what would he most likely say?

How can you affirm the apostle Paul's modus operandi?

ENCOURAGE CULTURALLY RELEVANT GIVING PRACTICES

An African man was once asked why he never put anything into the offering. He responded, "Because my cow won't fit into the offering bag." Gideon Kiongo, in his article, "An Open Letter On Giving In Kenya," shares the following:

> The very offertory plates and baskets we use suggest an idea of what our people are expected to contribute. These are designed to hold money (notes and coins) which limit giving other things to the church. However, when you look at giving in both the Old and New Testaments, you clearly see the giving of substance which of course included money but was not limited to that. I believe the early teachers in giving to the Church in Africa misunderstood the essence of giving from an African perspective. I would go further and state that their "theology in giving" was not biblically balanced either. The examples that they used were that of the "coin" that Jesus instructed Peter to get from the fish so as to pay the government tax and that of the poor widow who gave two mites. Each of these narrations are instructive in giving. However, we should be aware of the context as we draw out the teaching. We have basically carried on the misconceptions started by those who first brought us the Gospel.[10]

A retired missionary who lived in Burundi told Gideon Kiongo about the culturally relevant giving practices of the people of Burundi. Beyond giving money, the churches emphasized and developed ways people could give labor and substance. Their substance included animals, fruits, and vegetables. Additionally, they designed corrals for holding animals as their offertory "plate." Kiongo goes on to say:

> This all reminds me of the church as narrated in the first chapters of the book of Acts. This exemplifies a doctrine understood by the African Church within its customs and values. This is where I believe those who

brought the Gospel could have done better. What will it take to undo the wrong teaching? We must talk about it. We must talk about it especially in our homes and in the market places. We must involve the very people in seeking to understand what God requires of us in obedience.[11]

There are so many creative and expressive ways to give to God. I have heard of several examples of churches in which the members set aside a handful of rice at every meal to use in sharing the gospel. Some believers have supported their pastors by plowing their fields. In the Bible, the function of tithing was delivered through the form of bringing the firstfruits to God. Passing an offering plate is a man-made, Western form to fulfill the biblical function of giving and sharing. As missionaries, we stifle and limit the giving of local churches because we impose and lock them into our cultural forms. Missionaries have the rare opportunity to encourage churches to give in a manner that makes sense to their culture while abiding by the principles of Scripture.

How can you encourage culturally relevant giving practices?

FACILITATE PEOPLE TO MOBILIZE THEIR LOCAL RESOURCES

Over the years, I have done my share of exploring community development and have learned useful principles to apply to church planting as well. Asset-based community development (ABCD) has largely replaced the needs-based approach to community development. Why the need for a replacement? The needs-based approach presents development in a negative light—the facilitator of development starts with diagnosing what is wrong or what is lacking. The facilitator uses questions that invite participants to identify their problems. Development experts have pointed out the obvious fact that a needs-based approach starts with a premise that the community is deficient and needy. This approach only drives people deeper into a hole of despair and dependence on someone else to fix their problems. Corbett and Fikkert summarize the issue well:

Starting with a focus on needs amounts to starting a relationship with low-income people by asking them, "What is wrong with you? How can I fix you?" Given the nature of most poverty, it is difficult to imagine more harmful questions to both low-income people and to ourselves! Starting with such questions initiates the very dynamic that we need to avoid, a dynamic that confirms the feelings that we are superior, that they are inferior, and that they need us to fix them…

Pouring in outside resources is not sustainable and only exacerbates the feelings of helplessness and inferiority that limits low-income people from being better stewards of their God-given talents and resources. When the church or ministry stops the flow of resources, it can leave behind individuals and communities that are more disempowered than ever before.[12]

I once heard a Ugandan pastor make this statement: "Africans were not poor until we were told we are poor." I am not sure if Pastor Grace was quoting someone else or merely making a statement, but the impact is there. The pastor expounded by making an analogy: "A particular person may feel quite well. But when someone comes up to the person and says, 'You look sick today,' he suddenly does not feel too well." A needs-based approach starts the development process by saying, "You look sick today."

Unlike the needs-based approach, the assets-based approach starts with the positive: What is working? What assets and capabilities do you have? In this case, the facilitator of development builds upon that which is healthy, mobilizes local resources from within the local context, and allows the participants to develop synergy with each other. Through this self-sustaining approach, the developer stimulates a mindset that says, "We have assets and skills to contribute. We are capable of implementing growth and change. We have dignity." An assets-based approach empowers people and protects against paternalism and dependency.

Bill Strickland birthed a vocational training center in the inner city of Pittsburgh called Bidwell Training Center (BTC). The training they offer is market-specific and designed for underemployed adults. Below are excerpts from an interview with Strickland found in the online magazine *Trap Door Sun*:

TDS: You have made the distinction that Manchester Bidwell is not a poverty center but a center for success. How has this simple distinction changed people's perception of the center?

STRICKLAND: We start off with the assumption that people are assets, not liabilities. When you run a poverty center, the assumption is that everyone is a liability and they are treated that way. We believe that life is precious, that people are born into the world as assets. It is their circumstances that limit their opportunities.

So, by changing the opportunities, we can change the behavior. By bringing students into a first class facility, with world-class technology and world-class faculty, we have been able to demonstrate effectively that we can take people who are considered liabilities on a balance sheet and move them to the asset side of the balance sheet so they become contributing members to society and to themselves.[13]

Strickland believes that people are born into the world as assets, and he operates the BTC in such a way as to communicate that to the students. Strickland states that circumstances limit people's opportunities. I believe that one of the best ways to overcome circumstances is to facilitate people to believe that they are the assets to make change and to show them how to mobilize their resources for that change. (Please keep in mind that the BTC was not a North American ministry envisioned on the shores of America and then implemented in another country. BTC mobilized their local resources to develop the poor in their own local communities.)

Many of us have encountered a common missions practice in which a guest speaker at a conference provides the money for the facilities, meals, and attendee transportation. In regard to this practice, a story comes to mind. Pastor Kabutye, from Uganda, was invited to conduct a conference in another part of Africa. Those holding the conference communicated to Pastor Kabutye that they were very poor and needed his financial help to conduct the conference. The organizers of the conference sent Pastor Kabutye a budget of one thousand shillings. Pastor Kabutye told them that he would bring the money if they agreed to plan the conference and mobilize the people.

Pastor Kabutye brought one thousand shillings to the conference, but he intentionally waited to disburse the funds. His first order of business was to check and see if the hosts of the conference had indeed both organized the conference and mobilized the people. He was delighted to see that they had followed through with their commitment. He affirmed them for their hard work. Then he said something along these lines: "Let's see if we can mobilize the participants to come up with a creative way to provide meals." After some degree of dialogue, the participants agreed to bring their own meals, but eat together.

After three full days of a successful conference, the one thousand shillings was not needed. Pastor Kabutye implemented an assets-based approach which empowered the local facilitators of the conference to mobilize their own resources and complete a successful conference in a self-reliant manner.

Likewise, I believe we need to use an assets-based approach to church planting.

This approach includes conceptualizing and planting the church in a way that is sustainable for the local people. Furthermore, it includes encouraging the church to identify their own assets and mobilize their local resources. Instead of providing places to meet, instruments for worship, equipment for events, and resources for outreach, we can facilitate the church to ascertain what resources they need and provide those resources for themselves. May we endeavor to ensure that the goal is attainable and the people are capable, both components of sustainability. Their church experience may not look and sound like the missionary's church experience, but it will be their church. Churches with dignity will change the world; churches without dignity will be downtrodden by the world.

How can you facilitate those in your realm of influence to mobilize local resources?

AIM FOR LONG-TERM, SYSTEMIC CHANGE

Often, our approaches fix people's problems temporarily or leave them in worse condition than when we intervened. In Cambodia, I frequently saw tractors broken down, medical equipment shoved in a corner, and nonfunctioning wells. Family after family received bags of rice and supplies only to find themselves needing those very items three weeks later. For these reasons, more and more social action organizations are moving away from giving to others and doing for others.

I recall reading about two different well projects in Central America. The first project resulted in temporary relief, and the second project led to long-term systemic development. Bob Lupton shares about how his church from North America dug a well for a community in a village in Honduras.[14] The village cheered with exuberance when the well was completed and water was available. When the team from North America revisited the village one year later, they found that the well wasn't working and the people had returned to their old methods of hauling water. The team quickly repaired the pump and eventually returned home. I wish I could tell you that when the team visited for the third time the villagers were using the well, but that is not the case. The well project in Honduras is an example of temporary change with no sustainability plan in mind.

Lupton tells about another well project in Nicaragua that led to long-term systemic change. In this case, a local microlending organization hired a community developer from North America. The community developer did not make a plan for the villagers in regard to a well, but instead facilitated the members of the village to make a plan. The villagers invested some of their own money and provided all the labor. The community developer accessed a Nicaraguan engineer who trained the villagers in how to maintain the well, set fees, collect payments, and manage finances. Not only did the well provide that immediate village with water, but they were able to sell water to other villages. This well project in Nicaragua is an example of aiming for long-term systemic transformation.

One way of mobilizing local resources for the purpose of long-term systemic results is to facilitate income generation, which includes men and women using local resources to develop a livelihood. My coworker and I tried this with some Cambodian church planters. We taught the church planters an exercise routine called Tae Bo (a mixture of aerobics, boxing, and kicking). Upon learning the technique and several routines, the church planters conducted exercise routines for the public. They made an income, and the job itself was mobile. I learned a great deal in this income-generation experience, and I still have so much more to learn!

In their book *The Poor Will Be Glad*, Peter Greer and Phil Smith direct people away from traditional handouts and toward a new movement, Microfinance Movement (MF), which involves providing small loans to facilitate long-term self-improvement:

> This movement is radically different from traditional charity. It focuses on long-term systemic change and lasting employment patterns, not short-term quick fixes.[15]

In order to make such a loan program sustainable and able to be extended to others, loan repayment is essential. With this in mind, realize that there are certain ways of implementation that encumber loan repayment and other ways that facilitate loan repayment. To gain an understanding of effective microloans, I suggest you start with the books *When Helping Hurts* and *The Poor Will Be Glad*. More and more people experienced in microlending are facilitating the local people to provide their own initial funds instead of starting with the loan funds from the outside. Stimulating funds from among those who are poor may seem undoable, but there is evidence that it works and is all that much more healthy.

This whole approach is woven into a biblical understanding of people. God created human beings with a built-in work ethic. He invited humans to be a part of his creation stewardship by directing them to work and take care of his creation. Paul exhorted the Thessalonians with these words:

Make it your ambition to lead a quiet life, to mind your own business and to work with your hands, just as we told you, so that your daily life may win the respect of outsiders and so that you will not be dependent on anybody. (1 Thessalonians 4:11–12)

As people trying to fix poverty in others' lives, we can easily sabotage the process of cultivating self-respect in those others and allowing them to win the respect of outsiders through our gallant but uninformed efforts. May we commit to fostering healthy work ethic, long-term systemic change, and lasting employment patterns. In other words, may we mobilize people to labor for their own well-being instead of laboring for them.

How can you foster long-term systemic change and lasting employment patterns?

PRACTICE THE PRINCIPLE OF GEOGRAPHICAL PROXIMITY

Practicing the principle of proximity is another way to encourage local leaders and churches not to bypass local assets.

A church planting movement in India implements what they call "a theology of resources in the harvest."[16] In other words, they look for resources in the harvest field instead of outside the harvest field. Glenn Schwartz calls this same concept "the principle of geographical proximity." This principle encourages us to meet local needs from within the closest geographical proximity as possible. When there are needs, the idea is to find the resources to address the needs by starting with the individual, then the family, then the extended family, and so forth. Please see the diagram below.

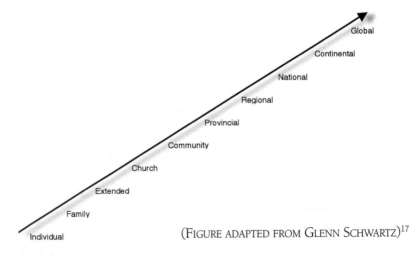

(FIGURE ADAPTED FROM GLENN SCHWARTZ)[17]

Local ministries and churches have been influenced by missionaries and Western churches to bypass the geographical proximity of the individual, family, extended family, church, local community, and provincial, national, regional, and continental resources in order to obtain resources from a global setting. If assistance is always or often provided through missionaries, churches, visitors, or organizations from the global context, the locals will rarely look to themselves, their families, their extended families, or their church or local community. Who would? For example, if the global community takes care of the local community's orphans, why would families or extended families or provincial services or national services bother to do the work of caring for their own orphans?

I am aware of the reasoning that says many of the provincial and national entities responsible for human needs are corrupt and have no intention of taking care of their own. While this is sometimes true, is it really a profitable solution to create a dependency syndrome by ignoring the principle of geographical proximity? Could it possibly be substituting a problem with another problem? I have many question marks in this paragraph because the issues are complicated, and I know there are no easy answers.

Better Care Network (BCN) is an organization that is trying to help people concerned about orphan care to research, discuss, and consider alternatives to the typical donor-driven, high-expense institutional orphanages. In order to stimulate more constructive thought, BCN requested that John Williamson (a senior technical adviser for USAID's Displaced Children and Orphans Fund) and Aaron Greenberg (chief of child protection for UNICEF) write a working paper on the topic of better care alternatives for orphans.[18] The authors express their belief that institutional and residential care are overused and seem to be the default method.

Interestingly to me, the authors explore alternatives that mobilize care in accordance with the principle of geographical proximity: family, extended family, and community. Some of the orphan-care alternatives suggested by Williamson and Greenberg are family support and strengthening, family reunification, kinship care, foster care, Kafalah (the Islam practice of permanently caring for an orphan while allowing the child to maintain his or her family name for lineage purposes), and adoption. I will not take time to explain each of these types of care, except to say that the alternatives are family-based instead of relying on foreign-driven, globally resourced orphanages.

Codrington Ntabeni worked as a local aid worker in Africa. He became disturbed by how the international aid organization he worked for completely ignored the principle of geographical proximity:

> This food aid organization seems to be perpetuating the problem in our community. Why do I say that? For one thing, I know this drought is severe, but they are virtually ignoring the people in our community who have resources they could give. Their solution is to bring aid by the lorry load from overseas. They also bring the money to pay, not only for the food and the lorries, but they also pay the people like me who help to distribute it. There are believers and non-believers alike in our community who could help with the food needed in the rural area. I wish we could mount a massive local campaign to get our people involved in meeting that need. But sometimes I wonder why we should. After all, this aid organization will pay people to do it for us. But deep down inside I know that's not right.
>
> Part of my frustration goes back to the day I joined this organization. At that time I asked what percentage of the aid we give will come from people in my country. I was given the impression that it is too frustrating to try to motivate local people in drought relief and that it was simply easier and more effective to get the aid from overseas. My frustration was further compounded when I learned that this aid organization for which I now work has a certain budget which must be used up each month or the people overseas will cut back on what they send the next month...
>
> Let me tell you what I think we ought to be doing. I think we ought to first look to our own people for as much as they can give to those in drought stricken parts of our country. After all, some of those needy people are relatives of those of us who live in towns and other parts of the country where food supplies are adequate. But frankly, how can we be expected to give sacrificially toward needy people in our rural areas when the aid organizations have a quota to be given away each month.[19]

Codrington Ntabeni's experience points to the neglect of the principle of geographical proximity. One can practically hear the exasperation in his words. In his case, as in so many, quick solutions have trumped long-term health. May we build on Ntabeni's ideas by using the principle of geographical proximity to deliberately plan for sustainability and self-reliance in our missions work!

How can you practice the principle of geographical proximity in your missions work?

PROMOTE LOCAL-LOCAL INTERDEPENDENCE

A timely "no" can actually serve as an act of compassion. That is what I learned when I met Williams, a resident of Zambia. Williams knows about sixteen languages. You might picture him as an interpreter for the United Nations, but Williams plants churches. He learns these languages as he befriends people within countries such as Malawi, Mozambique, and Botswana. His mother supports him by selling fruits and vegetables from her garden.

One day, Williams decided to build a house for his mother and sister so they would no longer need to live in a rented house. Glenn Schwartz, a coach in self-reliance, allowed Williams to benefit from local-local interdependence in regard to the completion of his mother's home, and he also teamed up with Williams to conduct a self-reliance conference in Mozambique.

In Africa, Glenn spent time with Williams in his home village. Williams explained to Glenn that he had built the walls of his house but did not have the means to put on the roof. I am sure that everything within Glenn wanted to help Williams finish the house. However, Glenn seized the opportunity to facilitate Williams to seek out fellow pastors or businesspeople to help support his church planting ministry. Glenn helped contact some of the local pastors and businessmen. Within a reasonable amount of time, a local African pastor took interest in Williams and his ministry. The local pastor assisted Williams in putting a roof on his house and with other needs related to his ministry. Furthermore, the local pastor and Williams have formed a supportive friendship and have joined hands in ministry.

What would likely have happened if Glenn had provided the resources to build the roof of Williams's house? Glenn would have met one need and gone on his way to America. He would have met that need with global resources and stripped the opportunity from someone locally to share resources and long-term, tangible friendship with Williams.

In the end, Williams received help from a local pastor and formed an ongoing partnership with someone who breathes the same air he does. Moreover, I imagine that a fellow citizen helping his neighbor created a more powerful testimony for the gospel than if a seemingly "rich American" had helped Williams. A painful "no" led ultimately to a healthier and more holistic outcome. Saying no often opens up opportunity for local believers and churches to fulfill the "one another" commands written in the Bible. Glenn says it best:

How does one deal with the question about not caring which I mentioned earlier? The most caring thing one might do is to think so highly of the gifts, abilities and privileges of local leaders that the outsider wouldn't under any circumstance want to interfere.[20]

Glenn promotes what he calls "local-local interdependence." In this case, he created an opportunity for a local pastor to support a local church planter. Supplying global financial resources often undermines local-local interdependence. Western churches try to fulfill their sense of global interdependence by pouring funds into provinces and villages across the globe, all the time destroying local-local interdependence.

In Acts 2:42–47, Luke writes about a community of believers who practiced local-local interdependence:

They devoted themselves to the apostles' teaching and to the fellowship, to the breaking of bread and to prayer. Everyone was filled with awe, and many wonders and miraculous signs were done by the apostles. All the believers were together and had everything in common. Selling their possessions and goods, they gave to anyone as he had need. Every day they continued to meet together in the temple courts. They broke bread in their homes and ate together with glad and sincere hearts, praising God and enjoying the favor of all the people. And the Lord added to their number daily those who were being saved.

What might have happened if someone from outside the community had offered this fellowship a generous amount of money? Local-local interdependence is a key ingredient to movements for Christ.

How can you promote or avoid hindering local-local interdependence?

AIM FOR PSYCHOLOGICAL OWNERSHIP, NOT FUNCTIONAL OWNERSHIP

I remember quite well when my parents would allow me to functionally drive their car. In other words, they owned the car, and they allowed me to occasionally drive it. One morning, I was washing the dishes and staring out the window. As my eyes scanned the car, I saw stems of grass and weeds sticking out of the hubcap of the front tire. "I am in trouble," I said under my breath. I ran outside and immediately tried to remove the grass. How had the grass attached itself in the hubcap? The night before, I was out with some friends. We were decorating the trees of our teacher with toilet paper. This outing involved some fast driving upon leaving the scene. I was the one driving, and I took a corner too fast, hence the weeds and mud.

Many years later, I bought a used car with my own money. And your automatic assumption is correct: I drove my own car with the utmost caution. (Oh, and by then, I was too mature to toilet-paper the trees of people's private residences.) I worked hard to earn money, and I bought the car myself. This effort created within me a sense of psychological ownership—I was a diligent steward of my own car.

Glenn Schwartz speaks about three types of ownership in his book *When Charity Destroys Dignity*: legal, functional, and psychological.[21] *Legal ownership* is merely the giving of a document that indicates the change of ownership from one person to the next. *Functional ownership* relates to being functionally placed in a role that serves another's objectives. *Psychological ownership* is a sense of ownership created by being a part of something from the very conception and contributing throughout every stage from one's own resources (time, effort, finances, skills, etc.). Below, I give two examples to help clarify the difference between functional ownership and psychological ownership:

Functional ownership: A missionary plans to go to Guatemala in about five months. He desires to work with city kids. While watching his son play basketball, an idea comes to mind: "Why don't I build a youth center to offer the kids something to do besides hang out on the streets?" Even before going to Guatemala long-term, the missionary raises funds for a youth center. Upon arriving, the missionary obtains permission and all the proper documents to begin building. Within six months, the spacious youth center is completed. The missionary announces job opportunities for youth counselors by way of the churches. Initially, he hires eight people to help him implement this youth ministry. The missionary builds a thriving ministry and has plenty of local people around him to make it a success.

Two years after the youth center is established, the missionary needs to return to the States for health issues. The missionary releases funds from his account to meet the expenses of the youth center, but eventually those funds dry up. The local staff and youth counselors care about the ministry, but not enough to dig in and rescue the ministry financially. Here and there, donations are sent, but the staff and counselors leave this ministry one by one. No one rises to serve as a local champion of the ministry.

Psychological ownership: A missionary is sitting with a group of young Thai believers. They have just finished an energetic game of football (soccer). They look over and see several young boys causing a ruckus. The football players dialogue about how they desire to minister to kids who have no role models in their lives. The missionary can think of all kinds of ideas. In spite of this, he keeps quiet. He asks the boys a couple of questions to stimulate their creative thinking. After much dialogue and a few jokes, the group decides to organize football teams and seek out volunteers from churches to serve as coaches.

Each Thai believer leaves with a delegated task to begin implementing throughout the week. As time passes, this enthusiastic group of believers develops an effective football ministry, and they even train other churches in how to do the same in their communities. Occasionally, the missionary plays football with the youth, but for the most part, he remains low profile. One day, the missionary dives into the dirt to protect the net from a possible goal. His leg catches the edge of the net, and he severely twists his leg. After medical care, he is mostly housebound due to limited mobility. His absence has no affect on the soccer ministry. Of course, they miss him, but the ministry excels without him.

Mission-established ministries in which the locals have only functional ownership usually cannot survive without the missionaries' drive and money. Those locals who serve out of a sense of functional ownership view their role as a job. They consider their contribution significant but feel they are helping someone else fulfill his or her ministry. If their needs are not met or a better opportunity comes along, they easily move on. If the missionary in the first example were to try to transfer the youth ministry to local people, they would expect him to finance it. In times of difficulty, those who have inherited the ministry may effortlessly walk away, concluding that it was not their dream in the first place.

As missionaries, I advise that we aim for psychological ownership, not functional ownership. Psychological ownership gives the local church the sense that a particular ministry is their responsibility under the lordship of Jesus

Christ. Psychological ownership is the fuel that drives the church to believe, to sacrifice, to share, to pray, to love, and to depend on God at all times. We create psychological ownership by refraining from organizing our own ministries in cross-cultural settings that later need to be transferred over to locals. Instead, we facilitate local believers and churches to dream, plan, and organize according to their passion, discernment, and ability to mobilize people and local resources.

James Avery and Bruce Avolio have developed a psychological ownership questionnaire (POQ) to assist organizations in measuring psychological owner-ship among their employees.[22] They suggest that there are four dimensions to "promotive psychological ownership," as they term it: self-efficacy, accountability, sense of belongingness, and self-identity. Let's look at these four dimensions in relationship to "doing missions."

- SELF-EFFICACY means that a person feels a sense of worth in his or her role. Self-efficacy cancels that feeling that one is merely a hireling of the foreigner.
- ACCOUNTABILITY ensures that a participant of any ministry or church recognizes that his motives, character, and actions are directly linked to those whom he serves and serves with. When a ministry or church is donor-driven and funded by foreigners, accountability among the local participants becomes impotent.
- A SENSE OF BELONGING causes people to view those around them as a community rather than an organization or a source to a paycheck.
- SELF-IDENTITY refers to a person being aware of his or her presence in the ministry and recognizing that he or she has the ability to influ-ence for the positive.

Self-efficacy, accountability, sense of belongingness, and self-identity all arise out of psychological ownership. Importing people into your ministry, or trans-ferring a ministry founded and funded by you to others, leads to functional own-ership but undermines psychological ownership. Without psychological ownership, a ministry will flounder.

Psychological ownership does not just happen. We need to intentionally sow psychological ownership as we implement the missionary task.

How will you sow psychological ownership in your missions work?

Avoid Creating Needs-Based Faith Due to Handouts That Accompany the Spread of the Gospel

While I was in Mongolia, I sat with about twelve members of a local church. They were trying to plant a church in a local district nearby. These church planters were experiencing some difficulties and asked for advice. As we dialogued, they shared about an experience in which they had bought and given a ger (a round, cone-shaped tent made with wood boards and wool) to a family within that district. The intention of the church planting team was to show compassion to a family that lived in crowded conditions by providing them with living quarters.

However, the benevolent act backfired. In a rather short amount of time, the family sold the ger and returned to living in tight quarters. They sold the ger to buy alcohol or whatever else they deemed more important than housing. Ultimately, the community members became jealous and antagonistic toward the recipients of the ger, and the ger was not used for its intended purpose. The story illustrates a common problem: handouts accompanied by evangelism often become counterproductive.

I am aware of a question that crosses many concerned minds: "How can a man or woman hear the gospel with an empty stomach?" My goal here is not to deny or affirm this rhetorical question. Rather, I want us to seriously consider that handouts—material goods and services given freely—along with the gospel often become the enemy of the intended goal of making sincere disciples of Christ.

The first shortcoming of combining incentives with the spread of the good news is that this method has the tendency to produce superficial conversions. Glenn Schwartz words it this way:

> When outside money and other material things accompany the spread of the Christian Gospel, sometimes people get the wrong impression about the Gospel itself. For example, if those to whom the Gospel is preached begin to receive material things that come with the Gospel, they may become more interested in those things than in the Gospel itself …When people come into the Christian faith for the material possessions they get, something goes terribly wrong in the spread of the Gospel. That might be the single most important reason why the dependency problem so often cripples the Christian movement and why it is so urgent that it be avoided or dealt with where it exists.[23]

The picture below shows a Cambodian man who received both a Christian booklet and bags of rice. This is an ideal picture to express the popular derogatory phrase "rice Christians." The very real problem of rice Christians is a result of people participating in Christianity at some superficial level to receive life-improvement perks. The perks often play a more significant role in their responses to the gospel than faith or commitment to be a disciple of Christ.

In a popular newspaper called *The Phnom Penh Post*, an interview with Cambodian Christians was published. Below are a few responses of those Cambodians who were interviewed:

> Thay admits she understands little of anything about basic Christian doctrine ("I can't remember any of the words we say in church," she says with a laugh) but she is convinced she made the right decision. "Buddhism taught me that I had to be responsible for myself, but with Christianity a community of people take care of you..."
>
> Buon Hari, Thay's 18-year-old daughter, is more explicit about the temporal rewards of the Christian faith she herself embraced six months ago. "The American missionaries give poor families like us $50 a month if we join their church," she told the Post...
>
> "In the border camps just about everybody was a Christian," Vouen says. People thought that by having a certificate of baptism it would make life easier in a new country."[24]

When I was learning the language in Cambodia, I taped a poster of the Cambodian alphabet on my wall. Due to the humidity, the tape lost its stickiness, and I often found the poster on the ground. Adhesion is temporary. A "conversion" made when a need is met along with the presentation of the gospel may adhere for a while, but when the troubles of life inevitably come and handouts are not readily available, the believer often detaches from God.

Ronnie Hahné and Wouter Rijneveld give us helpful insight to understand the difference between "adhesion" and "conviction" as it relates to conversion:

> One of the goals of mission work is conversion of people. Of course, the final goal is the glory of God and the establishing of churches comprises more than conversion of people. Still, this is the basis. Conversion is the work of the Holy Spirit, which He works by means of his Word.
>
> In sociology, conversion is usually distinguished in two levels: adhesion and conviction. At the first level, one changes his formal affiliation from one group or religion to another group. The deeper level of conversion is conviction, where the opinions of the new group or religion are really internalised (Nock 1933 cited in Gaventa 1992). We would like to define this second level of conversion as "being a dedicated and committed Christian," leaving the theological judgment about the "trueness" of the conversion where it belongs: to God. This description of the conviction level expressly includes the cost-aspect of being a Christian.
>
> It is clear for us, that in mission work, this second level of conversion should be our goal, since the first would tend to nominalism...
>
> From the perspective of incentives for conversion, we suggest that "money," "power," "status" offered can be incentives that lead to adhesion, while "exemplary living" and "contextualized evangelism and preaching" are incentives that lead to cohesion. This is another way of saying that rice-Christians are often weak and nominal Christians.[25]

In many cases, I do feel that the offer of betterment through the handouts, assistance, and jobs that come with the existence of missions organizations have replaced the hard work of "exemplary living" and "contextualized evangelism and preaching." We may have even elbowed out the Holy Spirit from his conviction work. We should be leery of speedily planting first-generation churches of conformity and not conversion.

Jay Moon, who served with SIM in Ghana until 2005, gives us something serious to think about:

> While the church in Africa is growing at a tremendous rate, the Scripture has not reached deeply into the worldview of the culture. Events like the 1994 genocide in Rwanda, considered by many as one of the most Chris-

tian countries in Africa and the center of the famous East African revival, reveal the tragic consequences when Scripture reaches only the surface level of culture but does not penetrate into the deeper worldview level.[26]

I am sure a variety of vital factors contributed to the genocide in Rwanda. Yet, I am also sure that "adhesion conversion" does not produce disciples of Christ who live out their faith at a level of innermost conviction.

Jesus himself experienced adhesion conversion when he filled the stomachs of five thousand people. After the miraculous feeding, those very people feverishly followed him to other places. However, Jesus saw through to their motives: "I tell you the truth, you are looking for me, not because you saw miraculous signs but because you ate the loaves and had your fill" (John 6:26).

Conformity weakens the testimony of Christ. People see through conformity, and it creates distaste in their hearts for the gospel. People observe that "adhesive believers" speak better English, wear better clothes, and have better jobs, but behave exactly the same as before they became Christians. This lack of credible testimony serves as a huge roadblock to a movement for Christ. In cases of conformity, missionaries hold just as much, if not more, responsibility than the conformer. We need to be aware of the reasons for conformity and form strategies to encourage true transformation.

Beyond superficial conversion, handouts that accompany the gospel create a needs-based faith. Such a faith causes believers to not give back to the community of Christ. Rather, they perceive the church as their patron and themselves as the client. In other words, they develop a mindset that the church's role is to meet their needs. Many Cambodian pastors have become troubled when members of the church expected the church to loan them money, pay their medical bills, give them gifts, and produce other material benefits, while giving or sharing very little with the church body themselves. People who experience a needs-based faith desire Christianity to benefit them and rarely develop a lifestyle of sharing.

Another drawback to handouts is that they can be interpreted as manipulation or buying converts. I must tell you that while many people want the handouts that accompany the spread of the gospel, there is another whole segment within any given society who will become more resistant to God because of those same handouts. Remember the response of Dorje and Pasang from Tibet:

Dorje and Pasang had heard that Christians were always trying to get people of other faiths to leave their own religion and become Christian.

Friends had told them that wherever the Christians go, they start Western style schools, hospitals, and development programs, and that this was the way they got people to convert to Christianity. Both Tibetans agreed that the Christians should not do this. From what they had seen, to become a Christian one would first have to stop being a Tibetan and become a foreigner. If that was the case then it was better to remain a Buddhist.[27]

When it looks as if people are becoming Christians to receive help, others in the community will think that Christianity attracts the cowardly and poor. Glenn Schwartz informs us that subsidy and handouts wreak havoc on the self-image and community image of churches—on how a church sees itself and on how outsiders see the church. Schwartz once spoke with a woman in Uganda who made this alarming statement:

> Do you know what people think of us when we become church members? They say to us, "Why do you join those Christians who are poor and beg for money from overseas? I don't want to do that."[28]

When the self-image and community image of the church of Christ suffers, there really is nothing to build on. May we keep in mind that our means to spread the gospel can actually become a hindrance to the gospel.

Another troubling aspect of using incentives to accompany the spread of the gospel is that this method is not reproducible, especially if the missionary uses materials and funds from his or her home country to provide gifts, helps, and services. The indigenous people may tend to believe that they need something in their hands to give away at all times. We may unknowingly teach them a new mindset: "Silver and gold I do have!" (Acts 3:6).

There is a common phrase spoken among those who promote microenterprise and workfare: "Give a hand up, not a handout." What does a hand up look like? We could try to pray, for starters. A miracle is a type of help, but the glory bypasses the missionary and goes to God. We could spur on local believers to creatively show love in action in accordance with their own culture, capabilities, and resources. That might be as simple as crying with someone or sharing a meal. Loving relationships, through thick and thin, provide for a need that is usually deeper than a physical need.

How can you avoid creating a needs-based faith?

UNDERSTAND HOW PATRON-CLIENT RELATIONSHIPS AFFECT CHURCH PLANTING

Missionaries can avoid creating a needs-based faith by understanding how patron-client relationships affect church planting and avoiding them. A missionary hired a Cambodian to serve as an interpreter for a ministry that worked with kids who lived on the streets. In a matter of days, the missionary shared his faith and invited the Cambodian interpreter to attend church. The interpreter regularly went to church and seemed to talk the same language as other believers in Christ. The missionary was so pleased that his interpreter had become a Christian. Eventually, this ministry to children living on the streets reached the end of their contract. Hence, the interpreter lost his job and needed to find another livelihood.

The interpreter had an uncle who worked at the post office as a supervisor. The uncle gave his nephew a job serving under him. The translator stopped going to church within two weeks of working at the post office. Why did he withdraw from church and other believers in Christ? In this case, his Christian experience was superficial and was tied to the missionary as his supervisor. The interpreter took on the interests, beliefs, and values of his Christian boss while working for him. Now that his uncle was the key to his well-being, he rather quickly aligned himself with his uncle's beliefs and values.

This whole experience was influenced by what is called a patron-client relationship. From my conversations with others, I understand that patron-client relationships exist in many parts of the world, which makes them worthy of consideration as we examine their influence on missions work.

Patron-client relationships define how social relationships are formed and conducted based on people's status within a society. Patron-client relationships are unspoken yet understood between the people on either end. The person with the higher status within the relationship is considered the patron, and the person with the lower status is the client. The patron and client have interrelating roles. The patron provides for and protects the client. In return, the client is loyal and serves the patron. The client will most often take on the beliefs, values, and views of the patron as part of his loyalty. This explanation casts light on the scenario of the interpreter and his quick exit from faith in Jesus upon losing his patron, the missionary.

In a patron-client method of church planting, the missionary sets himself or herself up in a role of being needed by the local people. He or she offers medical, linguistic, educational, or construction services that cause the locals (the clients) to need and depend on the missionary (the patron). The more social services and assistance provided, the more the missionary is perceived as the patron. Some see this role as worth capitalizing on, as it gives the missionary an edge to influence people for Christ. John Smith (a pseudonym) gives his perspective on patron-client mentalities based on his experiences in Bangladesh:

> For better or for worse the "patron-client" mentality has become firmly embedded in local Bangladeshi culture. Foreigners are often viewed as moneybags who must be praised and eulogized but manipulated shrewdly whenever possible. It has been said that a foreigner is like a faucet; he may not be flowing now, but if you stick around long enough, the money will eventually begin to flow.[29]

Those who practice the patron-client mentality did not come up with this seemingly manipulative behavior on their own; it comes from hundreds of years of outside patrons imposing themselves on people of other countries through colonization.

The reality is that patron-client mentalities and relationships are prevalent in many parts of the world, so missionaries need to be aware of the dangers of being cast in a patron role as it relates to dependency and paternalism. Dr. William Kornfield, in his article "Results of Paternalism and Some Viable Results," shares an example of how patron-client relationships affect the interchange between both parties:

> In many cases the Western cultural transplant is reflected in large evangelistic campaigns, usually financed by North America or Europe. In some cases the only cultural adjustment is the direct translation from English into the receptor language, thus negating major cross-cultural factors affecting decision-making. For example, Latin American evangelists trained in North America are usually people of a higher status—the upper middle class. The sociological lower class people of Latin America will often respond during an invitation—not necessarily because of the convincing power of the Holy Spirit calling them to repentance, but rather because their culture of courtesy obliges them to respond positively to a higher class person.
>
> In following up two major evangelistic efforts in Bolivia, I found that the number of people attending an evangelical church a year later was around 1% of the total number of professions of faith. Alfredo Smith, a noted Latin American pastor-evangelist with the C&MA, came

up with identical statistics. Statistics such as these have caused some Latin American leaders to rethink the value of Westernized evangelistic campaigns.[30]

It is possible that those who do missions from North America may have lost the ability to plant the gospel in other nations without setting ourselves up in a patron-client relationship. We use our expertise, services, and money to put ourselves in a position where people need us, and then we share the gospel from that patron platform. But in the long run, is patron-client evangelism reproducible for those who emulate us? Can they constantly bring the gospel to their cities and villages by providing goods and services? Furthermore, is this approach even biblical? Was Paul tossed out of so many places because he made himself needed by the people he ministered to? Why was the apostle Paul driven—often violently—from so many cities and towns? Did he not know about the patron-client method of church planting?

Phil Parshall is a missionary who served in Bangladesh and the Philippines for forty-four years. The Bangladeshis referred to Phil using two very different titles. At one point, they called him "Boro Sahib," which is comparable to the English acronym "VIP" (very important person). Phil earned this title due to his position as the boss of ten clerical workers in a correspondence office.

Phil explains the deeper meaning and ramifications of his title:

To me this was an uncomfortable designation signifying dominance as well as relational distance. To the Bengalis this was indicative of the fact that I was a power person from whom many good things could be obtained.[31]

In due course, Phil and his wife moved to a small town in Dhaka. In this case, the locals called Phil "Bhai," meaning "brother." Phil values this title:

With no employees and no trappings of ostentation, this "power person" had left behind vestiges of prestige. I was now much more one with the Muslim people I had come to incarnate among.[32]

Phil has given us a tangible way to grasp the difference between ministering out of a patron-client relationship and ministering out of a brother relationship formed out of mutuality. Ultimately, patron-client relationships between missionaries and locals most often create unhealthy dependency.

Patron-client relationships cannot always be avoided, as these types of relationships are a part of many different cultures, but missionaries have the responsibility to think and think again about how to conduct their cross-cultural ministry so they do not create unhealthy dependency through being a "Boro Sahib."

What can you do to avoid the pitfalls of patron-client relationships?

AVOID EXTRACTION

Extraction is a huge instigator of the unhealthy dependency syndrome. Often, extraction and its consequences unfold like this: Khan is a father, teacher, and farmer who has the respect of his community. The community appreciates how he guides his children and toils alongside them in the fields. Khan is not rich but has enough to support his family and help others here and there. He lives at the level of his fellow community members.

Missionary Bob is excited because Khan has so much potential to be a leader for Christ among his people. Bob invites Khan to study at a Bible school in the capital city. The invitation to study at the Bible school is an indirect invitation for Khan to sever himself from his livelihood as the head of his household. Now the missionary or Bible school must somehow provide for Khan, so they give him a scholarship.

Khan, in due course, becomes accustomed to institutional and city life. He makes weekend visits to home, but some of the community members notice a change in his lifestyle and become suspicious of his motives. Nonetheless, Khan is able to start a church with several families. Upon finishing Bible school, Khan has a difficult time supporting himself as he now serves as a pastor instead of a teacher or farmer. The missions organization agrees to pay his salary until the church takes over the responsibility.

This common pattern of support sounds feasible, but is it? Missiologist Gailyn Van Rheenen puts in his own words how Khan's story is not unusual:

> The American response, inbred by a pragmatic heritage, is to naively cast small doses of money to new converts to help and encourage: local preachers are quickly put on American salaries, service ministries created which can be maintained only by Western economic help, and Western-style training institutions developed.[33]

In Khan's case, the original idea was for the missionaries to wean him from subsidies while he slowly but surely encouraged his church to give. But from what I have experienced, the first seekers and believers in a church scenario such as this form a mindset that declares, "The missions organization is responsible for sustaining our leaders and church functions. Our giving pales compared to the mission's resources. What does our pastor do with all the money that comes his way, anyway?" Suspicion and indifference settle into the church: "We can't! Why should we? The pastor should do all the work; he gets paid for it."

The impression that there is an unlimited supply of resources from outside organizations stifles local giving and mutual support in every way. Over time, a mindset of dependency is created and grows its choking roots. To cut the choking roots, the local pastor speaks about giving, sharing, and tithing to his congregation, but to no avail. It is too late! They are already converts of dependency. "To pay the bill early will create dependence later."[34]

An alternative approach to extraction and outside subsidy is to encourage pastors and church planters to be bi-vocational and to allow the church to take the responsibility of giving, sharing, and supporting their leaders from the beginning. The dependency of Khan and his church started when Khan was extracted from his livelihood for training and subsidized throughout the process.

Although most extraction has to do with institutional training methods, missionaries also extract people to serve as personal workers or within ministry project roles. Ultimately, we need to discover and implement approaches that leave people connected to their livelihoods and cultivate churches that give and serve as stewards of their church.

What can you do to avoid extraction and the consequences of it?

WHY IT IS NOT WISE TO PAY CHURCH WORKER'S SALARIES WITH FOREIGN FUNDING

The testimonies and examples throughout this chapter reveal numerous methods that lead to unhealthy dependency and the consequences. However, many people appreciate referring to a list from time to time, so I've opted to include one here. Ronnie and Wouter, in their article called "Dependency," have created the following list of why it is not wise to pay church workers' salaries with foreign funding.

296 · JEAN JOHNSON

1) Once started, this cycle is extremely hard to break.
2) "Once a preacher or church leader is supported by outside Christians or agency, it becomes exceptionally difficult to transition to local support. The expectation is, 'Once supported by outsiders, always supported by outsiders'." Van Rheenen 2002
3) It motivates the church to resist transition to locally paid leaders. The need for outside support is always presented as real. Ott calls this a "mercenary spirit."
4) It brings the temptation for Christians to see the ministry as job-opportunity.
5) Lay involvement is hampered and restricted, since it is competing with official evangelism. If donors would realize that evangelism can be done without outside money, this would be dangerous. Thereby the (unbiblical) chasm between clergy and laity is made deeper. Naturally appearing leadership tends to be suppressed (Ellison calls this "the Saul syndrome") and initiatives for more sustainable structures for ministry are neglected.
6) It has no biblical support. Biblically, he who invests all his time in the gospel ministry should eat from what those he preaches to can give.
7) Local giving, actions of spontaneous love toward the pastor and faithful tithing is hindered.
8) It affects church growth negatively. Wayne Allen wrote his DMin thesis about the comparison of church growth between districts where at a time outside funding for church workers' salaries was introduced and other districts where such was not introduced and showed that in the latter, growth occurred in each case, while in the subsidized districts growth stagnated or even declined.
9) It makes the worker less accountable to the church he serves.
10) It makes the church worker less motivated to be devoted to his work.
11) It makes it difficult for the national church to exercise authority over such workers or to take action, since removing him from the subsidy system means "blocking one's progress" which is among the most grievous cultural offenses.
12) It creates or stimulates the idea that the church is a foreign organization and that church workers are actually paid agents of the foreign body. This decreases their credibility.

13) When transparency toward the church is limited, it can create the impression that church workers are rich people, whom you can go to for loans rather than to support them.

14) Western support of native workers is a model that national churches cannot reproduce.

15) Such a strategy is based on the assumption that the spread of the gospel depends on money.

16) This dependence on Western funds can reinforce feelings of inferiority.

17) It can rob the national church of the joy and blessing of being a truly missionary church and being part of the evangelization of the world.

18) It robs the dependent church of self-respect that comes from seeing God provide.

19) It hinders the expansion of the church, since this is now made dependent on outside funds coming in. Any decrease of money is translated into decrease of evangelistic activity.

20) If some do and some do not receive outside funding for their salaries it can create a great discrepancy between one pastor and the other and thereby jealousy. It can tempt the church to start looking for ways to also get the other pastors on the pay lists.

21) It exports and reinforces a materialistic mentality that is already rampant in the western church.

22) It discourages local initiative in designing culturally appropriate means and methods of evangelism and church life.

23) Outside funding may actually contribute to keeping dependent churches poor.

24) "During my years with WEF I traveled to 70 or 80 countries. I repeatedly would find that those who were supported almost exclusively from North America did not relate to the local church well. Their accountability was elsewhere." Howard 1997[35]

This list is an accumulation from various missions authors. Although it specifically relates to the pitfalls of supporting local workers with outside funding, I believe that many of the same consequences exist in relation to various forms of outside assistance.

It sounds like a lot of work to premeditate sustainability by mobilizing local people and local resources. But then again, maybe it is not. Think of how many fires we would not have to put out. Think about how, eventually, a healthy indigenous ministry could multiply exponentially. Imagine local churches working together in unity for a greater cause. Envision local believers plowing their pastors' fields and caring for their widows. Watch the workforce increase as volunteers abound. It is starting to sound worth the effort to me! My prayer for those of us who "do missions" is this:

> Dear God,
> Paul landed on the island of Malta, a prisoner bound for Rome.
> With nothing in hand but a snake bite and a prayer for the chief,
> A movement for Christ began.
> Remind us that our hands do not need to always be filled with stuff
> As long as we have a heart full of the Holy Spirit who empowers us.

CHAPTER SEVENTEEN

ORAL COMMUNICATION STRATEGIES IN ACTION

"One who sees something good must narrate it."

UGANDAN PROVERB

I am anxious to unwind the topical Bible lesson that I systematically prepared last night. The chalk feels grainy in my hands, a typical sensation for a teacher. As the church planters look on, I unravel the characteristics of church planting by both reading various Scriptures and creating an outline to guide our process. Feeling confident, I deliver the lesson with enthusiasm, so why do the Cambodian church planters look at me with that deep blank stare?

The reaction to my teaching has nothing to do with the humid and cloudy weather, or with a lack of sleep the night before. Rather, I don't get a good reaction because I prepared and presented biblical content in my Western logical style. I took the gospel story, which is naturally relevant, and served it like leftover rice. I completely ignored the Cambodians' method of both learning and processing and defaulted to my instinctive way of learning and teaching.

IDENTIFY AND USE RELEVANT ORAL METHODS OF COMMUNICATION

One day, as I traveled to a Cambodian village with a church planting team, I intently listened to their conversation. Throughout the entire trip, they communicated through conversation, stories, riddles, and songs. It dawned on me that I should train the Cambodian church planters using the very same communication modes that I observed them using. So, I trained them through conversation, storytelling, riddles, songs, and other oral means of communication that are relevant to Cambodians. Additionally, I encouraged them to use these same oral communication methods to plant their churches. I loved watching them do a question-and-response-style song to a drumbeat, asking how the world came to be.

Tom Steffen, who directs the Doctor of Missiology program at Biola University and served as a missionary in the Philippines, confirmed my communication revelation through his own experience:

> Then I came into contact with the Ifugao of the Philippines who reintroduced me to story. They wanted stories; I gave them systematic theology. They wanted relationships; I gave them reason. They wanted a cast of characters; I gave them categories of convenience. They wanted explorations; I gave them explanations. They wanted descriptions; I gave them definitions. They wanted stories; I gave them statements. The Ifugao challenged my take-it-for granted understanding of the way people learn, and forced me to reconsider the pedagogical "story" I had unconsciously accepted and biased.[1]

Steffen's experience gives us some insight into the preferences of oral-oriented learners: relationships, a cast of characters, explorations, descriptions, and stories. Some oral mediums are unique to a specific group; others are shared by many groups. Oral mediums that are shared usually have features unique to each specific group. For example, Mongolians use singing as a medium of communication, like many oral societies, yet their type of singing—"throat singing"—is unique to their culture. A throat singer starts with a low drone and manipulates his vocal tract to produce other tones simultaneously. Beyond the technique, throat singing is an integral part of Mongolians' spiritual relationship with nature around them. Through singing in this manner, Mongolians mimic sounds of nature and show their respect for their environment. Throat singing reveals the nomadic traditions of the Mongolians and their role as herdsmen of horses, sheep, camels, and yaks.

Oral cultures share many of the following methods of communication with unique variations: storytelling, narratives, folktales, drama, performances with audience response, public oration, dance, poetry, rhymes, riddles, parables, proverbs, songs, music, recitation, chanting, symbols, art, genealogies, communal interaction, relational events, concrete examples, conversation, rituals, participation, experiential learning, and apprenticeship.

The following methods of communication are in direct contrast to how oral people receive, process, internalize, and reproduce communication: linear thinking, reasoning, topical systematic presentations, categorizing, outlines, monologue preaching, preaching points, exposition, deductive Bible studies, fill-in the-blanks, abstract concepts, formal analysis, solitary assignments, and time-constrained experiences.

The very fact that I feel a need to present you with lists to reveal differences speaks of my own print-oriented experience. As this is likely your cultural background as well, lists enable effective communication between us. Yet my responsibility in another culture is to set aside my learning instincts if necessary in order to intentionally tailor my communication to the local forms, patterns, and processes of the receptor's culture. I take this Tibetan proverb to heart: "What is written in ink can fade away by a single drop of water; what is written on the heart will last an eternity."

Sit with families during the evenings, participate in community events, attend performances, and do whatever else you can do to identify the relevant oral communication forms of your host culture.

If you are working among an oral people or residual oral people, what are their common means of communication, and how can you use those means?

TAILOR APPROACHES TO THE WORLDVIEW CHARACTERISTICS OF ORAL SOCIETIES

Beyond oral communication methods, there are several worldview characteristics unique to oral societies. In other words, orality does not come down merely to methods of communication. Rather, orality is an integral and complex part of the worldview, which influences social structure, ethnic identity, religious beliefs, moral values, social obligations, roles, rites of passage, decision-making, trades, skills, and preservation of culture. Below, I give a few practical suggestions for cross-cultural communicators that correspond to worldview characteristics of oral cultures.

1. Foster communal-centered values.

Writing personal answers in a workbook, making personal decisions for Christ, and withdrawing to a private place to reflect are activities in conflict with oral cultures. Walter J. Ong, an expert in orality, explains in more detail:

> Primary orality fosters personality structures that in certain ways are more communal and externalized, and less introspective than those common among literates. Oral communication unites people in groups. Writing and reading are solitary activities that throw the psyche back on itself... If the speaker asks the audience to read a handout provided for them, as each reader enters his or her own private reading world, the unity of the audience is shattered.[2]

302 • JEAN JOHNSON

With this understanding in mind, cross-cultural communicators should avoid techniques, activities, and speech that isolate, individualize, or embarrass the participants. Rather, we aim to create unity, group identity, and mutuality. I suggest that cross-cultural communicators attend ample formal and nonformal community and family events to observe how communal dynamics unfold within a particular culture, and then implement what they learn.

For example, in Cambodian villages, I noticed that in some settings the speakers or performers would create harmony between themselves and the audience by interacting with them. Keeping this in mind, I would use humor, speaker-audience response, group memorization, and other means to create a flow between the group and myself when I served as a speaker in a ministry setting. These methods allowed me to accentuate the cohesiveness of the group.

Separating out and creating exclusive groups is a normal mode of operation for church leaders in North America (women's ministry and youth groups, for example). But among oral-dominated cultures, cross-cultural communicators should avoid strategies that undermine communal values.

In a society where the head of the household plays a key role, an outsider who creates separate groups may cause the head of the household to feel as if he has lost sight and stewardship of his family members. In this case, the head of the household will be resistant to the gospel and do all he or she can to make life difficult for others who are interested in it. When missionaries use methods that divide and separate, they are creating unnecessary persecution.

The fact that a particular group of people is communal in nature should be encouraging for church planters. In places like North America, churches spend years trying to create community. In communal cultures, if a missionary does not disrupt but rather emphasizes the organic communal interaction among oral groups, he or she will experience an inborn Christlike community.

Tom Steffen states that storytelling, an oral medium of communication, encourages natural group movements:

> ...naturally encourages group audiences rather than individual listeners. As clusters of believers (local fellowships) emerge they typically do so already grouped by existing, natural relationships. This contrasts with the traditional, individualistic information/reception/ response model which requires extraction and re-formation of these individuals into new, artificially grouped relationships (local fellowships).[3]

Communal values greatly affect how people relate to one another and make decisions as well. The group is necessary for survival; thus, loyalty to group members and group processes is invaluable. To stand out above others or to bring shame to others is considered harmful to the group. A cross-cultural communicator among the Hopi of Arizona misunderstood the importance of group dynamics:

> In class she assigned a task and told the students to raise their hands when they completed the work to see who could be first. When no student did so, even though they had completed the work, she became angry. She did not realize that the first one to raise their hand would be put to shame and would be treated by them as arrogant. Similarly, tribes that adopt competitive games such as soccer often make sure that each game ends in a tie so that no one is ashamed. Cooperation is valuable more than competition in a group.[4]

In accordance with this example of teaching among the Hopi, we realize how important it is to understand the individual's relationship to the whole group. Some cross-cultural communicators have expected instantaneous and individualistic responses as it relates to believing and following Christ. Revealing our worldview, North Americans often use the phrase "personal decision for Christ." But emphasizing individualism is an action that forces oral people to work against the natural flow of their group's harmony. Harry Box gives an example from Kevin Hovey's experience in Papua New Guinea:

> In most Papua New Guinean villages, the various decision making levels are:
> (1) Matters of no importance which affect no one else—made on a personal level.
> (2) Matters of importance but not affecting the whole village—clan or extended family.
> (3) Matters of major importance affecting the whole village—made at level of village.
> In any of the meetings (formal or informal) required to make decisions on levels (2) or (3), the pattern is fairly standard.
> Every man in the group has free expression on the subject while the women listen in (if they are present). Sometimes the women are allowed to voice an opinion they feel very strongly about.

> After the topic has been discussed thoroughly, one of the big men, who probably has been a silent listener up to this point will voice the consensus as a decision. Any worthwhile decision is made in this way.[5]

Not every community or group makes decisions in such a manner. But this example shows us how important and elaborate decision-making processes are among oral-dominated cultures that have communal values.

Mark Zouk is a missionary who lived and worked among the Mouk tribe of Papua New Guinea. Mark is a perfect example of working strategically within a communal culture. He used a method of sharing the gospel and leading the tribe to Christ as a unit rather than leading member by member to Christ over a period of time. He gathered the entire tribe together on a daily basis to hear chronological Bible stories from creation to the cross. During this three-month process, Mark purposely never led any individual to Christ. He patiently allowed the whole village to hear, understand, and respond to the gospel together.

When Mark had shared the Bible story of Jesus's death on the cross and tied the concept of the sacrificial lamb to several Old Testament stories, the tribe began to respond in unison: "Ee-taow! Ee-taow!" (It is true!). Mark had possessed incredible insight and patience as he worked among this oral, communal, and event-oriented people. We need more missionaries like Mark Zouk in the world—those who intentionally formulate their communication strategies to foster communal-centered values when working among oral-dominated societies.

What word usage, actions, behavior, and activities should you implement or avoid to foster communal harmony rather than discord?

2. Relate Through Heads of Households

A missionary enters a Burmese home and immediately addresses the children with pats on the head and hugs. Although this greeting seems harmless, it is in direct opposition to most oral-dominated cultures, who place significant value on the elders and heads of the household. Rather, I suggest that the missionary first greet the eldest members of the household, and then, eventually, give the children some minimal attention.

Relating to the heads of households goes beyond greetings. This intentional method carries over into various ministry settings. For example, when we present a drama, we include the heads of the household for as many main roles as possible, while giving children and youth more low-profile roles. Always be thinking,

"How can I include the heads of the households in every stage and every function of the church planting process?"

Many missionaries and visiting teams from abroad try to plant churches and establish ministries by starting kids clubs. The hope is that the children will bring back the enthusiasm and message to their families. Although sometimes a child or two will indeed influence their parents, the missionaries may actually be undermining a social tradition and causing thick (and unnecessary) resistance among the majority of families within the community. Among cultural groups that value the elders of the community and the heads of the household, cross-cultural communicators are challenged with the role of constantly considering how to support their host culture's social values.

In what practical ways can you relate through and show respect to the heads of the households?

3. Create a Bridge to Everyday, Concrete Life

Lately, I have become terribly weary of what I call "the filing game." I spend days creating the most organized filing system so everything will be at my fingertips as needed. The problem is that I can never remember what documents I actually have or what file they are in! This is a useful illustration of a reality in many cultures. Oral cultures are not accustomed to the abstract, or to tucking information away into files and categories for later usage. Rather, oral people interpret and apply their knowledge to immediate, concrete life.

Walter J. Ong, who has written extensively on orality, expounds on the fact that everything must be relatable to everyday life among oral cultures:

> In the absence of elaborate analytic categories that depend on writing to structure knowledge at a distance from lived experienced, oral cultures must conceptualize and verbalize all their knowledge with more or less close reference to human lifeworld, assimilating the alien, objective world to the more immediate, familiar interaction of human beings.[6]

Cambodian religious practices inform me that Cambodians emphasize the concrete—the here and now. Cambodians interact daily with the spirit world— at the least—by lighting incense, preparing offerings, and acknowledging the spirits' presence at their spirit houses, which are a common sight to every home and business. Technically, spirit appeasement is anti-Buddhist, so why the contrast between belief and practice? Buddhism is theoretical, philosophical, and ceremonial. Nirvana is lofty and out there somewhere—actually a state of nothingness and nonattachment. The eightfold path, which includes right view, right intention, right speech, right action, right livelihood, right effort, right mindfulness, and right concentration, is almost impossible to measure. Due to the abstract nature of Buddhism, the Cambodians create concrete bridges such as spirit appeasement, fortune telling, wearing fetishes, and other rituals that enable them to connect religion to everyday life. With that in mind, cross-cultural communicators in oral societies need to strive to connect truth and knowledge to the community's active lives and everyday concerns.

Jesus was a communication artist. He knew where each and every stroke and color should go on the canvas to create a masterpiece for the receptor. Jesus was a master teacher in relating his life and message to the receptors' daily lives. Take a pencil and a Bible, and circle every example in which Jesus connected his communication to the "human lifeworld" of his listeners. Jesus used everyday props to deliver a message relevant to everyday life: fish, sheep, wolves, camels, sawdust, trees, fruit, sand, rock, seeds, soil, lamps, wells, tombstones, fields, kingdoms, kings, moneylenders, children, farmers, victims, and so much more. On the spot, Jesus could use tangible objects, nature, and scenarios around him to communicate. He tied his message to the life and culture unfolding around him.

Ultimately, Jesus was receptor-oriented. Charles Kraft, in his book *Communicating Jesus' Way*, describes the qualities of a receptor-oriented communicator:

A receptor-oriented communicator, on the other hand, is careful to bend every effort to meet his receptors where they are. He will choose topics that relate directly to felt needs of the receptors, he will choose methods of presentation that are appealing to them, he will use language that is maximally intelligible to them.[7]

As receptor-oriented communicators, we have the opportunity to "bend every effort to meet the receptors where they are." Oral cultural groups are not so concerned with the existence of God, love, forgiveness, or righteousness, but rather whether this God works for everyday people in everyday life.

The British writer G.K. Chesterton told us, "Fairy tales are more than true: not because they tell us that dragons exist, but because they tell us that dragons can be beaten." In a God and gospel sense, let us show those people among oral cultures that dragons can be beaten.

As a receptor-oriented communicator, how will you relate your message to the receptors' concrete, everyday lives?

4.   Ensure Memorization and Relevance for the Sake of Reproduction

Oral learners rarely remember or internalize what they read or hear read to them. (Keep in mind that the ability to read does not exclude someone from being an oral learner.) Rather, they remember that which is presented in natural, oral forms, that which comes with tone quality—full of expression and conflict—and that which connects the participants to the concrete. Oral cultures consider history and ancient culture valid but maintain in their memory bank that which is relevant. Oral cultures will ultimately remember, pass on, and reproduce that which is significant for their present lives. Observably, Jesus understood and trusted this system of communication:

> This is one of the reasons that makes the oral teaching of Jesus so remarkable. Knowing full well this characteristic of the oral Jewish culture, He was prepared to risk His message of eternal life and salvation to the possibility of significant loss or erosion through the normal homeostatic processes of that culture. He did not provide a written back-up text, but trusted that His message would be perceived by people as sufficiently relevant and important that they would make the necessary effort to preserve it in their oral tradition.[8]

I recommend that we follow Jesus's example and tell his stories with an empathetic, expressive, and relevant manner. Jesus saw response, results, and reproduction. Remember the woman who spent time with Jesus, conversing at the well, and indeed never received a written tract?

> Then, leaving her water jar, the woman went back to the town and said to the people, "Come, see a man who told me everything I did. Could this be the Christ?" They came out of the town and made their way toward him. (John 4:28–30)

The Samaritan woman did not deliver a literate-oriented sermon to others in her community. Her words were concise, but full of expression and relevance: "Come, see a man who told me everything I did. Could this be the Christ?" Don't you wish you could make a group of people move toward Jesus with a sentence or two? Jesus's oral approach mixed with supernatural power led to the reproduction of his message about the messianic messenger—himself. The surroundings, the timing, the analogy to drawing water from the well, the dialogue about symbolic traditions, the connection to everyday life, and Jesus's empathy—all characteristics of oral communication—did not come up short.

For the sake of memorization, I suggest the use of formulaic styling and mnemonic patterns, both of which present ideas in a manner that are easy to remember and recall. The experts explain formulaic styling:

> To solve effectively the problem of retaining and retrieving carefully articulated thought, you have to do your thinking in mnemonic patterns, shaped for ready oral recurrence. Your thoughts must come into being in heavily rhythmic, balanced patterns, in repetitions or antithesis, in alliterations or assonances, in epithetic and other formulary expressions, in standard thematic settings (the assembly, the meal, the duel, the hero's helper, and so on), in proverbs which are constantly heard by everyone so that they can come to mind readily and which themselves are patterned for retention and ready recall, or in other mnemonic form. Serious thought is intertwined with memory systems.[9]

I have seen Cambodians use mnemonic patterns (memory techniques) in their chanting. This melodious chanting enables them to memorize and internalize important Buddhist doctrine such as "The Three Refuges," "The Five Precepts," and "Discourse on Loving Kindness."

I am not suggesting magical incantations. Rather, I am suggesting that we think out of the box so as to implement ways to memorize principles, Christ's mandates, and the Bible. A Thai follower of Jesus Christ taught people through formulaic phrases. Four different phrases each spoke of a component of the gospel message. Within each phrase, the second syllable rhymed with the first syllable of the consecutive phrase:

Kum-nerd (the beginning)
Gerd-baap (the origin of human sin)
Prap-tuk (the conquering of the suffering)
Kuk-kao (the kneeling down in prayer)[10]

In Cambodia, our team made sure every part of a Bible storying session emphasized one faith principle and accompanying application instead of conveying multiple principles. In addition, we created a mini-tune in which we sang the biblical principle. We also had participants retell the Bible story. All this intentionality was for the sake of memorization, recall, and reproduction.

How will you package and present information, ideas, and truths for the sake of memorization and reproduction?

MODEL AND EQUIP RELATIONAL-NARRATIVE COMMUNICATORS TO USE CHRONOLOGICAL BIBLE STORYING AS A CORE ORAL COMMUNICATION MEDIUM

I have merely scratched the surface in relating to you the characteristics of oral cultures. You may find it worthwhile to dig deeper in order to understand the inner workings of oral people. Oral cultures are made up of complex systems entailing many layers and facets of culture. If the cross-cultural communicator is of a literate experience, superficial changes such as using narratives here and there will not suffice. Rather, the cross-cultural communicator needs to intentionally and intimately learn and orient himself or herself to the oral culture.

Every major religion uses stories to teach doctrine, to pass on its distinctive beliefs from generation to generation, to train in moral conduct, and so on. In Cambodia, there is a story called "The Story of an Orphaned Monk." The story is about a boy whose family is murdered, and his contact with a passing cart leads to his adoption by a merchant and eventually his monkhood. This narrative is part of the school curriculum in Cambodia. The story, which is filled with symbolism and metaphors, teaches Buddhist morals and beliefs.

Storytelling is universal and knows no boundaries. People from diverse cultures preserve and relate wisdom, experiences, beliefs, counsel, and instruction through stories. Heather Forest explains the power and extent of the usage of stories, folktales, and parables:

A story can be a powerful teaching tool. In folktales told far and wide, characters may gain wisdom by observing a good example or by bumbling through their own folly. A story's plot may inspire listeners to reflect on personal actions, decision making, or behavior. Over time, a tale can take root, like a seed rich with information, and blossom into new awareness and understanding. By metaphorically, or indirectly, offering constructive strategies for living, ancient wisdom tales resonate with universal appeal...[11]

Before I go to a particular country or region, I read stories from that area. My audience has never been disappointed when I have related a truth or principle through stories that move them.

Tom Steffen tells us that people have an innate need to tell stories, as described by Walter Fisher:

Fisher (1987, 62) captures the reason why stories are told universally when he calls the human race homo narrans (lit. "narrative people"). People, by design, he claims, are storytelling animals because the great Storyteller created us. The human race, made in God's image, is homo narrans because the Creator is Deus narrans. God and narrative are insep-arable, therefore humans and narrative are inseparable.[12]

Steffen is suggesting that God is a "narrative God" and the people he created are "narrative people." Since the Bible is 75 percent narrative, it is fair to say the Bible is a "narrative Bible." Knowing that stories are universal, are prevalent among all cultures, and make up a great percentage of the Bible, I recommend that chronological Bible storying serve as the core oral medium of communication for missionaries. During my time in Cambodia, I used chronological Bible storying and reinforced the principle truths within those stories through other oral means such as cultural links, songs, poems, proverbs, and recitation.

Jim Slack and J.O. Terry developed chronological Bible storying (CBS) as a strategic communication approach among oral peoples. I initially tried using chronological Bible teaching (CBT) in Cambodia using the excellent resource *Firm Foundations* by Trevor McIlwain, which provides teaching through Bible stories in a chronological sequence. However, the Cambodians struggled with this format because the Bible stories were not presented as intact stories, but rather were examined through exposition and explanation. Chronological Bible storying and chronological Bible teaching serve different purposes. Among oral people, I suggest using chronological Bible storying, which is defined below:

A method of sharing biblical truths by telling stories of the Bible as intact stories in the order they happened in time. The person using this method leads hearers to discover truth in the stories for the purpose of evange-lization, discipleship, church planting, and leader training.[13]

There are three key components within this CBS definition. Let's look at these three components one by one.

1. "Intact stories…"

When storytellers relate an "intact" story, they tell the story as a whole without interruption. They allow the story and the listeners' interaction with the story to produce the outcome. A true storyteller avoids interjecting explanations or extracting points out of the story to present its contents in an abstract lesson or exegetical sermon. Rather, the truth is embedded in the story, and the story delivers the truth by engaging the mind, heart, and emotions. Dialogue provides a method to follow up the story for further internalization, understanding, and application.

Print-oriented people usually refer to a story, summarize the story, present the story in interrupted pieces, or begin a lesson with a story and move into a topical or expositional delivery. Tom Steffen says, "Telling a story and telling about a story are as different as telling about a particular ethnic group and living among them."[14]

2. " …in the order they happened in time."

Imagine picking up a novel and reading in the middle of the book. You would immediately need to make assumptions about certain characters and unwinding scenarios because you missed the beginning of the story, which built the foundation. Many literate-oriented learners have experienced the Bible through topical presentations, a little from here and a little from there. But how can someone truly receive and understand the Son when they do not yet know the Father? How can a Buddhist relate to Jesus if he thinks Jesus's beginning was after the birth of Gautama Buddha? The Bible is a story with stories. Each previous story gives insight into the next story and the overall message of the big story. Instead of trying to get people to cross a salvation line, chronological Bible storying makes disciples.

3. The Oral Bible…

A working definition of an oral Bible is "The accumulated Bible stories that have been told to an oral society."[15]

Some Christians may lament, "Yes, but how can people be true disciples of Jesus without the Bible?" We may want to ask, "How can people become disciples of a print-oriented faith?" Even though the Bible was initially oral, print-oriented learners cannot seem to fathom an oral Bible among the oral cultures of today. Those steeped in literate systems of learning are obsessed with storing information in technologies and organized systems (even though that information is not readily available to them as, for example, they encounter a wounded soul on the road).

Oral learners have a tremendous capacity to memorize. Creating an oral Bible among an oral group is a very real possibility. Someone recently told me about Bible translators among an oral group. These translators spent tears-upon-years translating the Bible for a particular indigenous group. Absolutely worthwhile! Yet, I never want us to think that we have to wait for translations of the Bible to disciple people among oral cultures. Literacy is not a prerequisite to discipleship or a part of the criteria to be a disciple. "The Word is near you; it is in your mouth and in your heart, that is the Word we are proclaiming" (Romans 10:8).

It took four hundred years to compile the Bible, and another one thousand years before the Bible was readily available due to the printing press—that's fourteen hundred years of communicating the Bible orally. Jesus commanded his disciples to preach the gospel to every nation. The disciples indeed successfully transmitted the gospel orally, for the Bible wasn't compiled until four centuries later!

I really believe that people are able to live in faith as obedient disciples of Jesus if they only hear, believe, and apply accumulated Bible stories from Old Testament to the New Testament. If you have time, watch the DVD *EE-TAOW*. This is an incredible story about how the Mouk tribe of Papua New Guinea came into a faith relationship through chronological Bible storying.

4. "...for the purpose of evangelization, discipleship, church planting and leader training."

Far too often, missionaries will use chronological Bible storying and other oral means of communication in the evangelization stage, but abandon this strategy for discipleship, church planting, and leadership training. Sometimes missionaries use CBS for church planting, but when the church is formed, they switch to analytical three-point sermons as their main means of teaching. In *Worldview Strategic Church Planting Among Oral Cultures*, a book I co-authored, I give a model of using CBS and complimentary oral forms through all stages of ministry development. Why do missionaries tend to make a shift from oral, concrete forms of communication to abstract, analytical forms? I think it goes back to the misconception that some missionaries have of church leadership. We think leaders need to be theologians who can juggle commentaries, preach articulate, expositional sermons, and administrate churches in a Western style. But for the sake of movements for Christ among people who are primary oral learners, we need to give local leaders permission and confirmation to use the existing communication formats that have worked for them in every layer of life, governance, and religion. The imposition of literate formats will serve like weeds trapped in the motor of a fishing boat.

How can you model and equip relational-narrative storytellers to use chronological Bible storying?

SELECT AND CRAFT STORIES THAT CONVEY THE ESSENTIAL BIBLICAL MESSAGE IN A WAY THAT IS SENSITIVE TO THE WORLDVIEW OF THE RECEPTOR'S SOCIETY

How do you go about selecting Bible stories and crafting them so as to address the worldview of the receptor? Allow me to walk you through an example of how we (the Cambodian church planting team and myself as a coach) chose our first story for pre-evangelism. Please keep in mind that in pre-evangelism, we did not present biblical stories in chronological order. However, once people showed interest through our pre-evangelism stories, we invited them into a chronological Bible storying experience.

First, we identified biblical truths that we discerned were vital for people to have a faith relationship with God. We allowed these biblical truths to guide our process.

Second, our team spent ample time identifying worldview barriers and worldview bridges to the gospel. A *worldview bridge* is any aspect of a people's worldview that instinctively connects to the gospel. For example, there is a Buddhist proverb that states, "A divine prophecy is required if an enlightened priest is to be born."[16] The content of this proverb serves as a worldview bridge to the gospel in the sense that the birth of Jesus, the high priest, is surrounded by divine prophecy. Thus, in a Buddhist cross-cultural setting, the communicator would be wise to include Bible stories that contain prophecy about Jesus.

A *worldview barrier* is any aspect within a cultural group's worldview that prevents the people from hearing, understanding, and responding to the gospel. A primary Cambodian worldview barrier to the gospel is a misconception held by most Cambodians that "Christians are required to hate their parents." For Cambodians, relationships do not end after death. The living and the deceased are connected to each other and responsible for each other. Living relatives have duties to fulfill for their dead ancestors, and dead ancestors have influence over the living. Thus, the process of relating, appeasing, and making merit for dead ancestors is extremely important. In light of this, Cambodians unwaveringly participate in a fifteen-day annual festival dedicated to making offerings for their dead ancestors. Cambodians do not welcome anything that seemingly threatens this festival or the traditions surrounding ancestral appeasement and merit-making. They are so protective of these customs that folk Buddhists in Cambodia started using a Bible verse out of context to support their notion that Christians were instructed by Jesus to hate their parents. These are merely one worldview bridge and one worldview barrier. We identified many more of both.

Third, we allowed these worldview bridges and worldview barriers to inform us of what Bible stories to include first and what stories to address later through layers of storytelling. Additionally, the worldview bridges and worldview barriers enlightened us as to what we needed to emphasize within the stories. J.O. Terry, a Bible storying trainer, summarizes it this way:

> For those using Bible Storying, knowing these worldview issues is most helpful in choosing the best stories and delivery to begin setting up the desired spiritual changes. There are some simple directives that can help to find those openings and clue us as to what stories might be a good beginning point, even how to tell the stories, and how to talk about the stories or lead a conversation regarding the stories.[17]

For our beginning point, we desired to dissolve the primary worldview barriers enough to cause the receptors to want to hear more. We discovered through our worldview profile that we needed to begin melting this most prominent worldview barrier among Cambodians: the misconception that Christians are supposed to hate their parents. With this worldview barrier in mind, the church planting team told the Bible story of Ruth and Naomi as their first introductory story. As they told or acted out the story, they emphasized Ruth's unconditional dedication and loyalty to her mother-in-law. They followed up the story by quoting God's command to honor our parents.

Other missionaries and Christians often wondered about the logic of starting with the Ruth and Naomi story in pre-evangelism. Our sole purpose was to start dissolving a key worldview barrier to the point that we could gain a second hearing, which signifies a softening. Several more key stories addressing other prominent worldview barriers led to an opportunity to meet regularly for chronological Bible storying.

Ultimately, we developed a story set for pre-evangelism and then repeated the process for evangelism, discipleship, leadership, and church planting. One Bible story cannot entirely dissolve a deeply instilled worldview belief. But throughout the chronological Bible storying process, we addressed each world-view barrier and bridge many times with various stories.

Often, people ask why we have so many Bible stories in our evangelism story sets. First of all, the worldview barriers guide how many stories and what partic-ular stories are included in the story sets, as well as how the stories are crafted. Second, the goal of these chronological Bible story sets is not merely to lead people to a one-time decision, but rather to lead them into a relationship with God that affects every aspect of their lives. We invite them on a journey *with* God, instead of merely to God.

For example, why include the story of Abraham finding a wife for Isaac in our evangelism story sets? First of all, the marriage story of Isaac and Rebekah serves as a bridge. The importance of marriage and cultural customs surrounding marriage in this story are shared by the Cambodians. Furthermore, we included this story and its accompanying biblical principle, "God is active in the lives of families," to help dissolve one of the barriers identified by the Cambodians: "It is difficult to comprehend a God who loves and who is involved in human lives." We intentionally include many Bible stories in our storytelling strategy that are typically left out of other evangelistic story track resources.

As I wrote these examples from my experience in Cambodia, I remembered another example from Africa. Dr. Grant Lovejoy interviewed two different mis-sions groups in regard to their chronological Bible storying sets and methods. Both of these entities were working among nomadic herdsmen in Northern Kenya. Dr. Lovejoy asked the two groups to share what stories they had been telling. One group said that they told the basic creation stories and skipped over all the Jacob stories to Moses. The other group shared that they included all of the Jacob stories.

Why the difference? One group didn't think that the Jacob stories added any-thing to the salvation message of Jesus and thus served as an unnecessary delay. On the contrary, the other group intentionally included the Jacob stories because those very stories were about nomadic herdsmen! The stories revealed to the Northern Kenyan herdsmen that God indeed could relate to them and their unique lives.

It may not be a good idea to rush Northern Kenyan herdsmen into a salvation decision by ignoring key components of their worldview. If they don't know how to relate to God in regard to their nomadic journey, most likely they will revert back to their own religious beliefs and practices. A much more beautiful outcome is when a herdsman falls to his knees in the middle of the grasslands and prays, "I know you are a God of the grasslands under my feet and the God who leads my nomadic journey. You are my shepherd and my herdsman."

J.O. Terry gives us another example from his experience:

Here are two examples from among Muslim women. I had prepared the God and Woman story lesson series. To make the stories simpler I took out most of the character dialog and simply narrated the stories. The women didn't like it. I had to go back and insert all the usable dialog into 90 stories. The women enjoyed listening to the characters in the stories speaking to one another. Then I discovered an even more serious flaw. As it turns out not many Muslim women are that interested in paradise. It is a place where faithful Muslim men go for their reward of a pleasurable life. So the stories and lessons were sort of moot as they really failed to connect.

I did a second set of story lessons that I called Heaven Is For Women and in it was more aggressively evangelistic and I dealt with salvation and eternal life as something that began now, not sometime in the unfathomable future, and that it was through acceptance and a relationship with the Father made possible through Jesus, the one who showed great concern for women and dealt with them compassionately. I thought that I was satisfied but then found that there were many very conservative Muslim women who were not interested in any "Christian" teaching.

Then I found a study that investigated how women in that part of the world would get together to share their misfortune stories in order to discharge their pent-up emotion. This led to the third set of stories (no lessons with "Christian" teaching) of Bible women who suffered misfortune in their lives. Then I added how God redeemed their lives. As it turned out, when a storyer would tell the stories, it provoked questions and discussion, so that in time as trust in the storyer built, opportunity came for "Christian" teaching, the very thing the women thought they didn't want. There are many other examples I could give you. I've learned my lesson in the value of knowing spiritual worldview issues before storying the Bible.[18]

J.O. Terry allowed these Muslim women's worldview and the expression of that worldview to guide him in selecting and crafting Bible stories. You can see that the process of storytelling in a worldview-specific way is not a program. Rather, storytelling is a dynamic way to share a relevant gospel with people. Therefore, the storyteller needs to be a forever student of the worldview, as J. O. Terry describes:

> For those of us who have used these directives in our ministries they have served us well. But I will admit that we never know all of a person's worldview issues and often find new ones we didn't know about as we began to tell our stories. It is usually a case of refining our understanding the longer we work with people of a particular group however it is categorized and incorporating the new knowledge into refining our methodology.[19]

Refining is the ongoing work of a missionary. As vibrant as the culture is, so must the missionary be. God, grant us a wisdom that never wearies. Through the Holy Spirit, allow us to be fluent in the language of worldview.

How can you go about identifying worldview bridges and barriers so as to shape your Bible storying?

REINFORCE BIBLICAL TRUTHS AND BIBLE STORIES WITH COMPLEMENTARY ORAL FORMS

Within oral cultures, redundancy and repetition increase reception and preservation of that which is communicated. In Cambodia, we purposely communicated one biblical truth in several oral forms. For example, when the church planting team conducted a dramatic presentation of the Ruth and Naomi story, they did it in such a fashion as to emphasize one main biblical truth and obedience to that truth (such as "honor our parents according to God's command"). Following the drama of the story about Ruth and Naomi, they communicated that same principle with common and complementary oral forms such as a proverb, a Cambodian-style song, a poem, conversation, and memorization using oral devices (rhymes, repetition, etc.).

During the Ruth and Naomi drama, Ruth sang a Cambodian-style song expressing her desire be with her mother-in-law. After the drama and dialogue, the participants sang this emotional song together. One elderly woman—on her own—substituted the name "Naomi" with the name "Jesus."

Along with storytelling, music and song are at the center of most peoples' culture. I recently saw a YouTube clip called "Shining Spirit: A Tibetan Family's Reunion Through Music." One of the brothers had left Tibet under refugee status and settled in Canada. Another brother was able to travel and see his brother in Canada. The two brothers decided to bring their family members together through recording a Tibetan song. Those who lived in Tibet taped their singing and playing of traditional instruments, and eventually the music was mixed in Canada.

As I watched the video, I could see that the Tibetan music was intimately tied to their emotions. I didn't just hear music: I saw tears, intensity, laughter, spirituality, communication, and bonding. Ethnomusicologists who understand the power of music and song refer to an ethnic group's music as "heart music." As much as we learn the heart language of a people, we also need to learn their heart music. At the least, we can build an understanding and appreciation of the heart music enough to celebrate and encourage the indigenous expression of worship.

In this section, I am going to lean on John Oswald—who has played a lute with a Tibetan song and dance troupe—to help us navigate the world of music. Oswald shares with us that music houses cultural values and demonstrates how people of a particular group interpret life. When I listen to a Cambodian song, I can decipher what Cambodians value or what they consider influential in their lives: rice, harvesting, nature, ancestors, spirits, reincarnation, kings, good karma, temples, Buddhism, parents, and honor. John quotes Nathan Corbitt:

> We sing to identify, express, or proclaim our viewpoint and loyalties. Songs function as guideposts to the deeper issues of life. They provide information that is otherwise inaccessible—the hidden or unconscious worldview. They are a map of worldview, telling the "basic assumptions the people have about the nature of reality and of right and wrong."[20]

Can you imagine what happens when missionaries ignore or override people's heart music with music that comes from a foreign context? This oversight and imposition creates a spiritual and emotional gap. I suggest that we learn people's worldview from their heart music and facilitate ethnic groups to compose their own music to express a biblical worldview.

Oswald gives an example of a Tibetan song that people responded to because of the nature of the song:

One day man went out (ya la so)
Saw a precious jewel in a field
(He) sold all, bought the field

In this world of beauty (ya la so)
Don't say there's no jewel (ya la so)
If the Savior Lord Jesus
Is not the jewel, then what is?[21]

So what makes this song uniquely Tibetan? Oswald tells us that the melody is Tibetan, and the lyrics are full of metaphor and symbolism. "Understanding has been gained through familiarity and well-loved word play. Repeated experience shows that songs like this easily open doors of authentic relationship and genuine discussion," writes Oswald.[22]

Cambodia has a style of music in which a man and woman sing questions and responses back and forth (sometimes in a comical manner). I so enjoyed listening to the Cambodian church planters explain the gospel through this question-and-answer technique!

When missionaries take their own cultural songs and translate them into another language, they create a huge disconnect between belief and heart. Oswald tells us that most translated songs do not transfer linguistically, culturally, or musically into Tibetan. Translated songs fall short of the following key characteristics of Tibetan music:

Fundamental to an understanding of heart music are musical style and tone and use of language. Tibetans define this as nyen po ("attractive to the ear," snyan po) and inbuilt into this are musical and linguistic expectations. Regardless of regional distinctives, folk song or modernized folk song that is nyen po usually has the following features: a) a "calm" quality (jam po, 'jam bo) of sound production (i.e. not harsh); b) flowing or "steady" (den po, brtanpo) melodic movement (not sudden); c) ornamentation and often glottalization (dring gu, mgrin 'gug) of the vocal line (not plain); d) poetic textual style (also not plain); and e) lyrical content that is sentimental and emotionally linked to ones identity.[23]

This Tibetan example is not a rare example, but is typical of how translated songs and imported music really undermine the culture and heart music. The cross-cultural communicator has the privilege and challenge to bridge the gospel to a people group through their music. Song and music are an oral-aural form that can serve as a medium of communication and reinforce biblical truth and Bible stories.

Another common cultural form is the proverb. A proverb serves as a family member of stories and songs. Proverbs not only reveal the worldview of a people to us, but they serve as stepping-stones to the gospel:

A Story is told[24] of a young man, sitting by the riverbank, discouraged since he could not swim across the river. An elderly man walked up, rolled up his pants, and then walked across the surface of the water. The young man was in disbelief until another elderly man arrived, rolled up his pants, and also walked across the surface of the water. Eventually, a third elderly man arrived and did the same thing! Finally, the young man decided to try for himself. He rolled up his pants and tried to walk across the surface of the water—only to sink and be carried away by the swift current. The three elderly men looked back and replied, "If only he had asked us—we could have told him where the stones were placed to cross over the river safely!"

When approaching oral cultures, proverbs can be regarded as these sturdy, time-tested stepping stones placed by the elders to move people from the riverbank of unbelief or young faith to mature faith. While these stones may not be readily apparent by literate learners at first glance, careful observation reveals that missionaries catch up on a conversation that God has already started.[25]

"Catch up on a conversation that God has already started"—I love that phrase! God has started a conversation with every people group. This statement echoes the phrase from Ecclesiastes which Don Richardson, a missionary who lived among a cannibalistic tribe in Western New Guinea, Indonesia, so loved to repeat: "Eternity in their hearts." God is not an absentee God. Missionaries do not bring God to a people. God is already present there working. Our role is to find out how and to join the conversation. Proverbs are a part of those "conversational nuggets."

Proverbs work together with other oral forms of communication. We used the Ruth and Naomi story to begin to dissolve a prominent worldview barrier among Cambodians: the misconception that Christians are supposed to hate their parents. We emphasized Ruth's loyalty to her mother-in-law to communicate the biblical principle of honoring our parents according to God's command. We affirmed the story and biblical principles with God's command from the book of Deuteronomy to "love and honor our parents," because Buddhists are fond of precepts. Additionally, we complemented the essence of the story with a Cambodian-style song of Ruth singing to Naomi about her level of commitment to her mother-in-law.

Our process was not proverbless. We actually started the whole process by quoting a Cambodian proverb: "Parents are more valuable than gold the size of a coconut." Then, we quoted Proverbs 23:22–25 back-to-back with the Cambodian proverb in order to bridge their worldview with the gospel. The proverb was used to show that God was already conversing with them. It served as a sturdy stepping-stone to move people across the river.

Someone once stated that proverbs are "short sayings based on long experiences."[26] It is true. Proverbs are pithy sayings which summarize long and impacting experiences. One could also say that worldview is a description of a people's long experiences.

There is an Ethiopian proverb that says, "If one is not in a hurry, even an egg will start walking." There is an urgency to spread the gospel. But let's not allow this urgency to cause us to bypass the hard work of making disciples in a worldview-strategic way. We want to see transformation at the core, not just at the surface.

What existing oral forms can you use to reinforce biblical truths and Bible stories?

One man said to Pastor Bhibuti, "Because you are telling us the stories, now we can understand everything. Before you were not telling the story, and we were not understanding anything."[27] Hearing, understanding, remembering, internalizing, applying, and reproducing are vital to making disciples among oral learners living in two thirds of the world. My prayer for those of us who "do missions" is this:

Dear God,
You never lacked a good story.
Your stories were full of heroes and villains, the loved and the scorned.
You were a storyteller and you are the Story;
Empower us to be in your story and to tell your story.

ENDNOTES

HEROES AND PREMEDITATION

1. Aisha Tyler, Brainyquote.com. http://www.brainyquote.com/quotes/keywords/idealistic.html

2. Steve Saint. *Missions Dilemma: Is there a Better Way to Do Missions?* Disc 1: Session 1. (Itecusa)

3. Margaret Wheatly and Deborah Frieze, *Walk Out Walk On* (San Francisco, CA: Berrett-Koehler Publishers, 2011), 5.

4. Joshua Project. "What Is A people Group?" Source: 1982 Lausanne Committee Chicago meeting. http://www.joshuaproject.net/what-is-a-people-group.php

PREFACE

1. *Ethnocentricity* is unconsciously believing that one's own culture is somehow superior to another's culture, interpreting life in another culture based on one's own culture, and conducting ministry from that interpretation (shoving one's culture down someone else's throat).

2. Jonathan Bonk, *Missions and Money* (Maryknoll, NY: Orbis Books, 2006), xxix.

3. David Livermore, *Serving With Eyes Wide Open* (Grand Rapids, MI: Baker, 2006), 61.

CHAPTER 1

1. *Missiology* refers to the theory and practice of missions. Alan Neely describes missiology as "The conscious, intentional, ongoing reflection on the doing of mission. It includes theory(ies) of mission, the study and teaching of mission, as well as the research, writing, and publication of works regarding mission" (Alan Neely, "Missiology," in *The Evangelical Dictionary of World Missions*, ed. Scott A. Moreau (Grand Rapids: Baker, 2000), 633.

2. Complete text at Afriprov.org, *African Proverbs, Sayings and Stories*. http://www.afriprov.org/index.php/resources/storiesdatabase.html?task=display2&cid[0]=4

3. Morris Kline, *Mathematics: The Loss of Certainty* (New York: Oxford University Press, 1980), 101.

4. Erwin Raphael McManus, *Wide Awake* (Nashville, TN: Thomas Nelson, 2008), 45.

CHAPTER 2

1. Jim Henderson and Matt Casper, *Jim and Casper Go to Church* (Carol Stream, IL: Tyndale House Publishers, Inc. 2007), 11.

2. Donald McGavran, quoted in Stephen Hawthorne, *The Perspectives Study Guide*, 4th ed. (Pasadena, CA: William Carey Library, 2009), 156.

3. David Garrison, *Church Planting Movements* (Midlothian, VA: WIGTake Resources, 2004), 22.

4. Alan Tippett, *Verdict Theology in Missionary Theory* (Pasadena, CA: William Carey Library, 1973).

5. Charles Brock, *The Principles and Practice of Indigenous Church Planting* (Neosho, MO: Church Growth International, 1981), 89.

6. Rebecca Lewis, "Promoting Movements to Christ within Natural Communities: Insider Movements: The Conversation Continues," *International Journal of Frontier Missiology*, Summer 2007, 75.

7. David Hesselgrave quoted in "Dictionary of Missiological Terms." *Missiology.org* http://www.missiology.org/missionsdictionary.htm.

8. David Garrison, *Church Planting Movements* (Midlothian, VA: WIGTake Resources, 2004), 21.

9. Rebecca Lewis, "Promoting Movements to Christ within Natural Communities: Insider Movements: The Conversation Continues," *International Journal of Frontier Missiology*, Summer 2007, 76, Endnotes.

10. Alan Hirsch and Dave Ferguson, *On The Verge: A Journey into the Apostolic Future of the Church* (Grand Rapids: Zondervan, 2011), 251.

11. Ibid., 40.

12. David Held, *A Globalizing World? Culture, Economics, Politics* (London: Open University, 2000), 6.

13. Hendrik Kraemer, quoted in David Phillips, *Peoples On the Move* (Carlisle: United Kingdom: Piquant, 2001), 85.

CHAPTER 3

1. The Khmer are the predominant ethnic group in Cambodia, making up 90 percent of the population. *Khmer* and *Cambodian* refer to the people of Cambodia and can be used interchangeably both for the people and the language.

2. Don Cormack, *Killing Fields Living Fields* (Borough Green, UK: OMF Publishing, 2009), 92–93.

3. Ibid., 107.

4. Ibid.

Chapter 4

1. I came across this explanation of a movement for Christ in Cambodia via a unpublished and non-formal document. I cannot remember the context, but do know that Dr. George Patterson penned these words.

2. Ed Tarleton, "Accelerate: An Application Combining CPM Methodologies & Inductive Bible Studies, 2004. http://www.heartforhungary.com/hope4ehu/ articles/accelerate.pdf

3. Steven Hawthorne, *The Perspectives Study Guide*, 4th ed. (Pasadena, CA: William Carey Library, 2009), 156.

4. Donald McGavran, "A Church In Every People," *Perspectives*, eds. Ralph Winter and Steve Hawthorne (Pasadena, CA: William Carey Library, 2009), 629.

5. Robert Coleman, *The Master Plan of Evangelism* (Grand Rapids, MI: Fleming H. Revell, 1993), 102–103.

6. Donald McGavran, quoted in Steven Hawthorne, *The Perspectives Study Guide*, 4th

ed. (Pasadena, CA: William Carey Library, 2009), 156.

7. B.D.B. Moses, "Church Planting Movements: Among Hindu Peoples," *Mission Frontiers*, March–April 2011, 19–20.

8. Mir-Ibm-Mohammad, "A Muslim Tribal Chief Is Bringing Jesus to His People," *Mission Frontiers*, May–June 2011, 19.

CHAPTER 5

1. Alan Chapman, "The England Football Story." Businessballs.com. http://www.businessballs.com/stories.htm#the-England-football-story

2. Marku Tsering, *Sharing Christ in the Tibetan Buddhist World* (Tibet: Tibet Press, 2004), 198.

3. Brian Hogan, *There's a Sheep in My Bathtub: Birth of a Mongolian Church Planting Movement* (Bayside, CA: Asteroidea Books, 2008), 125.

4. Rick Leatherwood, *Glory in Mongolia* (Pasadena, CA: William Carey Library, 2006), 164.

5. Ibid., 165

6. Alan Johnson, "Structural and Ministry Philosophy Issues in Church Planting Among Buddhist Peoples," *Sharing Jesus Effectively in the Buddhist World*, eds. Lim David, Steve Spaulding, and Paul De Neui (Pasadena, CA: William Carey Library, 2005), 263–264.

7. Jason Mandryk, *Operation World*, 7th ed. (Colorado Springs, CO: Biblica Publishing, 2010), 146.

8. Ibid., 159.

9. Ibid., 411.

10. Ibid., 612.

11. Larry Kreider and Floyd McClung, *Starting A House Church* (Ventura, CA: Regal Books, 2007): 96.

CHAPTER 6

1. Charles Brock, *The Principles and Practice of Indigenous Church Planting* (Neosho, VA: Church Growth International, 1981), 58.

2. Charles Brock, *Indigenous Church Planting* (Neosho, VA: Church Growth International, 1994), 125–126.

3. I am not the originator of these principles, but I cannot find any reference to where or whom these principles came from. I have had the principles in hand throughout my years in Cambodia.

CHAPTER 7

1. Glenn Schwartz, *When Charity Destroys Dignity: Overcoming Unhealthy Dependency in the Christian Movement* (Bloomington, IN: AuthorHouse, 2007), 169.

2. Kim Harrington, "Indigenous Missions." Master Builder Ministries, 1998. http://www.masterbuilder.org/tracts/indigmis.htm

3. David Marshall, *The True Son of Heaven: How Jesus Fulfills the Chinese Culture* (Seattle, WA: Kuai Mu Press, 2002), 2.

4. Gene Edwards, *The Silas Diary* (Jacksonville, FL: SeedSowers Publishing, 1998), 42–43.
5. Quoted in Jay Moon, *African Proverbs Reveal Christianity in Culture*, American Society of Missiology Monograph Series (Eugene, Oregon: Pickwick Publications, 2009), 2.
6. Marku Tsering, *Sharing Christ In The Tibetan Buddhist World* (Tibet: Tibet Press), The Complete Edition, 2004, 127–128.
7. Patty Lane, *A Beginner's Guide to Crossing Cultures* (Downers Grove, IL: InterVarsity Press, 2002), 19.
8. Mark Batterson, *Primal* (Colorado Springs: Multnomah, 2009), 63.
9. Gailyn Van Rheenen, "Money and Mi$$ion$ (Revisited): Combating Paternalism," Monthly Missiological Reflection #13. *Missions Resource Network*. http://www.mrnet.org/system/files/library/money_and_missions_revisited_combating_paternalism.pdf
10. Ibid.
11. Glenn Schwartz, *When Charity Destroys Dignity: Overcoming Unhealthy Dependency in the Christian Movement* (Bloomington, IN: AuthorHouse, 2007), 171.
12. Charles Brock, *Indigenous Church Planting* (Neosho, VA: Church Growth International, 1994), 89.
13. Robert Reese, Roots & Remedies of the Dependency Syndrome in World Missions (Pasadena, CA: William Carey Library, 2010), 92.
14. Quoted in Ibid., 98.
15. Ibid., 113
16. Children play a game in which one player chooses an object and then says, "I spy with my little eye something big and yellow." The other players are suppose to guess what the object is based on the clues.
17. Sam Kaner, with Lind, L., Toldi, C., Fisk, S. and Berger, D, *Facilitator's Guide to Participatory Decision-Making*, (San Francisco, CA: Jossey-Bass, 2007).
18. George Hunter III, The Celtic Way of Evangelism: How Christianity Can Reach The West …Again (Nashville, TN: Abingdon Press, 2000), 26.
19. Ibid., 26–27.
20. Ibid., 76–77.

CHAPTER 8
1. Ward Brehm, *White Man Walking: An American Businessman's Spiritual Adventure in Africa* (Minneapolis, MN: Kirk House, 2003), 16.
2. Ibid., 7.
3. Ibid.
4. Jonathan Bonk, *Missions and Money* (Maryknoll, NY: Orbis Books, 2006), 17.
5. Levy Moyo, *White Gloved Handshake: Christian or Christened Missions?* (UK: Chosen Graphics, 2006), 63.
6. Quoted in Rick Wood, "Fighting Dependency Among the 'Aucas': An Interview with Steve Saint by Rick Wood," *Mission Frontiers*, May–June 1998, 12.

http://www.adopt-a-people.org/articles/dependency.pdf

7. *Colonialism* is the process in which people from one territory claim authority over another territory. Colonists create an unequal relationship in which they become the prominent figure and authority, while the indigenous population becomes submissive and used by the colonists for their own gain.

8. Paternalism has similar elements to colonialism in that the outsiders impose and dominate in a cross-cultural setting. Paternalism is an attitude that says, "We know the best way."

9. Gailyn Van Rheenen, "Money and Mi$$ion$ (Revisited): Combating Paternalism," Monthly Missiological Reflection #13. *Missions Resource Network*. http://www.mrnet.org/system/files/library/money_and_missions_revisited_combating_paternalism.pdf

10. Steve Corbett and Brian Fikkert, *When Helping Hurts: How to Alleviate Poverty Without Hurting the Poor And Yourself* (Chicago, IL: Moody Publishers, 2009), 119.

11. William Smallman, *Able to Teach Others Also* (Pasadena, CA: Mandate Press, 2001), 25.

12. John Dekker and Lois Neely, *Torches of Joy: A Stone Age Tribe's Encounter with the Gospel*, 2nd ed. (Seattle, WA: YWAM Publishing, 1999), 185.

13. Patrick Lai, *Tentmaking: The Life and Work of Business as Missions* (Colorado Springs: Authentic Publishing, 2005), 158.

CHAPTER 9

1. Bob Lupton, "Vactionaries," *The Mennonite*, Feb 2011. http://www.themennonite.org/issues/12-12/articles/Vacationaries

2. Christopher Little, "When Two Bikes Split A Church." *Mission Frontiers*, November-December, 2000. http://www.missionfrontiers.org/issue/article/when-two-bikes-split-a-church

3. Ibid.

4. Ibid.

5. Robert Reese, *Roots & Remedies of the Dependency Syndrome in World Missions* (Pasadena, CA: William Carey Library, 2010), 1.

6. Glenn Schwartz, *When Charity Destroys Dignity: Overcoming Unhealthy Dependency in the Christian Movement* (Bloomington, IN: AuthorHouse, 2007), 1–2.

7. David Garrison, *Church Planting Movements* (Midlothian, VA: WIGTake Resources, 2004), 267

8. Hanok Tamang, "Be Aware! Dependency Will Destroy!" *World Mission Associates*, 2009. http://www.wmausa.org/page.aspx?id=83848

9. Robertson McQuilkin, "Should We Stop Sending Missionaries: Principles for Avoiding the Corrupting Power of Money." Mission Fest International. *Mission Frontiers*, 2007–2009, 2.

10. Peter Greer and Phil Smith, *The Poor Will Be Glad* (Grand Rapids, MI: Zondervan, 2009), 16.

11. Steve Corbett and Brian Fikkert, *When Helping Hurts: How to Alleviate Poverty Without Hurting the Poor And Yourself* (Chicago, IL: Moody Publishers, 2009), 28.

12. Niall Ferguson, foreword to Dambisa Moyo, *Dead Aid* (New York: Farrar, Strauss, and Giroux, 2009), ix.

13. Toby Mac, "City On Our Knees," *Tonight* (CD), ForeFront Records, 2009.

14. Jonathan Bonk, *Missions and Money* (Maryknoll, New York: Orbis Books, 2006), 17, xxvii, 1.

15. Joel Wickre, "Missions that Heal." *Christianity Today*, July 2007 (Web-only). http://www.christianitytoday.com/ct/2007/julyweb-only/128-52.0. html?start=1

16. Karim Sahyoun, "Footsteps: Planning for Sustainability," *TEARFUND*. No. 64, September 2005. http://tilz.tearfund.org/webdocs/Tilz/Footsteps/English/FS64_E.pdf

17. Assemblies of God World Missions, "Encouraging Church Planting," *The Intercessor & World Report*, June 7, 2011, Vol. 11, No. 25, 1.

18. Ibid.

19. Bob Lupton, "Vactionaries," *The Mennonite*, Feb 2011. http://www.themennonite.org/issues/12-12/articles/Vacationaries

20. Ibid.

21. Joel Wickre, "Missions that Heal," *Christianity Today*, July 2007 (Web-only). http://www.christianitytoday.com/ct/2007/julyweb-only/128-52.0.html? start=1

22. Jonathan Bonk, "Missions and Mammon: Six Theses." *International Bulletin of Missionary Research* 13, No. 4, October 1989, 174-180.

23. Peter Greer and Phil Smith, *The Poor Will Be Glad: Joining The Revolution To Lift The World Out Of Poverty* (Grand Rapids: Zondervan, 2009), 30.

24. Jerry Rankin, "Debilitating Dependence on Subsidy," April 22, 2010, http://rankin-connecting.com/2010/04/debilitating-dependence-on-subsidy

25. Ibid.

26. Peter Greer and Phil Smith, *The Poor Will Be Glad* (Grand Rapids, MI: Zondervan, 2009), 49–51.

27. Josphat G. Charagu is a bi-vocational pastor in Kenya. Josphat shared these words with a group of about 12 of us sitting around a table. We intentionally gathered in Karen, Kenya to dialogue about unhealthy dependency in 2008.

28. Shah Ali and Dudley Woodberry, "South Asia: Vegetables, Fish and Messianic Mosques," *Perspectives*, eds. Ralph Winter and Steve Hawthorne. (Pasadena, CA: William Carey Library, 2009), 717.

29. Peter Greer and Phil Smith, *The Poor Will Be Glad* (Grand Rapids, MI: Zondervan, 2009), 58.

30. Robert Lupton, *Compassion, Justice and The Christian Life: Rethinking Ministry to the Poor* (Ventura, CA: Regal Books, 2007), 22–23.

31. Glenn Schwartz, "Don't Chase Buffaloes." *World Mission Associates*. http://www.wmausa.org/page.aspx?id=83820

32. Glenn Schwartz quoted in Hahné, Ronnie and Wouter Rijneveld. "Dependency." *World Mission Associates*, April 2005. http://www.wmausa.org/ Page.aspx?id=109070

33. Glenn Penner, "Dependency: When Good Intentions Aren't Enough," *The Voice of the Martyrs*, April 25, 2002. http://www.farmsinternational.com/ pdf/dependency.pdf

34. Ralph Winter, "Why Sending Money Does Not Work As Well As Sending People," *Mission Frontiers*, September/October 1994, 1.

35. "A Congregation of Pilgrims: An Interview with Emmanuel Katongole," *Catalyst Groupzine*, Volume 3: Courageous in Calling, (Nashville, Tennessee: Nelson Impact, 2007), 69.

36. Ibid.

37. Ibid.

Chapter 10

1. Dr. Avery Willis, "Following Jesus: Making Disciples of Primary Oral Learners," Literate Communication and CBS. (Progressive Vision, 2002), Disc 2: Track 2.

2. Mark Batterson, *Primal* (Colorado Springs, CO: Multnomah, 2009), 53.

3. Trent Batson, "Web 2.0, Secondary Orality, and the Gutenberg Parenthesis," *Campus Technology*, 03/05/08. http://campustechnology.com/Articles/2008/03/Web-20-Secondary-Orality-and-the-Gutenberg-Parenthesis.aspx?Page=1

4. Dr. Grant Lovejoy in Dr. Avery Willis, "Following Jesus: Making Disciples of Primary Oral Learners," Impact of CBS on CPMs. (Progressive Vision, 2002), Disc 2: Track 1.

5. Annette Simmons, "The Power of Story: Dressing Up the Naked Truth," *ASK Magazine*, NASA, http://askmagazine.nasa.gov/issues/18/18_special.html

6. Heather Forest, *Wisdom Tales From Around The World* (Little Rock, AK: August House, 1996), 5.

7. Jeanne Choy Tate, "Studying the Bible across Cultures: Towards an Intercultural Hermeneutic." Prepared specially for the CANAAC-CANACOM Joint Assembly/Council meeting in Georgetown, Guyana, February 25–29, 2008. http://www.canaac.org/wpcontent/uploads/2009/04/studying_the_bible_across_cultures.pdf

8. Quoted in Alex Smith, *Communicating Christ Through Story and Song*, ed. Paul De Neui. (Pasadena, CA: William Carey Library, 2008), 11.

9. Askhari Johnson Hodari and Yvonne McCalla Sobers, *Lifelines: The Black Book of Proverbs* (New York: Broadway Books, 2009), 5.

10. Ibid., 33.

11. Ibid., 18.

12. Ibid., 84.

13. Ibid., 70.

14. Tokunbo Adelekan, *African Wisdom: 101 Proverbs From The Motherland* (Valley Forge, PA: Judson Press, 2004), 48.

15. Ibid., 72.

16. Ibid., 99.

17. Askhari Johnson Hodari and Yvonne McCalla Sobers, *Lifelines: The Black Book of Proverbs* (New York: Broadway Books, 2009), xiii.

18. Quoted in Joseph Healy and Donald Sybertz, *Towards An African Narrative Theology* (New York: Orbis Books, 1996), 18.

19. Gideon Kiongo, "An Open Letter on Giving in Kenya," *World Mission Associates*, 2009. http://www.wmausa.org/page.aspx?id=83856

20. Harry Box, *Communicating Christianity To Oral Even-Oriented People* (Ann Arbor, MI: UMI Dissertation Services, 2007), 35.

21. Dr. Walter Ong, quoted in "Orality," *Wikipedia: The Free Encyclopedia*. Oct. 9, 2010. http://en.wikipedia.org/wiki/Orality

22. Ibid.

23. Dr. Walter Ong, *Orality and Literacy*, (London and New York: Routledge, 1982, 2002).

24. Ibid.

25. Tom Steffen, *Reconnecting God's Story to Ministry: Cross-cultural Storytelling at Home and Abroad* (Waynesboro, GA: Authentic Media, 2005), 37–38.

26. Ibid., 41.

27. Ibid., 42.

28. Carla Brown, "Story and Song in Kepele-Dafo: An Innovative Church Planting Model Among an Oral Culture of Togo," *Lausanne World Pulse* 2006, 1–2.

Interlude

1. Quoted in Melvin Hodges, *The Indigenous Church* (Springfield, MO: Gospel Publishing House, 1976), 84.

CHAPTER 11

1. Charles Kraft, "Ethics of Change: A Reading for Cultural Anthropology." *Missions Mobilizer*. http://home.snu.edu/~HCULBERT/ethics.htm, 15

2. Tom Steffen, *Passing the Baton: Church Planting That Empowers* (La Habra, CA: Center for Organizational & Ministry Development, 1997), 4.

3. Erwin Raphael McManus, *An Unstoppable Force: Daring to Become the Church God Had in Mind* (Orange, CA: Group Publishing, 2001), 133.

4. Bob Roberts Jr., *The Multiplying Church* (Grand Rapids, MI: Zondervan, 2008), 30.

5. Donald McGavran, "A Church In Every People," *Perspectives*, eds. Ralph Winter and Steve Hawthorne (Pasadena, CA: William Carey Library, 2009), 629.

6. Ibid., 630.

7. Gavriel Gefen, "Jesus Movements: Discovering Biblical Faith in the Most Unexpected Places," *Mission Frontiers*, May–June 2011, 7.

8. Wolfgang Simson, *Houses That Changed The World* (Emmelsbull, Germany: OM Publishing, 1999), 12.

9. Rebecca Lewis, "Promoting Movements to Christ within Natural Communities: Insider Movements: The Conversation Continues," *International Journal of Frontier Missiology*, Summer 2007, 75-76

10. Bob Roberts Jr., *The Multiplying Church* (Grand Rapids, MI: Zondervan, 2008), 34.

11. Ibid., 29.

12. Tony and Felicity Dale, George Barna. *The Rabbit and the Elephant: Why Small Is the New Big for Today's Church* (Carol Stream, IL: Tyndale House Publishers, 2009), 72.

13. Erwin Raphael McManus, *An Unstoppable Force: Daring to Become the Church God Had in Mind* (Orange, CA: Group Publishing, 2001), 15.

14. David Watson, "Obedience-Based Discipleship." http://www.cpmtr.org/resources

15. David Watson, *Obedience-Based Discipleship: Field Testing Guide v1.5*. Texas, 2008 http://www.cpmtr.org/wp-content/plugins/downloadsmanager/upload/ 2008%20Obedience%20Based%20Discipleship%201.5.pdf

16. Jean Johnson and Diane Campbell, *Worldview Strategic Church Planting Among Oral Cultures* (Springfield: Life Publishers International, 2007), 132.

17. Tony and Felicity Dale, *Simply Church* (Manchca, TX: Karis Publishing, 2002), 111.

18. "Serve One Another in the Family of God." http://mentorandmultiply. homestead.com/ files/One_Anothers_pages_18_21.htm

19. Mark Batterson, *Wild Goose Chase: Rediscover the Adventure of Pursuing God.* (Colorado Springs, CO: Multnomah Books: 2008), 29

20. Neil Cole, "Organic Church," Perspectives, eds. Ralph Winter and Steve Hawthorne. (Pasadena, CA: William Carey Library, 2009), 644.

21. David Garrison, Church Planting Movements (Midlothian, VA: WIGTake Resources, 2004), 245–248.

22. Ibid., 224–225.

23. David Watson, "21 Critical Elements," *CPM Training Resources*. Download Power Point at http://www..cpmtr.org.

CHAPTER 12

1. Jonathan Bonk, *Missions and Money* (Maryknoll, NY: Orbis Books, 2006), 52, 56.

2. Ravi Zacharias, *Walking from East to West* (Grand Rapids, MI: Zondervan, 2006), 16.

3. Ibid.

4. Jonathan Bonk, *Missions and Money* (Maryknoll, NY: Orbis Books, 2006), 54.

5. Ibid., 55.

6. John Walker, *Costly Grace: A Contemporary View of Bonhoeffer's The Cost of Discipleship* (Abilene, TX: Abilene Christian University Press: 2010), 40.

CHAPTER 13

1. Charles Brock, *Indigenous Church Planting* (Neosho, MO: Church Growth International, 1994), 126–132.

2. Tony and Felicity Dale, George Barna. *The Rabbit and the Elephant: Why Small Is the New Big for Today's Church* (Carol Stream, IL: Tyndale House Publishers, 2009), 70.

CHAPTER 14

1. J.O. Terry in Dr. Avery Willis, *Following Jesus: Making Disciples of Primary Oral Learners* (Digital Publishers Discipling Nations, 2002), Disc 2: Track 3.

2. Ravi Zacharias, *Walking from East to West* (Grand Rapids, MI: Zondervan, 2006), 22–23.

3. Tom Steffen, *Passing the Baton: Church Planting That Empowers* (La Habra, CA: Center for Organizational & Ministry Development, 1997), 2.

4. I came across this explanation of a movement for Christ in Cambodia via an unpublished and non-formal document. I cannot remember the context, but do know that Dr. George Patterson penned these words.

5. William Smallman, *Able To Teach Others Also* (Pasadena, CA: Mandate Press, 2001), 10.

6. Tim and Rebecca Lewis, "Planting Churches: Learning the Hard Way," *Mission Frontiers*, January–February 2009, 16.

7. Ibid., 17.

8. Glenn Schwartz, *When Charity Destroys Dignity: Overcoming Unhealthy Dependency in the Christian Movement* (Bloomington, IN: AuthorHouse, 2007), 172–174.

9. Gailyn Van Rheenen, *Communicating Christ in Animistic Contexts* (Pasadena, CA: William Carey Library, 1991), 53.

10. Eric Bridges, "Worldview," *The Network For Strategic Missions*, 2004. http://www.strategicnetwork.org/index.php?loc=kb&view=v&id=15604&fso=c6b75511971b5eaa22ac0fab31efbed0&fby=0c6c62aba21d416689cb182a5202a2f2&

11. David Hesselgrave, "World-view and Contextualization: A reading for Cultural Anthropology," *Missions Mobilizer*. http://home.snu.edu/~HCULBERT/context.htm

12. Chris Hale, "Reclaiming the Bhajan: Ancient Musical Styles of India Transform Modern Worship of Christ," *Mission Frontiers*, June 2001, 16.

13. Ibid.

14. Sue Hall and Paul Neeley, "The Vaglas Sing A Song From the Heart," *Mission Frontiers*, June 2001, 21.

15. Paul DeNeui, "What Happened When Grandma Danced," *Mission Frontiers*, June 2001, 19.

16. Ibid.

17. Gilles, "What Happened to Oral Learning? Blame Plato," *Lausanne Global Conversation* Blog, 2011. http://conversation.lausanne.org/en/conversations/detail/11891

18. Brian Schrag and Paul Neeley, eds. *All The World Will Worship: Help for Developing Indigenous Hymns*, 3rd ed. (Duncanville, TX: EthnoDoxology Publications, 2005), 3.

19. Malcolm Hunter, foreword to David Phillips, *Peoples on the Move: Introducing the Nomads of the World* (Pasadena, CA: William Carey Library, 2001), XIII.

20. David Phillips, *Peoples On the Move* (Carlisle: United Kingdom: Piquant, 2001), 125.

21. Aubrey Malphurs, *A New Kind of Church: Understanding Models of Ministry for the 21st Century* (Grand Rapids: Baker, 2007), 77.

22. Ibid., 85.

23. David Garrison, *Church Planting Movements* (Midlothian, VA: WIGTake Resources, 2004), 243.

24. Josh Hunt, "Church Planting Movements (Read: The Amazing Power of Doubling Groups)." http://www.joshhunt.com/mail124.htm

25. Neil Cole, "Organic Church," *Perspectives*, eds. Ralph Winter and Steve Hawthorne. (Pasadena, CA: William Carey Library, 2009), 645.

26. David Phillips, *Peoples On the Move* (Carlisle: United Kingdom: Piquant, 2001), 125–126.

27. Neil Cole, "Organic Church," *Perspectives*, eds. Ralph Winter and Steve Hawthorne. (Pasadena, CA: William Carey Library, 2009), 645.

28. David Phillips, *Peoples On the Move* (Carlisle: United Kingdom: Piquant, 2001), 127.

29. Patrick Lai, *Tentmaking: The Life and Work of Business as Missions* (Colorado Springs, CO: Authentic Publishing, 2005), 154.

30. Josh Hunt, "Church Planting Movements (Read: The Amazing Power of Doubling Groups)." http://www.joshhunt.com/mail124.htm

31. Stephen Atkerson, *House Church: Simple, Strategic, Scriptural* (Atlanta: NTRF, 2005), back cover.

32. Quoted in Glenn Schwartz, *When Charity Destroys Dignity* (Bloomington, IN: Author-House, 2007), 171-172.

CHAPTER 15

1. Thomas and Elizabeth Brewster, "The Learner-Servant-Storyteller Posture." *International Bulletin of Missionary Research*, 1981, 162. http://www.strategicnetwork.org/pdf/kb11227.pdf

2. Tom Steffen, *Passing the Baton: Church Planting That Empowers* (La Habra, CA: Center for Organizational & Ministry Development, 1997), 50.

3. Patrick Lai, *Tentmaking: The Life and Work of Business as Missions* (Colorado Springs, CO: Authentic Publishing, 2005), 158.

4. Train and Multiply is operated by Project WorldReach. https://trainandmultiply.com

5. The terms "local champion" and "external saviors" were coined by Peter Greer and Phil Smith in their book, *The Poor Will Be Glad* (Grand Rapids, MI: Zondervan, 2009), 30.

CHAPTER 16

1. Gailyn Van Rheenen, "Money and Mi$$ion$," Monthly Missiological Reflections #2. http://www.strategicnetwork.org/index.php?loc=kb&view=v&id=3157&

2. Quoted in William Smallman, *Able to Teach Others Also* (Pasadena, CA: Mandate Press, 2001), 5.

3. Ken Stout, *Fostering Sustainability & Minimizing Dependency In Mission Finances*. An Integrative Thesis Submitted to the faculty of Reformed Theological Seminary, 2008. http://www.rts.edu/Site/Virtual/Resources/Student_Theses/Stout-Mission_Finances.pdf

4. Timothy Mitchell, "Western Missionaries in Africa: One Missionary's Encounter with Self-Reliance Thinking," *World Mission Associates*, 2009. http://www.wmausa.org/page.aspx?id=83847

5. Hahné, Ronnie and Wouter Rijneveld. "Dependence," *World Mission Associates* 2009. April 2005. http://www.wmausa.org/Page.aspx?id=109070

6. Glenn Penner, "Good Intentions Versus Best Practices," *World Mission Associates*, 2009. http://www.wmausa.org/page.aspx?id=84391

7. Phil Parshall, "Missions and Money," *Perspectives*, eds. Ralph Winter and Steve Hawthorne (Pasadena, CA: William Carey Library, 2009), 482–485.

8. The Waramajanna Project Proposal: A Self-Sufficiency Agro-Pastoral Project. http://www.arzouni.com/documents/WaramajannaProject.pdf 2

9. Christopher Little, "Partnerships in Pauline Perspective," *International Journal of Frontier Missiology*, Summer 2010, 9.

10. Gideon Kiongo, "An Open Letter On Giving In Kenya," *World Mission Associates*, 2009. http://www.wmausa.org/page.aspx?id=83856

11. Ibid.

12. Steve Corbett and Brian Fikkert, *When Helping Hurts: How to Alleviate Poverty Without Hurting the Poor And Yourself* (Chicago, IL: Moody Publishers, 2009), 125–126.

13. "The Jazz King: Improvising Hope, An Interview with Bill Strickland," *Trap Door Sun*, 2008. http://www.trapdoorsun.com/causes/bill-strickland.aspx

14. Bob Lupton, "Vacationaries," *The Mennonite*, June 16, 2009.

15. Peter Greer and Phil Smith, *The Poor Will Be Glad: Joining The Revolution To Lift The World Out Of Poverty* (Grand Rapids, MI: Zondervan, 2009), 30.

16. Patrick O'Connor, *Reproducible Pastoral Training: Church Planting Guidelines from the Teachings of George Patterson* (Pasadena, CA: William Carey Library, 2006), 137.

17. Glenn Schwartz, *When Charity Destroys Dignity* (Bloomington, IN: AuthorHouse, 2007), 145.

18. John Williamson and Aaron Greenberg, "Families, Not Orphanages," Better Care Network Working Paper, September 2010. http://www.crin.org/docs/Families%20Not%20-Orphanages.pdf

19. Codrington Ntabeni, "My Experience in Relief and Development," *World Mission Associates*, 2009. http://www.wmausa.org/page.aspx?id=83857

20. Quoted in Ronnie Hahné and Wouter Rijneveld, "Dependency." *World Mission Associates*, April 2005. http://www.wmausa.org/Page.aspx?id=109070

21. Glenn Schwartz, *When Charity Destroys Dignity* (Bloomington, IN: AuthorHouse, 2007), 12.

22. James Avery and Bruce Avolio, "The Measure of Psychological Ownership in Organizations," MindGarden.com. http://www.mindgarden.com/products/poq.htm

23. Quoted in Ronnie Hahné and Wouter Rijneveld, "Dependency," *World Mission Associates*, April 2005. http://www.wmausa.org/Page.aspx?id=109070

24. Phnom Penh Post. July 7–20, 2000.
25. Ronnie Hahné and Wouter Rijneveld, "Dependency," *World Mission Associates*, April 2005. http://www.wmausa.org/Page.aspx?id=109070
26. Jay W. Moon, *African Proverbs Reveal Christianity in Culture* (Eugene, Oregon: Pickwick Publications, 2009), 2.
27. Marku Tsering, *Sharing Christ In The Tibetan Buddhist World* (Tibet: Tibet Press, The Complete Edition, 2004: 127–128.
28. Glenn Schwartz, *When Charity Destroys Dignity* (Bloomington, IN: AuthorHouse, 2007), 110.
29. John Smith (pseudonym), "MBB church, Inc. in Bangladesh: Overcoming the Destructive Effects of Naïve Western Funding," *Hope Church*, 2006.
30. William Kornfield, PhD, "Results of Paternalism and Some Viable Results," *World Mission Associates*, 2009. http://www.wmausa.org/page.aspx?id=83849
31. Phil Parshall, "Missions and Money," *Perspectives*, eds. Ralph Winter and Steve Hawthorne. (Pasadena, CA: William Carey Library, 2009), 483.
32. Ibid., 484.
33. Gailyn Van Rheenen, "Money and Mi$$ion$," Monthly Missiological Reflections #2. http://www.strategicnetwork.org/index.php?loc=kb&view=v&id=3157&
34. Ronnie Hahné and Wouter Rijneveld. "Dependency." *World Mission Associates*, 2009. April 2005. http://www.wmausa.org/Page.aspx?id=109070
35. Ibid.

CHAPTER 17
1. Tom Steffen, *Reconnecting God's Story to Ministry: Cross-cultural Storytelling at Home and Abroad* (Waynesboro, Georgia: Authentic Media, 2005), 2.
2. Quoted in Harry Box, *Communicating Christianity To Oral Even-Oriented People* (Ann Arbor, MI: UMI Dissertation Services, 2007), 29.
3. Tom Steffen, *Reconnecting God's Story to Ministry: Cross-cultural Storytelling at Home and Abroad* (Waynesboro, GA: Authentic Media, 2005).
4. Paul Hiebert and Elosie Hiebert Meneses, *Incarnational Ministry: Planting Churches in Band, Tribal, Peasant, and Urban Societies* (Grand Rapids, MI: Baker, 1995), 129.
5. Harry Box, *Communicating Christianity To Oral Even-Oriented People* (Ann Arbor, Michigan: UMI Dissertation Services, 2007), 155.
6. Quoted in Harry Box, *Communicating Christianity To Oral Even-Oriented People* (Ann Arbor, Michigan: UMI Dissertation Services, 2007), 155.
7. Charles Kraft, *Communicating Jesus' Way* (Pasadena, CA: William Carey Library, 1999), 20.
8. Harry Box, *Communicating Christianity To Oral Even-Oriented People* (Ann Arbor, MI: UMI Dissertation Services, 2007), 54–55.
9. Walter Ong, *Orality and Literacy* (London and New York: Routledge, 2002), 34.
10. Miriam Adeney, "Feed Giraffes, Counting Cows, And Missing True Learners: The

Challenge of Buddhist Oral Communicators," *Communicating Christ Through Story and Song*, ed. Paul Neui. (Pasadena, CA: William Carey Library, 2008), 77.

11. Heather Forest, *Wisdom Tales From Around The World* (Little Rock: August House, 1996), 9.

12. Tom Steffen, *Reconnecting God's Story to Ministry: Cross-cultural Storytelling At Home and Abroad* (Waynesboro, GA: Authentic Media, 2005), 28.

13. Lausanne Committee for World Evangelization, *Making Disciples of Oral Learners* (International Orality Network, 2004), 123.

14. Tom Steffen, *Reconnecting God's Story to Ministry: Cross-cultural Storytelling At Home and Abroad* (Waynesboro, GA: Authentic Media, 2005), 21.

15. Lausanne Committee for World Evangelization, *Making Disciples of Oral Learners* (International Orality Network, 2004): 123.

16. Quoted in Dorji Thinley, *The Boneless Tongue* (Phuntsholing, Bhutan: KMT Publishers, 2005).

17. J.O. Terry, "The Important of Worldview in Witness and Storying," 2008. http:www.churchstarting.net/biblestorying/worldview.htm

18. Ibid.

19. Ibid.

20. John Oswald, "Gospel Communication in Tibetan Song," *Communicating Christ Through Story and Song*, ed. Paul De Neui. (Pasadena, CA: William Carey Library, 2008), 248.

21. Ibid., 250.

22. Ibid.

23. Ibid., 246.

24. http://www.oralitystrategies.org/files/resources/279/African%20Proverbs.pdf. Jay Moon adapted this story from Jack Maguire, the author of *The Power of Personal Storytelling: Spinning Tales to Connect with Others* (New York: Tarcher/Putnam, 1998), 137–38.

25. Jay Moon, "African Proverbs: Stepping Stones within Oral Cultures." http://www.oralitystrategies.org/files/resources/279/African%20Proverbs.pdf

26. Askhari Johnson Hodari and Yvonne McCalla Sobers, *Lifelines* (New York: Broadway Books, 2009), xv.

27. Paul Koehler, *Telling God's Stories With Power: Biblical Storytelling In Oral Cultures* (Pasadena: William Carey Library, 2010), 1.